Ulysses
by Numbers

Ulysses by Numbers

Eric Bulson

Columbia University Press

New York

Columbia University Press
Publishers Since 1893
New York   Chichester, West Sussex
cup.columbia.edu
Copyright © 2020 Columbia University Press

Library of Congress Cataloging-in-Publication Data
Names: Bulson, Eric, author.
Title: Ulysses by numbers / Eric Bulson.
Description: New York City : Columbia University Press, 2020. |
Includes bibliographical references and index.
Identifiers: LCCN 2020015071 (print) | LCCN 2020015072 (ebook) |
ISBN 9780231186049 (cloth) | ISBN 9780231186056 (trade paperback) |
ISBN 9780231546478 (ebook)
Subjects: LCSH: Joyce, James, 1882–1941. Ulysses. | Joyce, James, 1882–1941—
Literary style—Data processing. | Symbolism of numbers in literature. |
Criticism, Textual—Data processing. | Literature—Research—Methodology.
Classification: LCC PR6019.O9 U63215 2020 (print) |
LCC PR6019.O9 (ebook) | DDC 823/.912—dc23
LC record available at https://lccn.loc.gov/2020015071
LC ebook record available at https://lccn.loc.gov/2020015072

Printed in the United States of America
Cover design: Chang Jae Lee

For Kent Puckett
1 in 1,000,000

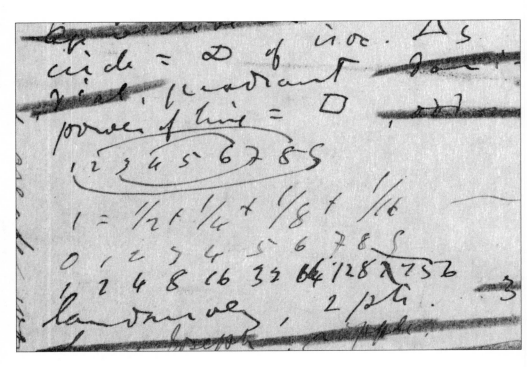

P.1 Notes for episode 17.

Source: Courtesy of the British Library.

C'ÉTAIT   *LE NOMBRE*
issu stellaire

EXISTÂT-IL

autrement   qu'hallucination   éparse   d'agonie

COMMENCÂT-IL ET CESSÂT-IL

sourdant   que   nié   et   clos   quand   apparu
enfin
par   quelque   profusion   répandu   en   rareté

SE CHIFFRÂT-IL

évidence   de   la   somme   pour   peu   qu'une

ILLUMINÂT-IL

Stéphane   Mallarmé,   *Un   Coup   de   Dés   jamais   n'abolira   le   Hasard*

Contents

Illustrations

Nº 1

Nº 2

Nº 3

Nº 4

Nº 5

Acknowledgments

I never imagined that I would write a book about numbers and definitely not one involving *Ulysses*. But it all happened largely because I was never left alone for too long with my ideas. From the start, I've been fortunate enough to have so many others offer support. Friends have been there, of course, but also colleagues, students, and acquaintances. Without all their questions, comments, corrections, and bouts of disbelief, I'm afraid the words that follow would never have counted for much.

Foremost among them, Philip Leventhal, not only for the encouragement to bring this all together as a book, but also for the direction necessary to help me gauge the scope and scale along the way. And then there are all the readers who provided critical assessments just as the counting got underway: Jean Day, David Weiss, Ian Gunn, Erik Schneider, Jean-Michel Rabaté, Hoyt Long, Richard So, Jim English, David Kurnick, and Jim Shapiro. As the counting continued, I could also depend on Edi Giunta, Kevin Dettmar, Franco Moretti, Michael Groden, Andreas Huyssen, Hans Walter Gabler, Evan Kindley, Aaron Matz, Josh Kotin, and David Kastan. For quick answers to the nitty-gritty genetic questions, I was fortunate to have Ronan Crowley to rely on. With all things related to copyright, there was Bob Spoo, a benevolent legal force in the scholarly community.

But a book like this doesn't get written without relying on the technical know-how of others. Among them, Nicholas Rougeux, a web designer and self-proclaimed data geek, who has a gift for making numbers beautiful. And then there is Warren Roberts, GIS-guru, who volunteered so much time to get these maps plotted and properly oriented. But none of this, of course, would have been possible without the data. For that I am indebted to Alyssa Krueger, my indefatigable research assistant, who collected and cleaned the numbers more times than either of us can really remember. The data collection was never straightforward and required not just remarkable patience but also a real understanding of the larger questions that were being asked.

Over the years, I received generous funding from the Digital Humanities Center at the Claremont Colleges and my own department of English at Claremont Graduate University. I owe a particular debt of gratitude to Ashley Sanders-Garcia, Dan Michon, Leigh Leiberman, and Aaron Hodges. Thanks are due as well to the National Endowment for the Humanities for a fellowship that gave me the luxury to write and research relatively uninterrupted for an entire year.

From the beginning to end of it all, there was Kent Puckett, a dear friend I could always count on to read drafts, ask tough questions, refine a phrase, and direct me to an unexpected source. This book is better because of him, but he also made it a lot of fun to write in the meantime. And, finally, I owe everything else to Finn, Leif, and Mika: the three people who keep reminding me that love doesn't have a number.

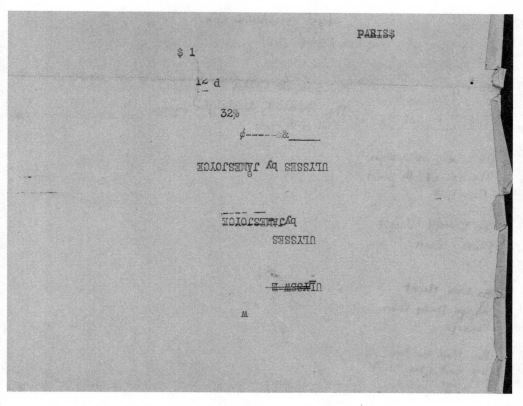

P.2 Notes for a prospectus of *Ulysses*, c. May 1921.

Source: Courtesy of the Manuscripts Division, Department of Special Collections, Princeton University.

Ulysses by Numbers

NUMBERS AND SYMBOLS

0: 663.27
2 1/2%: 702.04
4%: 708.01
5%: 702.02 702.34
1/8: 632.02
.15: 703.06
1/6th: 701.40
1/4: 732.29
2/7ths: 704.37
1/3rd: 702.03
1/2: 761.08
90%: 656.34
1 (51)
1st (9): 685.21 688.01 708.15
  733.14 736.21 756.25 761.15 763.38
  765.15
1 1/2: 661.15
2 (44)
II: 511.21 632.38 660.15 667.34
2nd (7): 685.26 707.26 708.12
  708.15 733.41 739.23 762.16
2/-per: 659.18
2 1/2: 632.33
2.59: 702.21
3 (21): 632.29 655.37 672.26 695.27
  702.19 705.18 705.39 706.02 706.11
  727.02 732.29 736.12 740.07 744.17
  744.34 749.24 754.11 755.19 757.31
  760.07 766.26
3rd: 733.09
3.15: 699.09
3.33: 670.01
4 (19): 107.32 265.18 478.21 632.27
  632.29 668.14 669.13 672.26 693.20
  697.35 702.24 727.02 736.16 744.12
  748.08 754.11 756.10 757.16 766.26
4th: 652.07 707.11
4.46: 692.08
5 (26)
5 5/11: 679.08
6 (10): 655.20 663.24 677.13 680.27
  697.24 704.21 709.14 709.20 760.18
  765.28
6th: 721.26
7 (8): 230.37 298.11 652.08 699.22
  712.13 738.31 765.40 766.38
7th: 685.06 760.06
8 (11): 334.11 659.33 659.33 660.03
  677.13 702.19 720.06 720.33 720.33
  732.12 760.08
8th: 732.13 733.41

8.29: 670.02
8.35: 584.24
8 1/2: 706.25
9 (13): 334.11 631.35 632.27 653.01
  660.03 684.07 695.04 706.24 706.25
  720.06 720.39 721.09 730.24
9th: 684.07 684.07
9.15: 69.09
9.20: 69.10
9.23: 69.10
9.24: 69.11
9 1/2: 712.15
10 (15): 334.11 660.03 680.28
  683.13 685.18 699.04 706.25 706.25
  720.06 720.35 721.01 730.24 730.42
  756.15 760.06
10th: 694.12 734.13
10.20: 669.06
11 (6): 107.32 661.36 706.25 721.01
  759.36 759.37
12: 293.15 298.14 706.25 706.26
12.25: 497.03
12 1/2: 655.11
13: 287.35 456.16 653.01 693.20
13 1/2: 663.27
14 (7): 245.15 308.36 653.15 654.02
  660.04 662.19 680.04
14A: 327.29
14h: 699.19
15 (11): 60.22 633.11 654.15
  655.19 677.18 720.34 721.08 734.12
  747.40 752.41 760.17
15th: 677.37
16 (11): 226.11 615.33 654.19
  663.23 663.24 663.27 687.06 695.35
  747.22 757.12 767.20
17: 135.01 669.07 695.07 695.33
17 1/2: 663.27
18: 668.03 721.02
18th: 635.33 720.32
19: 652.32 668.15 684.23
20 (12): 478.20 632.29 702.03
  702.07 704.37 734.41 746.09 750.41
  757.37 760.18 762.30 764.11
21: 670.01 692.08 693.19 715.21
22: 655.08 663.31 715.21 752.26
23 (5): 668.13 695.28 698.38
  715.22 760.19
24: 693.30 760.19
25: 707.30
26: 655.07 662.36 680.08

P.3 Miles Hanley, *Word-Index to James Joyce's "Ulysses,"* 1937

Overture

P.4 "Shakespeare & Co. Bookstore."

Source: Courtesy of Getty Images.

J ust opening a copy of *Ulysses*, you may have already missed the first number. And there's a good reason: it is not one you can actually see. Instead it's the sum you get when counting the letters of the title on the cover:

$$U + L + Y + S + S + E + S = 7$$

Thrilled by the idea that printed texts enabled "the sheer detachment that permits such counting," Hugh Kenner was the first reader to take notice, and it was a discovery, he believed, that anticipated the other unwritten 7 appearing on the last page between 1914 and 1921, the two years Joyce used to identify the beginning and end of the composition.[1]

Another set of numbers (escaping Kenner's notice) awaits us on the title page, this time identifying the address of Shakespeare & Company (12, rue de l'Odéon, 12) and the year of publication (1922). Though it looks like a conventional publisher's note—one that received the *bon à tirer*, ready to print, from Joyce during the proof stage—the two 12s surrounding the *rue* where *Ulysses* was getting wrapped for distribution just don't add up. The first identifies the building number of Sylvia Beach's bookstore, but the second gets the arrondissement and the numerical formatting wrong (VI[e]). Or does it? A pair of 12s could be found painted on the outside of Beach's bookstore, as was customary in Paris at the time (figure p. 4). But we also can't forget the date when the novel itself arrived in the world.

"The entire printing house is pleased to offer you the first copy on the date of 2 February" ["[L'officine toute entière] est heureuse de vous offrir le premier exemplaire à la date du 2 Février"], Maurice Darantière, the owner, wrote to Sylvia Beach, the publisher.[2] First copy on the second day of February: this title page, normally intended to identify the author, publisher, address, and date of publication, has been recoded here as a bibliographical birth certificate: the four 2s contained in the sequence 12, 12, 1922, mirror the 2.2.22 marking the day, month, and year of Joyce's 40th birthday and the publication of the novel.[3]

Twenty-two, it turns out, is also the age of Stephen Dedalus when *Ulysses* opens, the number of books in the Old Testament (according to Flavius Josephus) and the letters in the Hebrew alphabet, and it was also the original number of episodes (before Joyce settled on 18), the number of hours in *Ulysses*, and the letters in the Irish alphabet.[4] If you keep counting, you will discover that 22 is the number of words printed *en francais* on the copyright page. It is the same number, in fact, that Kenner counts in the opening sentence of the novel, one mirroring the sum of syllables that can be found in 2 lines of hexameter, the meter of Homer's *Odyssey*.

The next page announces a run of 1,000 copies, each one with a printed N°, or number, that would be stamped in by hand, and it was followed by an announcement identifying an unspecified quantity of "typographical errors" (201 of them in the first errata list). All that stands now between the publisher's paratext and "Stately, plump Buck Mulligan" is an enlarged roman numeral on an otherwise blank page.[5] This *I* represents the complete merging of number and letter; a pronoun in English and the first digit in a numerical sequence, it was part of a counting system dating back to the ancient Etruscans who adapted it from the Greeks: a fitting line of influence given the fact that it appears in a novel with a translated Greek title. Without a table of contents there to map out the structure ahead, the *I*, which also marks the first official page number (left blank), was the earliest indication that *Ulysses* even had different sections, III of them. But as evident from the other details in these pages, it was also a powerful reminder that numbers can be found where you least expect them, and with the opening finally in sight, one set ten lines down from the top of the page and free of any heading, it's time to jump in. Unless you skip ahead, though, you wouldn't know that the plot actually begins on page 3, Joyce, Dante, and Homer's favorite number, one associated in different ancient cultures with the concept of "1, 2, many" and in the age of the ancient Greeks with "beginning, middle, end."[6]

INTRODUCTION
Ulysses by Numbers

All is from Number. Number is the source of all things.
—Ezra Pound, *Guide to Kulchur*

I

Numbers are all over *Ulysses*: on the inside, the outside, and everywhere in between.[1] They appear as roman or arabic numerals; they are spelled out as words; or they are quantities that can be added, subtracted, multiplied, or divided. You can hear the numbers in the rhythm of certain lines, see them in the patterns generated by recurring words or phrases, and feel them in the bulkiness of the book itself.[2] Choosing to take notice of these numbers, whatever their frequency, form, or feeling, does not mean that you're letting yourself get distracted from what really counts. To the contrary: numbers are not just another set of convenient correspondences scattered across the pages of *Ulysses*. *Numbers are* Ulysses. They structure, organize, and give this novel shape; they set the pace of the plot and regulate the rhythm of the city, the movement of its inhabitants, and the size of the crowd; they organize our experience with lines, paragraphs, and pages, as well as the cast of characters and the passage of seconds, minutes, and hours. So crucial are numbers to *Ulysses* that this novel is unthinkable without them.

Yes, unthinkable. Readers, of course, want the words when they pick up a copy, and who can blame them? But consider the simple fact that Joyce needed numbers to write *Ulysses*. More than an assemblage of carefully curated words, his novel is also an elaborate structure, and the process of transforming a narrative about a single day in Dublin into an object that could be distributed to others involved coming up with ways to organize all that material into paragraphs, pages, and episodes with hundreds of characters circulating in between. Readers have tended to avoid the numbers because the critical tradition treats them only as empirical facts or mystical symbols. The truth is in between: the numbers are both/and, empirical and mystical, and scrutinizing the friction that exists between these interpretations is, you might say, a way to ground numerical intuition and reenchant quantitative thinking.

In the numbers there is a productive tension between part and whole, particular and the general, detail and totality, and it was something Joyce needed to bring the disparate elements of his modern epic together. The same is true for readers if they have any interest in accessing the novel's genetic code. By getting the sequences identified, we come to learn about the structure and design of *Ulysses*; but, more importantly, we come to discover how much the qualitative experience has a quantitative dimension. You probably never thought too hard about how many characters or words there are in an episode, but computational reading asks you to consider the many aspects of *Ulysses* so easily missed: Why does Stephen Dedalus think in blocks of sixty paragraphs when he's walking down Sandymount Strand? Why does the average length of episodes spike with the sixth one and then double with those that follow? When exactly did the writing happen? Exact numbers can be generated for all of these questions, but they are not the answer—at least not entirely. They turn our attention back to the pages of the novel, asking us to consider, in turn, how creation has a computational component. All works of art have to begin and end somewhere, and it's not just the assembly of the various parts that makes them come to life for the author: it is the act of reading.

Reading *by numbers* is not a practice that many literary critics take too seriously. And it probably doesn't help that the phrase evokes memories of the mass-marketed painting kits, which began appearing in the 1950s—the founder, Dan Robbins, capitalizing on an idea he claimed to have borrowed from Leonardo Da Vinci. The first official patent for painting by numbers dates back to 1923, a year after *Ulysses* appeared, and it describes a process of using an outlined image with a numerically organized color scheme that could be filled in by any aspiring artist.[3] "Every Man a Rembrandt," was the slogan. With *Ulysses*, that canvas is already filled in with words, but to take the analogy one step further, the outline, or form, is still there in, around, and behind them. With his eighteen episodes, each one lasting one hour or thereabouts, over the course of a single day, Joyce was writing by numbers to keep all the parts together, but he also encouraged friends and admirers to read by them precisely so they could follow along. *Every Man a Joyce*, it seems, for those who are keen to know how he pulled it off.

What follows is an attempt to use numbers as a primary means for interpretation and is focused on three things: *Ulysses* as a novel, computation as a method, and close reading as a critical practice. Most of us would feel comfortable identifying what *Ulysses* is and what it's about, but complications would arise and divisions ensue once we tried to explain just *what it is* and how it developed over time. There are lots of answers out there already, but instead of providing one more biographical, historical, social, psychological, linguistic, or genetic spin, using the content of the words or their variation as a starting point, I treat this novel as a quantifiable object that can be measured, and I do so precisely so that we can address a whole range of related questions involving its scope, scale, size, design, and proportion. Some of the numbers were put there deliberately, the result of individual choices and practical material constraints, but so many others are there, if not by always by chance, then certainly by preconscious forces that are not attributable to a single will, the rules of genre, or the conditions of literary production or reception.

But if the numbers are, indeed, there, we still need to locate them. Computation is not something that most literary critics find particularly valuable and, if anything, there is widespread suspicion that a borrowed method, more at home in the physical and natural sciences, is anathema to the close reading of literary works and the careful elaboration of their historical, social, and cultural contexts. This perspective, though certainly understandable given the complex formation of the disciplines over the centuries, is becoming increasingly strained both because of technological discoveries shaping the digitization, storage, transmission, and search of literary texts but also because of the wider availability and potential affordances of computational tools and resources used for text analysis, data mining, network analysis, mapping, and timelines.

Right now the divide between the computational and noncomputational is clear: you do it or you don't. It is a fraught relationship, the antagonisms increased by anxiety about the future of the discipline. It can seem cataclysmic at times; the history of criticism has been filled with such conflicts, though under different names and as a result of specific historical pressures. The difference now is that there have never been tools powerful enough to make that exploration of quantitative questions about literature as expansive or accessible. A century ago, all of the computation was done by hand, sometimes taking years to collect the data and perform calculations, but now it is not only more efficient than ever but also there are tools that facilitate the visualization so critical to the analysis.

I am by no means recommending we read all literary texts by numbers. I am suggesting, however, that we continue to think about this computational turn less as an ominous threat to the very foundations of literary criticism, something that will destroy the integrity of all humanistic endeavors, and more as an opportunity to reflect on what it can do to the way we engage with the texts we already love. Numbers certainly won't kill the reading experience, and, following Thomas Kuhn, it's worth pointing out that they don't actually mean anything on their own: interpretation and context count in the analysis.[4] That's obvious: just counting the number of coffee cups in your cabinet or books on your shelf does not actually make them mean anything. It's only when you figure out what question guides the interpretation of the number that you might actually arrive at a productive place for thinking about what your coffee cups or books say about where they are, who they are for, what they are made of, and why you might have so many or so few.

It's no different with *Ulysses*. Once you begin to see the numbers, then you are in a position to consider how it is a *work of art*, something made by a human being at a moment in history that continues to recede into the past. We'll never get back to 1922, but by taking the measurements now, we are able to assemble a set of facts about its dimensions that can then be used to consider the singularity of *Ulysses* and help explain how it ended up one way and not another. Which brings me to the close reading. This critical activity has a long and varied past, at least a century old, and one that has seen, in more recent decades, the rise of competing methods that are keen to question and perhaps upend its dominance. The truth is that close reading is here to stay, and, if anything, the so-called distant, surface, and postcritical approaches will only serve a supplemental role in the discipline. But if our desire for closeness with the words of literary texts remains stable, we do not have to imagine that encounter between reader and word in the same way. Close reading might be more or less the same in theory, but in practice, other media are helping transform what and how literary works are being read. To read closely with numbers, using computational tools and digital formats, enhances the interpretation since it begins with and works through basic facts. Of course, none of it will matter much if the motivation for collection and interpretation is not subordinated to a bigger idea, working for and against the various theories already in circulation but also with the goal of determining what new ones can be considered and, whenever possible, proven or discredited.

Which raises a few pointed questions: Is computation really so diametrically opposed to close reading? Is it a method that only takes us further away from the *thingness* of the literary object, stripping it away from any historical context or aesthetic essence? Indeed, these are big questions deserving of much more space than I can devote to them here. But for now, I raise them to make a point that I will develop throughout this book: computation is already close reading; close reading is already computational. Whatever individual readers choose to focus on when they read closely, it is a process that involves identifying the small details, assembling the presence of patterns whenever possible, and then addressing their significance to the work as a whole. Close readers might not calculate an exact number for the quantity of details they assemble, but in their approach lies the tacit acknowledgment that they are countable: computation becomes a precondition for closeness.

One year before the publication of I. A. Richards's *Principles of Literary Criticism*, a book largely responsible for codifying close reading as a disciplinary practice, T. S. Eliot had this to say: "Comparison and analysis . . . are the chief tools of the critic. It is obvious indeed that they *are* tools, to be handled with care, and not employed into an enquiry into the number of times giraffes appeared in the English novel. They are not used with conspicuous success by many contemporary writers. You must know what to compare and what to analyse."[5] What Eliot sees at this moment is the danger of imagining close reading *only as computation*. Though counting giraffes in a novel might sound frivolous enough when done for its own sake, he does not dismiss the possibility that facts, numerical and otherwise, can be useful for literary interpretation. *The number of giraffes* can provide a starting point for analysis and comparison of the text, and in this way, Eliot, like Kuhn with his history of measurement in the physical sciences, emphasizes that computation needs context, and it is the act of close reading that brings the disparate facts to bear on much larger questions about how the universe and the book as universe work.

II

A novel and its numbers: a novel *as its numbers*. And why not, if, as Pound puts it, "number is the source of all things." It was the Pythagoreans who first started suggesting that an elaborate system of numerical resemblances exist between nature and the cosmos. The Pythagoreans believed that numbers not only possessed attributes (reason, opinion, harmony, and justice) but also, Aristotle writes, "since it seemed clear that all other things have their whole nature modelled upon numbers, and that numbers are the ultimate things in the whole physical universe, they assumed the elements of numbers to be the elements of everything, and the whole universe to be a proportion or number."[6] A lot happens to get numbers from the cosmos of the fifth century BCE to the computer of the mid-twentieth CE, but the basic idea that a number is something to be seen, heard, and read remains to this day. And that's just one part of the equation. We also need to remember that at one point in human history, numbers were only spoken words; the rhythm of a nursery rhyme an example of the unity between the two (*Eenie meenie minie mo; One two, buckle my shoe*; and so on). For Friedrich Kittler, the complete separation of number and numeral occurred with writing, and it remained that way until Alan Turing imagined a universal computing machine that could process an infinite set of coded instructions made of ones and zeroes.[7]

The novel is not a computer built to generate calculations or solve complex equations. It is a precoded machine, part of a much more expansive "media history of numbers," as Kittler once called it, that can help us understand how literature can be computable and cosmic, practical and mystical, lettered and numbered all at once.[8] Though filled with words, novels also carry numbers (sometimes in the form of letters), and no matter how elaborate or incomplete the fictional worlds inside them, these numbers are there behind the arrangement. Stuart Gilbert was the first reader to apply this idea to *Ulysses*. In his 1930 study, he treated the novel as a sequence of thematic variables that could be put into an equation to help decode "the structure of the book as a whole." "*Ulysses* is like that of all epic narratives, episodic," he explains on the first page. "There are three main divisions, subdivided into chapters or, rather, episodes." The meaning contained within these subdivided episodes, he continues, is "implicit in the techniques . . . in nuances of language, in the thousand and one correspondences and allusions with which the book is studded."[9] As much as Gilbert's numbering here and elsewhere included passing statements about the structure, the network of allusions, and events and timeframes of the plot ("Mr. Bloom's day begins, like Stephen's, at 8 A.M., when he is preparing his wife's morning tea at their house, No. 7, Eccles Street"), all of it was backed up by a schema that Joyce passed on to him, one identifying the Homeric title and character but also the hour, organ of the body, art, color, symbol, and narrative technic.[10]

For John Kidd fifty years later, this schema was evidence enough that a more elaborate numerical pattern lay in waiting. In his preface to an abandoned Dublin edition from the 1990s, he wrote: "It should surprise no one that Joyce, who assigned a reigning color and organ of the body to each chapter of *Ulysses*, and constructed a huge scaffolding of Homeric correspondences, would count letters, words, sentences, paragraphs, and pages."[11] Kidd never ended up publishing the results of his theory, and his plan to recuperate the original layout was abandoned. But if Gilbert's publication of that schema made it impossible for readers to ignore the extent of Homer's presence after the 1930s, the reverse was happening to the numbers since each resetting of the novel, beginning with the fourth impression in 1926, effectively erased any patterns encoded in the lines, pages, and paragraphs of the original.[12] Facsimile editions are now widely available in print and digital formats, but that impulse to go a-counting has not gained traction in the meantime.

The practice of reading *Ulysses* by numbers that was recommended by Gilbert, promised by Kidd, and mastered by Hugh Kenner is not new of course. Numbers have long played a role in the production and reception of literary works and have been part of a numerological tradition prizing their allegorical and symbolic value for millennia.[13] Take Dante's intense admiration for nine as one powerful example. Looking back on the meaning of events in his life, as he does in *Vita Nuova*, he discovers the number everywhere. He is nine years old when first setting eyes upon the nine-year-old Beatrice, his intercessor, and though Florence is a small town, he only sees her again nine years later, long enough to change the direction of his life, before she dies on the "ninth day of the month."[14] According to Dante, the nine heavens counted by Ptolemy were in perfect alignment on the day of her earthly birth making her a miracle. And here is his proof: "the number three is the root of nine, for without any other number, multiplied by itself it gives nine, as we plainly see that three times three is nine. Therefore, if three is the sole factor of nine and the sole factor of miracles is three, that is, Father, Son, and Holy Ghost, who are three in One, then this lady is accompanied by the number nine so that it may be understood that she was a nine, or a miracle, whose root, namely of the miracle, is the miraculous Trinity itself."

Dismiss it, call it nonsense, refuse to buy into the logic, and still, for Dante, this number is a fact, not just a figure: Beatrice, the embodied number, nine, is a miracle.[15] Literary history is filled with all kinds of numerological puzzles, some more elaborate than others, and they can be found in works by Homer, Catullus, Vergil, Dante, Petrarch, Boccaccio, Spenser, Shakespeare, Milton, and Pope.[16] R. G. Peterson, in fact, has identified four distinct phases in the history of literary numerology—Alexandrians (ancient world), Aristotelians and Thomists (Middle Ages), Platonists and Pythagoreans (Renaissance), and Palladians (eighteenth century)[17]—but he acknowledges, as do several others, that there was a rapid decline at the end of the eighteenth century, inspired by a rationalism and empiricism suspicious of the mystical charge numbers can carry. But if listeners and readers have been trained at different moments over the millennia to recognize the presence of numbers in different literary works, it was not a skill that carried over into the discipline of literary criticism until the middle decades of the twentieth century when numerological criticism was in its heyday and led to the uncovering of a wide range of symmetrical constructions with the critics Alastair Fowler, A. Kent Hieatt, and Marie-Sofie Røstvig leading the charge.[18] Not only did they take the numbers seriously, but their intensely close readings of some major, mostly English poets, revealed that it was irresponsible to ignore them any longer. The motivation to write by numbers may change over time, along with the audience's ability to decode them, but R. G. Peterson is right to suggest that the literary use of measurement and the desire for symmetry is bound up with "deep human feelings about number, centers, circles, and limits—from the writer, like the early Greek philosopher, responding to the immediate circumstances of nature."[19]

In the 1960s, at a moment when numerologically minded critics were searching for symmetry, others were looking ahead to a future of machine-assisted reading. This newly emerging field of so-called humanities computing was planning to use computers to uncover patterns, symmetries, structures, and correspondences of several works at once. A few attempts were made to apply computers to the study of style, but the most successful results were confined to the compilation of concordances and word lists. Computers, in other words, were saving time through their capacity to compute, but they were not going to revolutionize the interpretation of literature or modify anyone's perspective on literary history.

Fast forward to the early 2000s and Franco Moretti's ambitious call for *distant reading*. By that time, humanities computing had already begun to evolve into a mode of computational criticism interested in conducting quantitative experiments on corpora that contained thousands of works with the goal of going even bigger. *Operationalizing* was fast becoming a new keyword for quantitative literary analysis, and it described the process by which concepts could be transformed into a series of operations that allow us to measure objects.[20] To know the concept required having the measurement to test it, and it could involve the sentence or paragraph but also work across genres and archives.

Living in a quant-obsessed computer age, it's tempting to think that numerology belongs somewhere in the cabinet of literary-critical curiosities: fun to show off now and again but nothing to take too seriously. And it's no surprise to discover that the Digital Humanities community pretends it never existed. That is a mistake because it would require ignoring a legitimate practice in a shared literary critical history and also one that we need nowadays to remind us that numbers have a qualitative dimension. To confront a number and to decipher what it means is not, strictly speaking, a quantitative exercise. There are values, some of them empirical, but history has taught us that they can have a mystical or aesthetic connotation.

Yet instead of seeing these two critical traditions as somehow opposed to each other, it can be more productive to consider what they share. For starters, numbers. Numerology is, in effect, a mode of computational reading adapted from a much earlier tradition of biblical exegesis that not only recodes words, lines, pages, and paragraphs as discrete and sequential units but also involves counting them to discover sequences, ordinal and cardinal positions, and sums. In addition, the numerological approach believes that the meaning of a text cannot be found only in what the words or the structures that contain them say. The numbers, both alone and together, can speak. The possibility of a message hidden within them requires that someone is there who can identify, decode, and interpret.

That same impulse drives computational literary analysis (CLA). In the most basic terms, CLA counts literary texts. The major difference involves the fact that these texts are digitized, which means they can be coded by an extensible markup language (XML) and fed into different processing programs. Like numerology, CLA believes literary works are not made of words alone or, to put it another way, that the words in literature mean more than they say. And whether analyzing syntax, genre, style, or narrators, a computational approach treats literature as data for all kinds of formal and statistical analysis. I am not arguing here about the validity of numerology, and I have no interest in trying to convince anyone that CLA is really numerology in a digital age. Rather, I want to reorient how we understand the relationship between the two precisely because *Ulysses* is a novel that holds them both in suspension—the symbolic and the empirical, the qualitative and the quantitative, the abstract and the concrete, the mystical and the rational. The numbers of *Ulysses* are never just numerological or computational: they are both. And that is precisely the reason that the numerological and the computational can inform each other whenever reading by numbers is at stake.

Take "*number 7* Eccles Street" by way of an example.[21] It's the address of Leopold and Molly Bloom, but does that exact number really matter? What if it were 6, 14, or, why not, 9? For the numerologist, that number 7 might correspond with the days of creation and rest, but so what? How far does this connection take us in our interpretation of a fictional day in Dublin? A computational reading, on the other hand, would instead see that seven as a quantitative fact. Molly and Leopold live in the seventh unit located on Eccles Street, a real street in Dublin. And that's of potential interest for someone interested in the historical or topographical dimension of the novel, who might want to know that there was actually a 7 on that street in June 1904. But why argue over the validity of one or the other when they're both correct? Seven is a number *in a novel*, and it can have a qualitative and quantitative dimension. So even if it is charged with symbolic meaning, this digit also serves a quantitative function that contributes to the realism.

Ulysses may seem like a strange choice for anyone going in search of numbers. For one thing, it is a *modernist* novel, which means it belongs to an ironic moment in literary history that largely lacked any patience for sacred correspondences even if they came from an author who had renounced Catholicism but whose numerical sensibility kept his appreciation for its rituals and symbols. But *Ulysses* is also a *novel*, belonging to a genre without a particularly strong numerological tradition. A lack of rigorous rules for formal composition may be one reason, but Alastair Fowler has argued that prose is also to blame since it teaches readers "to move relatively quickly along the semantic line."[22] If readers of verse are conditioned to meditate on words and lines in search of mathematical patterns, novel readers can be found speeding along into nothingness. Perhaps that's a fitting end, given György Lukács's definition of the novel as the "epic of a world that has been abandoned by God." But if God is absent from *Ulysses*, critics such as Ernst Robert Curtius have claimed that number has a "form-bestowing factor in the divine work of creation" making Dante's *Commedia* an obvious precursor, with Kidd arguing that the "numeric patterns" make *Ulysses* as "consummately ordered" as Spenser and Dante.[23]

All of this numerical ordering makes *Ulysses* seem like a literary relic from a bygone age. Some of his contemporaries may have been steeped in the mysticism of Eastern religions, but Joyce builds primarily on Greek, Christian, and Hebrew models with a specific literary lineage. Dante's influence looms large, but that's also part of an intertextual strategy for advertising his own oversized ambition. To write by numbers by 1922 was one way to insert yourself into an established tradition. Numbers, then, were not simply ornaments or offhand allusions. They could be adapted to set the foundation for a fictional work and insert the novelist into a preexisting literary-historical chronology.

III

"A man can learn more music by working on a Bach fugue until he can take it apart and put it together, than by playing through ten dozen heterogeneous albums."[24] That was Pound's recommendation, and it served as a warning to others that vast reading does not automatically lead one to knowledge. You first have to decide which examples to choose and how best to read what's already available.[25] Here's the reason for my choice: *Ulysses* is a "morphological nightmare" (Franco Moretti) and a "memorable catastrophe" (Virginia Woolf) in the history of the novel.[26] Nothing quite like it existed before 1922, and its arrival in the world marked both a beginning and an end in literary history. So radical were Joyce's experiments with language, literary form, character, and narration that it forced generations of readers, writers, and critics to wonder not only *what literature can be* but also what it may end up becoming.

But can these numbers from *Ulysses*, and *Ulysses* alone, really teach us anything if we don't also draw comparisons from a more expansive sample? Such a reduction in scale may be a way to learn about one nightmarish novel in literary history, but it is not how things tend to get done in quantitative fields in the natural and social sciences or in an emerging humanist one that includes CLA.[27] Working with a variety of computational tools, CLA emphasizes that big data can be drawn from corpora (often digitized and available in online archives) and then run through different statistical models before the empirical results can be visualized and interpreted. Reading at such a scale is done in the hopes of trying to answer some of the foundational questions in the field of literary criticism (What is a poem? Who reads novels? What is the life cycle of genres?), and any data point in the sample is meaningful insofar as it fits within the clearly defined parameters of the specific quantitative measurement whether it involves a search for hidden haikus, the number of topics per paragraph, gender imbalances, or the semantic uniformity of characters.[28]

That is not the approach I am taking in the chapters that follow, and it's not just because of the reduced scale. The distant reading of literary data is being conducted in search of large-scale *patterns*, but in the broad sweep, it is a practice that has so far ignored the qualitative value of literary numbers, both as it exists in the printed numerals contained within specific literary objects and, more problematically, in the transformation of these same literary objects into data. CLA, then, may need the numbers for interpretation, but to get them, it employs quantitative methods that erase granularity and nuance, thereby defusing the interpretive charge that these numbers can carry. So even as CLA will, no doubt, continue to compile datasets from different literary samples in the hopes of proving or disproving the validity of various concepts, there's a downside we need to be aware of: generating more numbers should not make us forget that we are dealing with *literary objects*. Whatever measurements get taken, there is a qualitative dimension to the numbers that necessarily influences how the data itself gets defined, used, and interpreted (more on that later).

So, as much as I share CLA's affinity for numerical thinking, my approach is different. For one thing, I use the data from a single sample so my conclusions are not replicable, meaning they do not automatically apply to the same question being asked of other literary texts or concepts.[29] So when I focus on word counts, for instance, connecting them with the material pressure of serialization and narrative experimentation, I am not recommending that the same conclusions should inform our understanding of all serialized novels. And when I count characters to foreground Joyce's gradual discovery of the dimensions of the crowd, the results cannot be extrapolated to discuss trends in novelistic crowd control across the twentieth century. Others may, indeed, follow my example, applying these same small-scale methods to different works, but if comparisons are going to be drawn between samples, context will be critical and need to account for the ways a literary work is produced and circulated at a particular moment in history.

My approach to numbers is different for another reason: the data sets in this book are relatively small and the computational methods basic. In two of the five chapters (involving the collection and counting of words, paragraphs), the data was run through statistics-based text-analysis programs (Voyant and R). Someone could potentially use punch cards or some other manual indexing method (as done in the precomputer processing days), but the amount of time required is often enormous and the data, once sifted and structured, would not be as easily manipulated when searching for different results. In two other chapters (collecting and counting subscribers and characters), I relied on more sophisticated computational tools (ArcGIS and Cytoscape) that made it possible to visualize the data in different formats. Again, someone could potentially generate network diagrams and maps by hand, but these programs also made it possible to employ different filters. In both cases, the diagram and the map were modified during the research process as new avenues for critical investigation emerged.

Quantitatively inclined critics may scoff at the simplicity of the sample, tools, and methods, tempted perhaps to imagine *"Ulysses" by Numbers* as something akin to CLA-light or low-res Digital Humanities, but that's only because there has been a great deal of confusion about what counts as computational *literary* analysis in the first place. When Moretti recommended that his fellow critics develop new strategies for distant reading, supporters—and even some detractors—agreed that the big data and statistical models made the best sense, but that was largely because the whole enterprise was driven by fantasies about macroanalysis and a desire to uncover the laws of the literary universe.[30] Nothing of the sort has taken place—not even close—and most quantitative critics are becoming more accustomed to the limits that kill the fantasy but also seem more resigned to work with what they've got, which regularly translates into what's already digitized (or digitizable), archived, and not protected by copyright.[31]

I begin from the simple premise that a computational approach does not have to involve distant reading at dizzying scales to be valuable as literary criticism. In the past few decades, Digital Humanities has been tracing its lineage to the concordance building of Father Roberto Busa (beginning in 1946 when he enlisted IBM to assist in the compilation of an *Index Thomisticus*), and the tendency is to emphasize the impact that computers have had on the relationship between scholar and text.[32] Quantitative philology can certainly benefit from computers, but it does not depend on them. Instead, it emphasizes a reading practice once anchored in the stylistic analysis of Leo Spitzer, Ernst Robert Curtius, and Erich Auerbach during the same period as Busa, and it was adapted in the 1960s for the computational stylistics of Karl Kroeber, Louis Milic, and others.[33]

If the computer-generated index could facilitate the search across texts, philology had its eye on style—that most elusive quality defining the essence of authors and the periods and places in which they live even if it can be difficult to pinpoint. In his defense of the scientific nature of stylistic analysis, Spitzer writes:

> From the surface to the "inward life-center" of the work of art; first observing details about the superficial appearance of the particular word (and the "ideas" expressed by the poet are, also, only one of the superficial traits in a work of art); then, grouping these details and seeking to integrate them into a creative principle which may have been present in the soul of the artist; and, finally, making the return trip to all the other groups of observations in order to find whether the "inward form" one has tentatively constructed gives an account of the whole.[34]

Part to whole, inward to outward, detail to idea, form to soul: these are the categories that define stylistic analysis. It is not a practice that only moves in one direction, generalizing from the small details, nor is it a mode of reading that seeks to draw broad conclusions across literary history. Stylistic analysis is itself a way to access the *literariness of a specific work*, a vast and complicated topic, but it is central to how we define the very object of analysis and the task of the literary critic.[35] Literariness is what separates the *Iliad* from the newspaper, *To the Lighthouse* from a laundry list, and there seems to be no end to the reasons why the two should ever be confused.

Yet with the arrival of machine learning, statistical analysis, and algorithmic reading, this is precisely what can happen. I'm not suggesting that CLA is part of a sinister plot to erase literariness, but it is making that literariness difficult to recognize. And this is not just because of the scale. Rather, it has a lot to do with the assumptions about what makes literary data, well, data. Consider the case of *Moby-Dick*. Someone working in CLA could throw this novel into a corpus of 500,000 others to try and define the genre of the American novel between, say, 1851 and 1951. Once the words were assembled into a collection of types (number of unique words) and tokens (total number of words), it would be possible to search for frequency, number of words per sentence, categories of words, and so on. The data will eventually get visualized, showing fluctuations over time, perhaps even indicating shifts in word usage, sentence length, or gendered pronouns, and that will be followed by an argument about the possibility that there are generic trends and conventions that can be discerned over several decades in the history of the novel.

But where is *Moby-Dick*? That's Ahab's question, of course, but in this case, it reminds us what's getting lost in this sea of big data: the novel itself. No one will take the empirical results about genre and read Melville's novel differently. Instead, the quantitative data is there as a collection of facts about a larger category to which *Moby Dick* may or may not belong, the kind that weigh and measure Moby Dick as if he would ever be caught dead hanging on a hook. And here's the problem: this approach tends to treat the data as something that can be detached from the literary work itself, as if *Moby-Dick* and Moby Dick are not mutually constitutive. But the truth is that the data in this work, or any other literary work for that matter, is immanent, something deeply embedded in every aspect of the object itself, not just the words or their arrangement and rhythm or their selection or mobilization though different narrative techniques and modes of representation but everywhere. To reduce it to words that can be removed, cleaned, and measured along with thousands of other samples might tell us something about processes in literary history or even about some of the ways techniques and narration work, but they are not to be confused with the thing itself. Instead of taking apart the Bach fugue and putting it back together, CLA surveys the ten dozen heterogeneous albums without ever making all the details add up.

At whatever scale, and regardless of sample size, computational work in the humanities has come to depend on making literary data visible. In one of the few sustained investigations of this trend, Moretti and Oleg Sobchuk point out that the presence of scatterplots, timelines, diagrams, and histograms are the "one feature that immediately distinguishes Digital Humanities from the 'other' humanities."[36] Pervasive, maybe, but still undertheorized, which is a problem since the transformation of literary data into statical two-dimensional images is not just done for the sake of illustration: it is a necessary stage in the interpretation. Computational literary analysis has come to depend upon graphic design for its display of quantitative information. But the more that data visualization in the humanities moves beyond simplistic graphs, bars, diagrams, and charts, the more it needs to consider how the visual experience plays an important role in the interpretive process. Visualizations may *reveal* data, as Edward Tufte once put it, but they are also conceptual—the shape, structure, and layout part of a vocabulary meant to communicate a message that is not, strictly speaking, in the data itself.

Take, for example, my discussion of characters in *Ulysses* (chapter 3), in which I am concerned, above all, with trying to understand the scale both at the level of the episode but also in between and across all episodes. The critics who already work on character systems or spaces are accustomed to thinking in terms of time-based narrative structures consumed by readers forced to wade through sequences of words. But what happens when the network makes these same characters visible at a glance? Meet *Ulysses* (Figure 0.1). Using Cytoscape, an open-source network analysis platform,

0.1   Character network of *Ulysses*.

I generated a visualization that includes all the characters that make at least one appearance in the novel.[37]

Seeing the character space as a diagram is an opportunity to capture some of the wonder that the sentences and paragraphs conceal. Taken together, these 592 nodes are beautiful, capturing a wholeness that no reader ever experiences when working at the level of the individual word or line. What we get instead is a two-dimensional image identifying character quantities and relations, but it is one that draws our attention to a symphony in progress, all of these parts woven together to generate a harmony that can be felt even when the prospect of imagining it as an image might seem impossible. More than a symphony for the eyes, though, the network diagram is there to make us question what's happening in the structure of the novel itself. In short, it is the record that documents the building of a countable community. Joyce never had a master list of all the characters who would make an appearance. The network was a gradual process, one that he continued to modify on the fly as the plot unfolded. Seeing the novel as a network helps us to imagine character less as a mimetic problem and more as a quantitative one. With the arrival of each episode, characters were added, subtracted, and rearranged, but the process of determining how to make a room, street, or pub feel crowded had to be resolved. The network image doesn't provide the resolution, but it does generate an estrangement that lets us approach the literary object differently, moving between time and space, up above and down below, to explore the creative process accompanied by quantitative information that anchors our analysis and comparisons.

Data to visualization to interpretation: the character network is itself an opportunity to wrestle with some of the fundamental questions about how *Ulysses* was made. Instead of keeping us at a distance, gazing at the distribution of nodes and edges, the interpretation requires diving back in for context, which in this case demands knowing when certain quantities of characters appear in the plot and what stage in the compositional process they may have arrived or recirculated. But there's another qualification to make as well, and it is one that informs how to approach the visualizations appearing in the pages that follow. Though built from literary data, they are by no means an attempt to reduce the complexity of the novel or pretend as if visualizations alone are the answer. Instead, the interpretation works against the grain, making it hard to ignore the fact that the qualitative experience we have with this novel exceeds any and all the data we can collect. Still, it's worth trying, if for no other reason than that the decoding might bring us closer to understanding some of the intellectual and emotional effects of *Ulysses* that continue to elude empirical and mystical explanations alike. And if we're lucky, it will belong to the kind of criticism that can make the "preconscious," as R. P. Blackmur once called it, *consciously* available."[38]

IV

"Limited to the text alone and without a guiding set of directions, how would we read Joyce's *Ulysses* if it were not titled *Ulysses*?" Though he was never one to count the letters of the title, it's a question Gérard Genette asks in an attempt to explain what's really going on in the pages of any novel's paratext.[39] The paratextual details assembled in the overture are part of an authorized commentary on *Ulysses*, telling readers at the outset that the meaning of this novel is not going to be found in the words only. Numbers abound as well, and they have a charge that is symbolic, structural, material, historical, economic, literary, and political. Ignore all of the ways that they get woven in and around the words, and you miss out on a message spelled out for all readers to see.

Opportunities for finding numerical correspondences and making calculations continue as soon as the paratext ends. And in what follows, I want to tackle some of the more prominent ones. That first sentence of twenty-two words is certainly a good start, but Kidd, second only to Kenner in numerical wizardry, believed that it should be joined with the first lines of the other two sections, one with fourteen words, the other with seven. Add them all up, Kidd argues, and you will find your way to a literary allusion: " 'Stately, plump Buck Mulligan' is introduced in three sentences of forty-three words stopped with a colon. Then follow the first four words spoken in *Ulysses*, themselves from the opening of the Mass: *Introibo ad altare Dei*. Turning to that fount of English letters, the Protestant King James Bible, which Joyce drew on more than the Catholic Douay version, we find at *Psalms* 43:4, 'then I will go unto the altar of God.' "[40]

Like Kenner, Kidd was fascinated by the *numberiness* of *Ulysses*.[41] Examples of numerical puzzles can certainly be found in other novels, but the effort is never as sustained or deliberate, and they include the fact that Milly Bloom's fifteen-line letter (excluding the postscript) was written on her fifteenth birthday, there are three 3s in the thirty-third line of a section of episode 7, page seventy-seven has a reference to "Seventh heaven," and eight words are added to page eighty-eight during the proof stage.[42] As entertaining as these numbers can be for the most attentive readers, they also provide a structural clarity, giving some of the most fleeting details a numerical charge and position within an overwhelming mass of material.

"Numbers are definite": that's Kenner again, who goes on to explain that "Whatever is sufficiently definite attracts correspondences, and *Ulysses* with its thousands of clear-cut stipulations, a book in which each separate word seems thrown into relief, attracts them like burrs."[43] *Ulysses*, in Kenner's formulation, is all *numburrs*, a novel that invites readers to notice them even if their full significance remains obscure. The first reviewers scrambling to get a handle on the novel would regularly reference the number of pages and the years of composition as if they were meaningful in their own right. "It contains 730 pages," reads one unsigned review, with another reporting "seven hundred big pages."[44] "It has taken Mr. Joyce seven years to write *Ulysses*," Edmund Wilson pointed out in the *New Republic*, "and he has done it in seven hundred and thirty pages [*sic*] which are probably the most completely 'written' pages to be seen in any novel since Flaubert."[45] Seven years with what was really 732 pages of print and 736 if you count the ones left blank at the end: What, other than the repetition of the number seven, would compel anyone to mention these details? There are novels with durations and dimensions that far exceed these, and yet getting the number of years and pages nailed down seemed like an effective way to make *Ulysses* tangible.

Though these particular numbers would eventually come to mean something—both to Joyce and to his audience—*Ulysses* was a work in progress for seven years and 732 pages, one with a structure that was changing *as the writing, revising, and creating was being done*. Readers are invited to contemplate its conception through computation, and that, to draw on Kenner once more, is possible because it is a "printed book whose pages are numbered."[46] Printing didn't just get the words down on paper: it separated them into line breaks, paragraphs, and page breaks. Numbered pages worked like the cardinal points on a compass for Joyce during the composition process, one that was made all the more difficult by the fact that placards were arriving unpaginated. "Mr Joyce asks us what was the number of the last page actually printed" ["M. Joyce nous demandait quel [sic] était le numéro de la dernière page actuellement tirée"], was a question Joyce directed repeatedly at Maurice Darantière's office. No surprise given the fact that after episode 5, when they moved from using placards to proofs and back to placards because of the repeated revisions, it was common enough to have several episodes getting revised simultaneously and sent back and forth out of order.[47] A hastily sketched calculation by Joyce on Darantière's letter a few weeks later, for example, reveals that he wanted to know where the printing of placard 20 left the overall count. Turns out the printers had reached the end of episode 12, but given the fact that they were also setting up episode 18, it appears Joyce would have had, for the first time, a more definite sense of an end point, a detail, as I'll explain shortly, that factors into one of Kidd's most fantastic, if uncorroborated, theories about Joyce's page puzzles (figure 0.2).[48]

Ending up with 732 printed pages required a great deal of effort from everyone involved: Joyce writing and revising, Sylvia Beach paying and mediating, and Darantière and his team setting and resetting. In the negotiations that took place in late April 1921, 592 pages was the original projection and it included thirty-seven leaves of sixteen pages each using nine-point Didot typeface. Joyce preferred the other option, Elzevir 10, which raised the estimate to 720 (using forty-five leaves), but the increased paper costs were the obvious downside. After a meeting in Paris, of which no record exists, Elzevir 11 was chosen; but a month later Darantière was still under the impression he could keep it all under "six cents" if he added more lines per page and increased the number of words per line.[49] With the mass of corrections Joyce was sending back and telephoning in, he was clearly not helping the cause—forcing Beach to change the page count on the flyers by hand (figure 0.3). By September, a frustrated Darantière was warning Beach that the "très grande nombre de corrections" were not only making the novel longer, they were threatening to carry the work over into another year.[50] By the end, these additional corrections ended up costing as much as the original estimate for paper.[51]

Given how many possible variables were at play in the ten months between the original negotiation and the final date of publication, it is remarkable to discover that *Ulysses* only ended up requiring one gathering

Maurice Darantiere
maistre imprimeur
A Dijon

2.440

trois novembre
mil neuf cent
vingt et un

Miss Sylvia Beach
P a r i s (VI°)
Rue de l'Odéon I2

Ulysses --- Le retour des signatures I9 et 20 nous est nécessaire pour
la continuation de la mise en pages,signatures 2I et suivantes. Nous
possédons ici les placards 37,38 et 39 bons à mettres en pages.

Daignez agréer, Mademoiselle,l'expression de mes respectueux hommages.

Maurice Darantière

252 — 288 — 17°
288 — 304 — 18°
304 — 320 — 19°
320 — 336 — 20°

6/2/2
1/2
96 ⌐16

0.2 Letter from Maurice Darantière to Sylvia Beach, November 1921, with Joyce's marginalia.

ULYSSES suppressed four times during serial publication in "The Little Review" will be published by "SHAKESPEARE AND COMPANY" complete as written.

This edition is private and will be limited to 1.000 copies :

100 copies signed on Dutch hand made paper. . . . . **350** fr
150 copies on vergé d'Arches. . . . . **250** fr.
750 copies on hand made paper . . . . **150** fr.

The work will be a volume in-8° crown of 732 pages.

Subscribers will be notified when the volume appears, which will be sent to them by registered post immediately on receipt of payment.

All correspondence, cheques, money-orders should be addressed to :

Miss *SYLVIA BEACH*

" SHAKESPEARE AND COMPANY "

*12, RUE DE L'ODÉON, PARIS — VI*ᵉ

0.3   Prospectus for *Ulysses* with correction to number of pages.

more than the original forty-five that Darantière issued in his estimate and more as a warning than a desirable option.[52] If there were actual negotiations about the paper increase in the final months, no record exists. The printing would go on even while the novel remained unfinished and the costs increased. But there was one significant downside: the inside of *Ulysses* was a mess. Peter de Voogd explains that more words per line and more lines per page generated a cramped layout that violated the proportions of harmonious book design. In an effort to make it all fit, Darantière extended the line farther into the margin, resulting in what John Ryder calls an "ill-conceived book."[53] For Wim van Mierlo, this unsymmetrical page was the material expression of the novel's difficulty, which ended up intimidating readers and annoying critics.[54] Joyce, at least, didn't care: all the episodes were made to fit into 732 pages, with the added serendipity that the last page, containing the late addition of so many *yeses*, added up to twenty-two lines of text.

1,000 is another number that's not quite what it seems. Prominently displayed on the limitation page I mentioned earlier, it only accounts for the copies intended for public distribution. There were another twenty unnumbered ones that Joyce originally designated for friends and reviewers in England (six), France (six) and across the Continent (five), with another three for family members back in Ireland (none reserved for the Irish press). Once Darantière began printing copies out of order in February and March, there was a change in the plan. Joyce wanted to add another forty in an effort to generate more promotional buzz, but it was never to be: there were too many damaged copies (including the ones nailed through during the crating of one shipment) and the type was also getting worn out. Darantière recommended adding another one hundred or two hundred copies with the molds, but it was expensive, and there was already talk with Harriet Shaw Weaver about a second impression through the Egoist Press in the fall of 1922.[55]

By the time *Ulysses* appeared, the dimensions no longer corresponded with the ones laid in the spring of 1921. But how much material was really added during this final push? "*Ulysses* grew by one-third in proof" has been a common refrain for decades, a line repeated verbatim that can be traced back to Sylvia Beach, who, in turn, claims to have picked it up from the man himself.[56] Anyone who compares the word counts in the Rosenbach manuscript and those with the final episodes as printed in Gabler's edition, however, will discover that this quantity is more fiction than fact: *grew by one-fifth* is more like it.[57] Still, the phrase "grew by one-third" is as much a qualitative designation as it is a quantitative one.[58] And what if this phrase has been more useful as a rhetorical gesture than a genetic fact? It wouldn't be the first time a number that sounded accurate turned out to be misleading. Such is the case, for instance, with the mathematical conundrum appearing in episode 17 about a number so large that it would yield "33 closely printed volumes of 1,000 pages each." Kenner actually did the calculation and discovered that the math was all wrong: the yield is thirty-seven and not thirty-three. Still, he argues, this number "has the ring of rightness."[59]

With "grew by one-third," we find ourselves in a similar situation. The ratio may be wrong, but there is still a rightness if we follow the logic of threes in this novel: three sections, two of them bookending the novel with three episodes. For Joyce to write one-third of the novel on the proofs is another way of suggesting this was part of a longer plan. Without that addition of one-third for the final four episodes in their complete form (roughly 86,000 words), *Ulysses* would have ended up as a more modestly-sized 150,000 word novel, which would mean that the page count would have been closer to five hundred with the composition completed well before 1922.[60] A shorter novel, a shorter timeline but a different set of numbers for a different object. One-third does not mean anything on its own, but in the context of all the other numbers mapped onto the narrative of its becoming, it has evolved into a *ratio of rightness* that is, indeed, free from the burden of accuracy.

The number of episodes is more definite; but as with the previous example, there's a twist. What began as twenty-two distributed across the three sections as 4+15+3 ended up as eighteen with a sequence of 3+12+3.[61] It's a more symmetrical arrangement that has strong similarities with the ring composition of Homer's *Iliad*, one in which the episodes at the end have strong structural similarities with the first three (1/24, 2/23, 3/22). But what does it mean to know that *Ulysses* is comprised of eighteen episodes or that it can be further subdivided into three sections of three, twelve, three? Do these quantities, selected and arranged by Joyce in that order, shape the reading of the novel in any significant way? The quick answer is yes. There is an interpretive charge for the numbers of individual episodes as they appear in sequence (1, 2, 3, 4, and so on), and it works because there is an overarching structure giving them coherence. Together, they generate a series of correspondences extending far beyond Dublin or the twentieth century.

In Jewish mysticism, eighteen corresponds with the value of letters in the Hebrew word for *life (chet+yud=chai)*.[62] Twelve is known as the "great astrological and scriptural number" identified with the months in a year, the hours in a day and a night, the principal parts of the human body. It is also a number that can be divided further into three 4s or four 3s (4x3). That is one of the reasons seven (4+3) and twelve (4x3) are "rightly considered" another form of each other, both of them numbers underpinning the quantities of time and space of the universe (seven planets, seven days, twelve signs of the zodiac, twelve hours of the day). Three has been around since "the dawn of history," embraced by Christianity for the Holy Trinity, and four counts the cardinal points, phases of the moon, and the elements.[63] The habit of using Homeric titles in reference to each episode has effectively obscured these numerical foundations. Going back to them, as I do throughout this book, may actually refocus our attention on their ordinal and cardinal significance allowing us to understand the cross-referencing that also occurs between numbers.

An ordinal set of numbers are contained *in the episodes* as well. *Ulysses* begins twice at 8 A.M. (in episodes 1 and 4), with the hours of the clock synchronizing at noon in episode 7, with 9 o'clock absent, and then continuing until 2 A.M., with the hours between 9 and 10 p.m. unaccounted for. But if a ticking clock helps to unify the events on a single day in Dublin 1904, together they correspond with all time, all space, all life. That tension between the micro and the macro, the universe and Dublin, is what makes Kidd's theory about the middle of *Ulysses* so tantalizing, and it is only one part of an argument about a more extensive "numeric pattern" concealed within the novel itself.[64] If there are eighteen episodes total, we would expect the middle to be somewhere between episodes 9 and 10. It's a logical supposition that explains why Joyce would have written the words "End of First Part of *Ulysses*" on a fair copy manuscript after episode 9. It is halfway if you're counting episodes, but it's only around 2 or 3 p.m. if you're keeping track of the clock in the plot. Kidd locates the other middle in episode 13, using the evidence of a passing phrase planted in one of Bloom's monologues: "Done half by design." Turns out that this phrase appears on page 366, the exact middle of the novel if we're measuring pages, but also the number of days in 1904, a leap year.[65]

Kidd never did end up publishing the evidence that would definitively prove Joyce knew the last page number of his novel when he wrote this phrase, but it would have been a stunning authorial feat.[66] And still, there it is: "Done half by design," on the very same page that Bloom prepares to leave the beach before returning to a now darkened Dublin, which will dominate the second half of the plot (and the five episodes that remain in the next 366 pages). This division in the middle of the novel reorients the time and space: *Ulysses* is two halves now, day and night, but also a single year, since the day itself, represented as 366, also condenses the time of the year in which it appears. According to Kidd, 732 was the number you get when adding the days in a leap year to the number of nights.

V

The examples I discuss in this book are a powerful reminder that the numbers of *Ulysses* may have a distinct material history, but the relevance of all these sums, ratios, sequences, and single digits is still anchored in the belief that an intention lurks behind it all, leaving readers with two options: either there is archival evidence to prove that a numerical correspondence was deliberate or arguments get made to try and establish degrees of plausibility. In a book devoted entirely to the subject, John MacQueen seems to think so. "Literary numerology," he argues, "may be defined as the theory of verse and prose composition in terms of which an author *deliberately incorporates in the text* of his work numerical patterns which he regards as conveying precise significance."[67] By this definition, whatever claims critics make about the meaning of specific numbers—the twenty-four books of the *Iliad*, the "double center" in *Paradise Lost*, the one hundred Cantos of the *Commedia*, and the eighteen episodes of *Ulysses*—there is the implicit assumption that they were put there on purpose. But if computation in its search for quantity leads us away from intention, it is not as remote from qualitative claims as it may seem.

By way of an example, consider the word counts of *Ulysses*. Once
you know that Joyce stays around a six-thousand-word limit for the
first three episodes (as was recommended by Ezra Pound for something
short), what does that tell you? And what can be learned once you discover that Joyce doubles and then triples the word count per episode as
the novel progresses? The answer is not to be found in the significance of
six, twelve, or eighteen thousand. In fact, these specific numbers mean
nothing at all here in numerological terms. Instead, it is the relationship
between the various quantities that can help us understand how the proportion of the novel was achieved. Joyce may have had a sense of scale in
and across episodes, but there is a numerical unconscious at work, and
it is one that helps us to demystify the process by which the novel was
built over time.

Trying to pin down what *Ulysses* is nowadays can be tricky. Out of copyright in the European Union since 2012 (and almost never in copyright in
the United States), it is in the process of being *remade*.[68] The book will
continue to circulate in printed editions, of course, but the digital versions
are becoming more widely available—the most ambitious one includes
Gabler's XML upgrade to his critical and synoptic edition.[69] And while
digital versions such as this one do away with the original line counts and
pagination, they are encouraging readers to try out different computational procedures.[70] Using his 1922 edition, Kidd may have been able to
track down a Biblical allusion in the first five lines of episode 1, but just
imagine what he would make of the following:

```
<div type="episode" n="01">
<p rend="inset"><lb n="010000"/>I</p>
<p><lb n="010001"/>Stately, plump Buck Mulligan came from the
   stairhead, bearing a
<lb n="010002"/>bowl of lather on which a mirror and a razor lay crossed.
   A yellow
<lb n="010003"/><distinct type="nonstandard-compound">dressinggown
   </distinct>, <distinct type="archaism">ungirdled</distinct>, was sustained
   gently behind him on the mild
<lb n="010004"/>morning air. He held the bowl aloft and intoned:
<lb n="010005"/><said who="bm">-<quote xml:lang="la">Introibo ad
   altare Dei.</quote></said></p>
```

Joyce's words are still there, but they are now a dataset described using XML.[71] XML allows for the creation of a specific set of tags to identify paragraph breaks (<p>) and line breaks (<lb>) but also the character speaking ("bm" for Buck Mulligan), the presence of foreign words ("lang=Latin" in this case), and the creation of new ones (<distinct type="nonstandard-compound">). Indeed, the lines above may represent a version of *Ulysses*, but they are definitely not *as Joyce wrote them*.

That, however, is not the point: this digital *Ulysses* is there *to help us read the words by having the computer count for us*. And there's no getting around the fact that reading by numbers is the new normal in the digital age. The computer does not recognize words. It follows a series of commands, made possible by the markup that can be used to conduct different kinds of searches on a *datafied* novel. Number is now impossible to miss. It is there in the all-pervasive "n," a tag that identifies page, line, and episode number, serving as a reminder that this sum of more than 263,000 words had to be distributed somehow.

In order to compare multiple copies electronically for his edition, Gabler and his team keyboarded all the relevant documents word by word, generating an electronic file that contained a cleaned-up final version. By making the output files public and searchable, Gabler is paving the way for a whole range of computational readings in the future. I say *future*, of course, but Kenner was using them back in the late 1980s at a time when they still had to be transferred by floppy disk.[72] Not a surprise given that he once described *Ulysses* as "data thrust into a computer and whirled through permutations baffling to the imagination but always traceable by careful reason."[73]

Getting his hands on "the master tape," Kenner was only interested in what he could do with the result: count. "I can tell you how many exclamation marks pepper the opening episode of *Ulysses*," he reported without any irony. Sixty-one is the answer, but Kenner didn't stop there. He followed it up with the number of shriek marks in episodes 3, 7, and 11 (38, 86, 103), the presence of *-ly* terminations in episode 1 (120), and the observation that the swine references in episode 15 include "twenty-four pigs, six hogs, three swine, six instances of 'pork' even one of 'porc.'"[74] For Kenner, the computerized *Ulysses* has the potential to enhance our experience with the printed version by allowing us to search through more than a quarter of a million words with unprecedented speed and accuracy. "Silicon elves," he writes, can "keep count of punctuation marks and word terminations" much faster than us humans.[75] Fast or not, the numbers don't become meaningful just because they had been discovered, and the twenty-four pig references are a far cry from the twenty-two words echoing the rhythm of Homer's hexameter.

But even if Kenner's early results were less than revolutionary, they provide some more clarity on the distinction I mentioned before between numerology and CLA. The numbers Kenner finds are by no means intentional. So while Joyce may have been aware that he was laying on the pork references in episode 15 precisely in order to play off the idea that Odysseus's men were turned to swine, that final number, twenty-four, does not fit into an extraliterary system for signification. What Kenner discovers instead is the efficacy of a search tool capable of measuring aspects of *Ulysses* that are simply unknown. Getting the measurements can make the language and syntax concrete, but the goal should be conceptual; that is, it should make us question how they are built into a more elaborate structure that holds them together.

Counting *Ulysses* is a way to read it. It is a situation not unlike Bloom's as he stands alone amidst all the pebbles on the beach. "Who could count them," he wonders, "Never know what you find" (*U*, 312). Kenner didn't know either, but his playful experiment with a computerized version was significant for its predictive power, even if the results were less than compelling. A more substantial event in the computational history of *Ulysses* involved a word index first compiled by Miles Hanley, who was doing research for a *Linguistic Atlas of New England*, and Charles Kingsley Zipf, who had been conducting statistical investigations into word frequency. *Ulysses* was an ideal sample for both because of its length and diversity (260,430 total words by Hanley's count using the 1934 Random House edition).[76] Zipf had been working on smaller samples to try and demystify word distribution, but not long after getting his hands on the word index, he made a major discovery: *Ulysses* was "harmonically seriated." That means that the word frequency across the corpus follows a pattern and is evenly proportioned. In fact, after testing the results against a variety of other literary works—including the *Iliad*, *Beowulf* and the plays of Plautus—Zipf concluded that it was "the most clear-cut example of a harmonic distribution in speech" he had ever encountered (figure 0.4).[77]

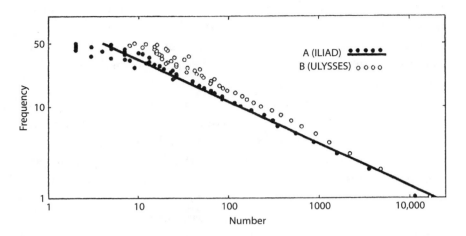

o.4   George Zipf, "The number-frequency relationship of words. (A) Homer's *Iliad*; (B) Joyce's *Ulysses*."

Source: Courtesy of Pearson Company.

In this first systematic attempt to read *Ulysses* by numbers, Zipf was able to prove that the frequency of words is inversely proportional to their rank. The most common word will appear twice as often as the second, five times more than the fifth, and so on. Given that *Ulysses* has 260,430 total words, 29,899 of them unique (by Hanley's count), this doubling occurs every tenth word. So if, for example, the tenth most common word appears 2,653 times, then we could expect that the twentieth most common word to appear approximately 1,300 times, the one thousandth most common word twenty-six times, and so on down the list.[78]

Most readers of *Ulysses* would have a difficult time imagining the novel as a statistical equation, but that's precisely what makes this example so fascinating: Zipf abstracted the literary object to test a theory about the distribution of unique words across a large corpus, and it worked. Preliminary investigations were also made by one of his students to test whether or not the frequency and rank were inversely proportional to the interval between repeated words across pages: for the limited sample tested (involving frequencies of twenty-four or less), it was.[79] Though Zipf's law would eventually get applied to a whole range of other nonliterary phenomena (height, urban density, earthquake magnitudes, the structure of the internet), he did have one specific takeaway for *Ulysses*: Joyce, he believed, "systematically tended to avoid repeating words."[80] Which words? Zipf doesn't say, but it is a compelling point of departure for anyone curious about word diversity. It also shows how the numbers derived from computational analysis provide a qualitative perspective that would certainly elude the author but also the index or word list. Hanley couldn't see it, Zipf could, and that's more or less where things ended.

Out of a word index to *Ulysses* a law about language frequency was born.[81] But as momentous as this encounter was for linguistics and statistical probability, it didn't do much to the way anyone actually read the novel—not least of all Hanley and Zipf, who were really just in it for the data. That is not the case with the chapters that follow. In fact, I want to make it clear from the start that the data is used to generate, complicate, and, at times, resist the interpretation of the novel. Numbers alone don't lie, but they can mislead, and so any attempt to read *by them* requires a healthy degree of skepticism about the methods and assumptions even when the results seem objective and verifiable.

Another point: I have been examining how two different critical approaches to numbers can be used to guide our interpretations of poems, novels, and plays. But I want to make one obvious declaration: these are *literary numbers*. Emphasizing the literariness is not a way to discredit the empirical or the symbolic and allegorical. Rather, it is a warning that we need to keep in mind where the numbers are appearing, to whom and through what means they are becoming available, and to what end they can be used. Our lives are saturated in numbers, and literature— because it is not real life—can use them differently. They do not have to be facts, they do not need to add up, they do not even have to be correct. It's not that literary texts don't count. Rather, it's that they don't have to count the same way and for the same ends. And that is what makes the entire literary numerical enterprise so fascinating. Something like a novel can be written and read, all the while making readers forget that there is always a limit to what can and cannot be told (in so many words), who can and cannot be there, how long events can and cannot last, and where the plot can and cannot go. Melville made an entire novel out of this premise, and in a stroke of genius, he managed to construct a plot convincing readers to keep their eye out for *one white whale* while so many other pods were swimming by.

VI

The idea for this project began with the novel, not the numbers. In fact, I can trace it back to the moment when I began asking a very simple question: Why is *Ulysses* as long as it is? "A book, even a very long book," René Wellek reminds us, "has to have some limits."[82] But as true as that statement may be, finding those limits requires that we approach the literary object not as something fixed but in flux—a work in progress with coordinates that had to be calibrated and recalibrated during an attenuated creative process. My interest in the actual numbers emerged once I realized that the word counts would give me a concrete sense of the proportions across the eighteen episodes, thereby making it possible to focus on the differences and the similarities, including the drastic spikes, averages, and deviations. Readers, even the most casual ones, will have a vague sense that some episodes are longer or shorter than others, but they would be less inclined to consider when episodes shared dimensions or consider why a specific set of dimensions might change, sometimes dramatically, from one section of the novel to another.

I may have started with a simple question about length, but with these numbers, I was in a position to see the novel from an entirely different perspective—the actual counts letting me think about *Ulysses* less as an accumulation of words with a message and more as a machine engineered to say something we're not accustomed to hear. Beginning with six thousand words in episode 1 and ending with twenty-four thousand in episode 18 was the end result of an organic process, the proportions of the episodes, both individually and in aggregate, resulting from choices made along the way to accommodate experiments with narrative techniques and shifts in plot but also the many different representations of time, space, and interiority. So just as it would be strange now to think of *Ulysses* opening with a twenty-four thousand word episode, try to imagine Molly Bloom tucked in bed with only six thousand or so words to spare. These aren't just different lengths: they would belong to a different novel. Length, then, is a quantitative barometer of sorts. It records what is happening to time, space, and narrative more generally in the novel, but it is also one of the most significant indicators documenting what was happening during the composition, and later the revision process, and would come to define the experience of every reader navigating one page at a time.

Each of the chapters that follow begin with a question about *Ulysses*—Who wrote it (chapter 1)? How long is it (chapter 2)? How many characters are there (chapter 3)? Who read it (chapter 4)? When was it written (chapter 5)?—using different datasets to try and find an answer. "Making Style Count" examines how paragraphs can be used for stylometry, a practice that relies on statistical analysis (word usage, frequency, and sentence structure) to decode authorial identity. Focusing specifically on the number of paragraphs per episode—but also as they evolved at various stages—this chapter argues that more than containing words, paragraphs were an opportunity to imagine what thought—realized narratively as interior monologue—looks like and the ways it could be modified to accommodate different experiences with time and space. This interest in the basic building blocks for the novel is the impetus for the next chapter, "Words in Progress." It takes the word counts from the episodes serialized in the *Little Review* but also, at times, compares them with the book versions to explore how limits on length can be used to understand the creative process and also considers what they tell us about the material conditions of its production and reception. "One or How Many?" turns our attention to those fictional beings who pass through these same words and paragraphs, asking a specific question: What makes a character count? The answer is not as straightforward as it might seem—especially once you begin to differentiate between degrees of *being there* whether as a major or minor character, as someone present in the plot or mentioned, or even dead or unborn. But even when we make the numbers speak to what's happening inside the novel, the question of where it went in the early months of 1922 is still a mystery. Using the data collected from lists, notebooks, subscription forms, and other records, "GIS Joyce" maps out the distribution of the first subscribers in order to understand, as much as possible, not just who read *Ulysses* but where. The final chapter, "Dating Ulysses," turns to the one number everyone thinks they know, the same one that tells us when *Ulysses* was written. Using the dateline Joyce left on the last page, this chapter explores, more broadly, if and how literary time can be represented quantitatively, especially when there is ambiguity regarding the point at which the literary work begins and ends.[83]

There's always going to be more to count, but *"Ulysses" by Numbers* is one attempt to recover a dimension that had to be lost long before it could ever be found. Getting the numbers down will enhance our appreciation for how *Ulysses* happened in the same way that the discovery of a first star in the sky can make us feel the vastness of the universe and the sound of a few passing musical notes the immensity of time. You could say that the numbers locate *Ulysses* in time, and working through them now by collecting, cleaning, visualizing, and interpreting the data, we get to discover the words, characters, paragraphs, pages, and first readers at scales we never quite noticed before. Doing so, we get to think of reading less as a critical effort to master the meaning of the words and more as a creative activity in which writing and reading by numbers converge and the novel itself comes to life over and over and over again.

These numbers in *Ulysses* are not just data: they're music. "Seven times nine minus x is thirtyfive thousand. Falls quite flat," Bloom observes in his imaginary equation, before admitting what's behind the magic: "It's on account of the sounds it is" (*U*, 228). And it will come as no surprise to discover that when Stephen and Bloom use the word *number* themselves, they're referencing a musical composition. That's just one more reminder that counting can help us hear the sounds on every page, each of the chapters that follow motivated by the spirit of the phrase that passes through Bloom's endlessly curious mind:

Numbers it is.

N.º 1
Making Style Count

Still if he works that paragraph.
—Leopold Bloom

I

Who wrote *Ulysses*? Probably not the question you were expecting at this point, but before responding (or dismissing it entirely), consider what evidence you'll draw on. All of it will be based on the firsthand or second-hand testimony from friends, colleagues, and acquaintances who knew the person responsible for creating it; then there will be the estimation of critics, some of who have worked closely with the relevant authenticated documents. This kind of authorial proof was not available to Homer, of course, and very little of it was around for Shakespeare, a writer still hounded by suspicions of authenticity.[1] Still, we know enough about the worlds in which they lived that we feel comfortable identifying the works they composed with distinct styles and personalities (even if for Homer it is a collective one). Questions about authorship are significantly less common for modern authors—in part, because they tend to leave so much material behind, and eye-witness testimony abounds. Joyce, the one born on February 2, 1882 in Dublin, is among them: his major works at the center of a vast constellation of secondary sources. But before getting sidetracked by how difficult it may be *not to know an author* nowadays, let's return to that original question: I'm not asking *who* is James Joyce or even *what* is *Ulysses*. Instead, I want to know *who* wrote *Ulysses*.

Style is the category that gets used to try and answer such questions, though the approaches vary widely. There is no single way to prove how style is the man or woman, and this is especially true when we're talking about *literary style*. Joyce can sound like Joyce, yet it's not always clear what the source of the singularity may be: word choice, sentence structure, characterization, modes of narration, or even subject matter. If following the experiments of Harry Mathews, you were to take the structure of *Ulysses* and insert a different plot with different words, would it still sound like Joyce?[2] Or what if you kept the same words and plot but then added a different structure? When it comes to literary style, it may not be possible to boil it all down to a single element, yet, what is true for this novel is true for so many of the others we read. Something about *Ulysses* sounds like Joyce and vice versa. Part of his style is unconscious, shaped by the period in which he was writing, other parts intentional, emerging out of a deliberate interest to use language and syntax differently. In any case, style is not biographical, by which I mean we cannot pin it down to an event in Joyce's life or to the circumstances of his upbringing. Style is something else. It is infused into the writing, making it possible to sound authentic even when all the words are borrowed.

Conspiracy theories about the authorship of *Ulysses* do exist, including one claim that Ettore Schmitz (a.k.a. Italo Svevo) is behind it all. But in the 1960s, the study of literary style was fast becoming a subject of immense interest for statisticians thanks to the arrival of computers that could analyze lexical diversity on a large corpus of texts and across a wide range of genres and authors.[3] One of the more successful early examples involved the *Federalist Papers* written by Alexander Hamilton, James Madison, and John Jay between October 1787 and May 1788. A majority of these pamphlets were published anonymously under the name "Publius," inspiring two statisticians (Frederick Mosteller and David Wallace) to examine the frequency of noncontextual words (conjunctions, prepositions, articles such as *upon, enough*) and nonfunctional words (*by, of, to*). Once they determined the thirty words that most clearly distinguished Madison and Hamilton from one another, they built a statistical model and plugged the code into an IBM 7090 computer three thousand words at a time. Relying on Bayes' theorem, which calculates probability based on previous events, they were able to solve this stylistic whodunit: Madison, they determined, is the principal author.[4] The bigger takeaway, however, was the proof that the computer-assisted statistical analysis of lexical diversity could be used effectively to authenticate literary identity.

Not all of the computer-assisted stylistic experiments in the early 1960s were as successful. A. Q. Morton, a Scottish minister, used computer analysis to decode the style of St. Paul, leading him to the conclusion that only four of the fourteen epistles can be attributed to him with any certainty (the others belong to five other hands).[5] The problem wasn't the computer: it was Morton's method. By focusing on such things as first and last words in the sentences (a technique he called "positional stylometry"), he didn't account for the fact that Greek manuscripts in prose tended not to have marks of punctuation, so the whole idea of where a sentence begins and ends can be difficult to establish. One of the most scathing responses came from John W. Ellison, already established for his work producing a concordance to the Revised Standard version of the Bible with a RAND Univac I computer, who threatened to use Morton's own method against him.[6] But in order to show just how misguided Morton was about St. Paul (even claiming it an abuse of scholarship and computers), Ellison brought *Ulysses* into the argument. A *New York Times* columnist, who was among the room full of conference goers at Yale University, reports: "The rector said that by using the method, he thought he could 'prove that five authors wrote James Joyce's *Ulysses*,' and that none of them wrote *Portrait of the Artist as a Young Man*. At least six authors could thereby be assigned to the two novels."[7]

Five authors, one *Ulysses*, and no *Portrait*: if it were possible to transport *Ulysses* to a world where Joyce was entirely unknown, that conclusion might not seem so outlandish. Still, there are a few other points worth making. For one, Ellison never actually performed any stylistic analysis on *Ulysses* with a computer (probably because of the amount of labor involved), so his comment is entirely hypothetical, simply meant to foreground the absurdity of ever thinking that literary style could be measured by sentence length and positional stylometry. The second, however, is that he uses this particular novel to make the point. Ellison's joke is funny because it assumes that *Ulysses* could only have been written by one person, and the mere thought of suggesting otherwise would be an insult not just to Joyce and his readers but also to stylometry.

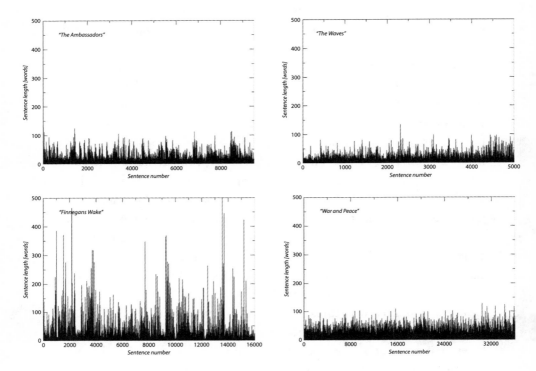

1.1 A variety of multifractal sentence arrangements in *The Waves*, *War and Peace*, *The Ambassadors*, and *Finnegans Wake*.

Source: Courtesy of Professor Stanislaw Drożdż.

Ellison may have dismissed sentence length as a reliable indicator of style, even if it was a hot topic for literary-minded statisticians in the precomputer days of the 1940s, but more recently a group of nuclear physicists used it as the point of analysis for a corpus of 113 literary works in English, French, German, Italian, Polish, Russian, and Spanish.[8] Their conclusion: *Finnegans Wake* is a multifractal (fractal of a fractal), which means the word counts within sixteen thousand sentences form a consistent pattern across the work as a whole (figure 1.1).[9] More surprising, out of this sample *Finnegans Wake* was the closest to a mathematically pure fractal, more so than Woolf's *The Waves*, John Dos Passos's *U.S.A. Trilogy*, and Roberto Bolaño's *2666*. Why a group of nuclear physicists would be working on this particular problem is unclear, but their conclusion reveals that multifractal structures can, indeed, be a useful indicator of style. It's not the content or diversity of the words that tip them off: it's the variation in sentence length (more than sixteen thousand) across an entire work.[10]

Strange to think that in all this time, and with so many different studies of styles and languages, no one has ever tried *to prove* by computer who wrote *Ulysses*.[11] The most ambitious computer-assisted experiment so far involved Gabler and his specially designed TUSTEP program, but that was for the production of an edition, and the handlist Steppe and Gabler generated was more of an alphabetized afterthought intended for word searches. There's still time, but I make this observation if only to highlight that the style of *Ulysses* seems so self-evident, so obvious, so basic, so singular that no machine and no statistical or computational model could ever teach us things we don't know already.

But for the sake of *Ulysses*, and the potential value of literary computational methods more generally, what would happen if we were to take this question seriously and approach it as a novel without an author? What would we choose to focus on if we wanted to examine style quantitatively? In the century or so that stylometry has been around, units for analysis have included the length and frequency of words and sentences, and they work rather well with models involving statistical probability. Authors become identifiable not only by word choice but also by word adjacency and lexical diversity.

Another option, one foundational to the organization any literary structure in prose, will involve the one element that few, if any of us, take much notice of: the paragraph.[12] As unmemorable as the paragraph may seem, it works behind the scenes to keep all of the words and sentences in order. By using the term *order*, I mean to suggest that the paragraph has a design, it does not just appear because of a predetermined decision made by a machine. Instead, it is chosen by the author, left there to perform a great deal of semantic work, bringing ideas together and also breaking them apart. In addition, the paragraph is there to be counted, and anyone who pays attention begins to realize just how formative the paragraph is not only to the pacing of an argument or plot but also to the arrangement on the page. Having too few or too many paragraphs is something readers will notice, but it's that in-betweenness, often a combination of short and long, that can slip by without much fanfare. Still, paragraphs, though extraordinarily common, actually do something, focusing attention with

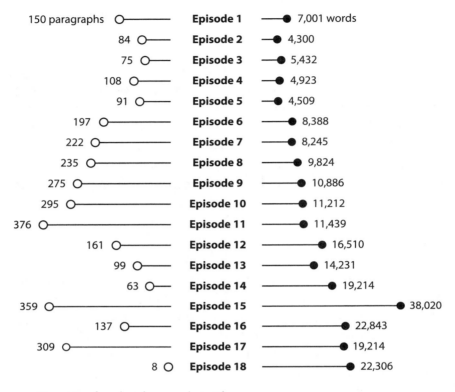

1.2　Quantities of words and paragraphs in *Ulysses*.

an enforced pause or straining attention by withholding one, thereby forcing readers to hang on as the sentences pile up.

If the paragraph can have a style, it is also in the quantity, one that gets defined by the number of starts and stops that an author decides upon (figure 1.2).[13] But if everyone agrees that the paragraph can be defined by what it does, there is no consensus on how often this process should occur or whether the variation in size or sum even matters. Gertrude Stein seemed to think so. Even more than the sentence, paragraphs, she argues, have an "emotional" content not because of what they say, but rather because of how "they register or limit an emotion."[14] That limit is precisely where they derive their power: the paragraph, in other words, has to begin and end (usually in a sequence), but no matter how long it may wander, this unit is finite. It's the finitude, in fact, that makes the paragraph, that "understudied scale of prose writing," measurable from a wide variety of angles, some of them I'll address in this chapter.[15]

But if paragraphs can have a thematic or material limit, they also have the power to ground narrative experiments so that they don't short-circuit by running on for too long. So no matter how surprising the words, sentences, or episode structures become, the paragraph remains. Not even Molly Bloom could kill it off with her extended monologue or the headline-obsessed narrator of episode 7 or the cheeky narrator from episode 10 with its sudden temporal and spatial displacements separated by asterisks. And if Joyce found himself at the end of the English language with *Ulysses*, he held on to that paragraph for dear life and never let go even after surrendering to the dreamscape of *Finnegans Wake*, which begins in the middle of a sentence that culminates in—what else?—a final incomplete paragraph.

Powerful or not, the paragraph is still one of the more overlooked organizational units in *Ulysses*. This has not been the case for Marcel Proust. Fredric Jameson, for example, has called the paragraphs from *À la recherche* Proust's "most striking innovation," and that's for a writer who brought the madeleine, and by extension the flood of memory, to the modern novel. Part of this innovation comes from the fact that Proust was using paragraphs to "organize human experience," inserting so much material in them during the revision process that Jameson wondered "how, under such conditions, any sense of completeness or totality is possible."[16] The answer, as Jameson knows, is irrelevant. There is no totality in the Proustian paragraph because the content of the memory as documented on the page always exceeds the act of remembering. The paragraph, then, is fundamental to the construction of a memory-theater put there to demonstrate the impossibility of ever fully capturing the human experience with an ever-receding time.

Joyce's paragraphs may not be as monumental an innovation, but they were certainly an innovation. When consulting the piles of manuscripts and drafts, Jean-Michel Rabaté and Daniel Ferrer noticed that Joyce, like Proust, had a tendency to stuff his paragraphs with words, sentences, and phrases during the revision process, but it was seldom the case that he added new ones.[17] These so-called paragraphs in expansion not only

meant the size of the novel would increase, but also there was the implication that the process could continue so long as there was time left, the
finishedness of the paragraph only imposed by the necessity of publishing
deadlines and death. The paragraph remains the perfect unit for anyone
eager to take a close look at Joyce's creative process, and depending on
which example you choose (and the number of revisions that followed),
the results can be pretty revealing.

The other side of the genetic equation, however, deserves our attention
as well. *What do we make of the fact that paragraphs expand in size during
the revision process but rarely in quantity?* For some episodes, the answer to
this question will depend on where the episode falls on the genetic timeline. If the earlier episodes, once proofed, were more or less off limits to
further revision, the later ones, still in process, were an opportunity to
weave in recurring words, themes, and motifs. That, Kenner suspects, is
one reason why the novel gets more complicated as it goes: later episodes
were more available to tinkering, the kind that tends to happen inside the
paragraph.[18] As a general rule, the quantity in the episodes remained more
or less stable.

Such was the case, for instance, with episode 12, which went through
nine different proof stages. Michael Groden noticed that the encyclopedism of this episode was the result of late-stage additions, but with
only "two entirely new paragraphs added."[19] The effect is significant.
"The additions," Groden argues, "change the episode's pace, as they give
the passages of gigantism an increased life of their own."[20] And then
there's episode 14. This is the one with sixty-three paragraphs that are
meant to correspond with the arrival of the sperm to the egg, the weeks
of gestation, and the exit of the baby from the womb. Given such a rig-
idly defined structure, there was really no room for new paragraphs, but
the number, for those who counted, was evidence that the quantity was
integral to the overall effect and meaning of the performance. Add one
or two more paragraphs to episode 14, and the correspondence between
language, birth, history, time, and creation collapses—even for the readers who never kept track.

And here we are, already sixteen paragraphs into this chapter, and I
still haven't even defined the term. In the *Oxford English Dictionary*, a
paragraph is defined as "a distinct passage or section of a text, usually
composed of several sentences, dealing with a particular point, a short

episode in a narrative, a single piece of direct speech, etc."[21] No surprises here, but consider all of the quantifying that the *paragraph* brings with it: *several, particular, short, single*. In order to define the paragraph, it becomes necessary to imagine how it can be distinct, something that can be extracted from a larger body of text, and still connected, something comprised of sentences and parts of speech. The point is that a paragraph can have its own identity, but that doesn't mean it can, or even should, exist on its own. So while it might be possible to condense the stories "worth writing" into a paragraph, William Faulkner, at least, was someone unwilling to recommend one-paragraph stories.[22]

Before deciding whether or not paragraphs can even have style, we should be clear about what we mean by *paragraph*.[23] The *Oxford English Dictionary* definition fails to indicate that the concept of the paragraph was around long before moveable type. In ancient Greek manuscripts, *paragraphos* identified interlinear markings made in the left margin to signal a change in speaker.[24] As this typographical convention circulated over the centuries, scribes developed other symbols that could be used to mark a new speaker or topic (*K* for *kaput*, or head), and it came to be called a pilcrow. Eventually, scribes would keep the space of pilcrow blank so that rubricators, the ones in charge of inserting the first letters, could provide elaborate designs by hand. With the arrival of the printing press, scribes and rubricators alike were left with less time to complete their tasks, and before long the paragraph was transformed from a stylized symbol in the margins into a blank space. By the nineteenth century, the distance of that blank space was standardized, and it would measure one em dash.[25] And so it is that the paragraph defined as a line break followed by an indent with a capitalized first sentence is still with us today both in print and on screen.

If only things were that simple. "The internal length and organization vary infinitely" ["Sa longueur et son organization internes variant à l'infini"], one theorist of the paragraph writes.[26] The paragraph may be a printer's convention, but it is the writers who get to decide not only on length and internal organization but also frequency. Joyce was among them. *Ulysses*, then, begins like any other novel with an indented first line, and if you follow the sequence of the next few sentences, it ends with a colon, followed by an indented em dash preceding a Latin phrase, and then another indented line, another colon and another em dash accompanied by a line of dialogue. On the page, it looks like this:

> Stately, plump Buck Mulligan came from the stairhead, bearing a bowl of lather on which a mirror and a razor lay crossed. A yellow dressinggown, ungirdled, was sustained gently behind him by the mild morning air. He held the bowl aloft and intoned:
> —Introibo ad altare Dei.
>
> Halted, he peered down the dark winding stairs and called up coarsely:
> —Come up, Kinch. Come up, you fearful Jesuit.

Seven lines of *Ulysses* with four indented sentences. Nothing particularly unique here, but this example raises an important question, and it is one that will affect the analysis that follows: Does an indent always signify a paragraph break? You can see how it makes sense for the first line, but why is the dialogue indented as well and then followed by an indented single line in third person? Can a line of dialogue be a paragraph? And what about a single line of third-person narration? Is that a paragraph as well?

In other words, what counts as a paragraph? If it's the indent, then any line of dialogue can fit the bill, but it's even more complicated if you consider the way Joyce formatted dialogue in his manuscript drafts, putting each dialogue dash flush left so that it was in line with the unindented part of the preceding paragraph. In order to format the computerized version of *Ulysses* in the 1980s, Gabler needed those line breaks for dialogue, using the same command to create separate narrative paragraphs. In preparing the extensible markup language (XML) version though, he decided to *deparagraph*. Here is what you find (hint: <p>= paragraph):

```
<p><lb n="010001"/>Stately, plump Buck Mulligan came from the stair-
   head, bearing a
<lb n="010002"/>bowl of lather on which a mirror and a razor lay crossed.
   A yellow
<lb n="010003"/><distinct type="nonstandard-compound">dressinggown
   </distinct>, <distinct type="archaism">ungirdled</distinct>, was
   sustained gently behind him on the mild
```

<lb n="010004"/>morning air. He held the bowl aloft and intoned:

<lb n="010005"/><said who="bm">–<quote xml:lang="la">Introibo ad altare Dei.</quote></said></p>

<p><lb n="010006"/>Halted, he peered down the dark winding stairs and called out

<lb n="010007"/>coarsely:

<lb n="010008"/><said who="bm">–Come up, Kinch! Come up, you fearful jesuit!</said></p>

What was once four paragraphs is now two. The <p>, also known as the paragraph element in HTML, is exactly where it should be in the first line—that is, before the indented narrative paragraph. You'll notice, how-ever, that the lines of dialogue are also included. The *deparagraphing* has combined the dialogue with the paragraph preceding it.[27] That is not how it appeared in the 1922 version or so many of the editions that followed (Gabler excepted).

To paragraph or not to paragraph may not seem particularly urgent, especially for those readers who prefer to imagine this unit as a convenient prose container. But it's definitely an issue for anyone concerned with the relationship between narrative frames, which includes those blocks of text organized by paragraphs and the extranarrative elements (including dia-logue but also snippets of song and other bits of text) that often follow in between. Once you begin paying attention both to the structure and quantity of paragraphs, it makes perfect sense. The line of dialogue is an extension of the narrative preceding it but not automatically the one that follows. Take, for example, the moment when Hynes walks up to Bloom at Dignam's funeral. "No: coming to me," Bloom thinks before a line break followed by a few lines of dialogue: "I am just taking the names, Hynes said below his breath." The conversation continues, but breaks again into another paragraph, this time about M'Coy (*U*, 92). We may clearly see the blocks of dialogue on the page but, they are not a self-contained para-graph. With few exceptions, they follow from the paragraph that precedes it.

With interior monologue, things will get a lot more complicated, but for now, I want to keep the focus on that leap between line break and indent, one we barely register as we make our way from the top of the page to the bottom. Buck Mulligan holding up his bowl and intoning *Introibo ad altare Dei* is part of a sequence: first the bowl, then the words. And this formula gets repeated more times than anyone would probably want to count. But then consider what this tells us about the paragraph. For one thing, it is not defined by the indent alone: it contains spoken words that are still technically placed outside of it. To define the paragraph in this way, then, requires acknowledging that it is an elastic unit, one with the capacity to incorporate words that are, strictly speaking, external to it.

But if adding dialogue to the preceding narrative can help keep paragraphs organized by topic, there's one problem: it's hard to know exactly how to count. For Kidd, every line of dialogue represented a paragraph, and using this definition, he counted one hundred of them in episode 3, which, he believed, corresponded with the one hundred cantos in the three canticles of Dante's *Commedia*. What's more, he singled out paragraph 33 for containing the phrase "The grandest number . . . in the whole opera" and paragraph 100 for its references to a "threemaster ship" and "crosstrees," both of them, he argued, allusions to Christian symbols. In Kidd's reading, the paragraph can be *symbolic in its quantity.*[28] So as much as we know about numerology's deep roots in words, sentences, sections, lines, chapters, and pages, never before has the paragraph been among them. But here it is: a sum of paragraphs with epic ambitions and mystical intentions.

And maybe this particular example shouldn't be so surprising given that Joyce got into the game himself with episode 14. As Kenner explains, this episode opens "with eleven paragraphs that get Bloom into the Mater. It closes with eleven paragraphs outside again. Eleven is Joyce's inception-number, re-creation number. And between this pair of elevens, inside the Mater, we may count exactly forty paragraphs: forty for the forty weeks of gestation."[29] And then there's another example in episode 18. Though critics tend to refer to the sentences of Molly's soliloquy, they are ignoring the indents. Episode 18 is actually comprised of eight paragraphs made up of two sentences (marked by two periods), and if we're willing to factor in a reference to this episode from *Finnegans Wake*, that's how Joyce came to think of it too: "thank Maurice [Darantière], lastly when all is zed and done, the penelopean patience of its last paraphe."[30] *Paraphe* is the French word for "initials" or "signature," but it's also a reference to the very unit upon which the episode was built. And if the number 8 is a heavily charged symbol, invoking the day of her birth and the infinity sign, it's the paragraph that set the limit, giving episode 18 a structure that changes topic and pace even if it's only the readers in Molly's head who would notice.

"Paragraphs contained style but they did not *shape* it." That's what the Stanford Literary Lab, following the paragraph-oriented criticism of Erich Auerbach and Ian Watt, concluded in their own work on the subject.[31] But if we take into account these three examples, isn't *Ulysses* an exception? Aren't these paragraphs doing more than containing style? Though the dimensions of the individual paragraph may change, it's the quantity that defines the content *over the course of an entire episode*. The significance of what's happening inside the paragraph, then, is dependent on the sum (100, 63, 8), and readers who do not know the number miss the symbolism that holds it all together. In saying that, of course, I realize that each of these symbolic correspondences can be stretched to the realm of absurdity—yet, they are still foundational to the overall structure as it exists in this novel. What's more, they provide different answers to the question: How many paragraphs are enough for an episode? It depends on what the content demands. And in this eccentric system of signification, sixty-three paragraphs can mirror embryological development, eight paragraphs can signal eternity, and one hundred can contain an entire cosmos.

Consider, though, how these examples would also complicate any computational project that uses big data sets to arrive at broader conclusions. These counts might tell you how the paragraph works in *Ulysses*, but they would not be particularly useful for anyone working across a much larger sample with hundreds or thousands of novels. I bring this up now to emphasize the specificity of the unit itself, especially given that it is less than likely to attract much attention. And if using the paragraph to isolate a few lines of prose or break up a thought is one thing, assembling an entire collection of them in order to structure an episode is quite another. Paragraphs do have style once you figure out how to count them.

Counting paragraphs brings its own set of complications. That has a lot to do with Joyce's experiments with page layout, punctuation, em dash dialogue, and the inclusion of extraliterary material (including the printed matter in newspapers, songs, advertisements, etc.). In the process of trying to keep these numbers as straight as possible, I have established a few rules (with exceptions): the paragraph must have an indent (but not all lines with indents are necessarily paragraphs); dialogue is counted along with the body of the main paragraph preceding it (as was laid out in the original 1922 edition); bits of songs or remembered quotations are generally not included as separate paragraphs. A handful of episodes still required more inventive solutions: I count the 59 lines of the overture in episode 11, for instance, as one paragraph; in episode 15, the paragraph unit includes speaker plus stage directions and dialogue; in episode 17, each "paragraph" is a combination of question and answer. Some may not be entirely satisfied with these rules (and their occasional exceptions), but the main point of the chapter still stands: the standard definition of a paragraph as a unit marked off by an indent doesn't work if you are interested in exploring larger questions involving the overall proportion and design. The quantities and dimensions of the paragraphs were made to accommodate a whole range of experiments with time, space, narrative, character, and, in general terms, world-building.

II

In the introduction, I identified the tension that exists between the long history of literary numerology and the more recent emergence of literary computation. If the figures of numerology are symbolic, traceable to an authorial intention, the ones for computation are not, which means they are the building blocks for a proportion that can *feel about* right even if the number does not have any secondary valence and the exact measurements remain unknown (or perhaps unnecessary). The three examples I mentioned so far belong to the numerological mode of criticism, and they are each a provocation to the interpretive process because they ask us to consider why one episode may be more worthy of a number than another. And can a paragraph still have style when it lacks symbolism?

To try and answer the question, we need to expand the category to accommodate different ways of measuring paragraph size and structure. In the most comprehensive book on the English prose paragraph dating back to 1894, E. H. Lewis uses quantitative measurements to explain how the paragraph has evolved over the course of three centuries, focusing on such things as average sentence length and the average number of words per paragraph and per sentence. In the process, he discovers that those long, single-sentence paragraphs so beloved by Bunyan, Sterne, and Defoe fall out of fashion (he suspects because sentences get shorter), but the turn toward shorter sentences, which coincides with a decrease in conjunctions, also ends up reducing the average length of paragraphs. It is in the relative differences of paragraph size (including sentence length), however, that Lewis identifies a style that is understood collectively.[32] An author, in other words, can be singular, but he or she is using paragraphs in a way that he identifies with a trend at a specific moment in time and place.

Lewis draws on a wide variety of prosaists for examples but also includes one novel by Charles Dickens and another by George Eliot for comparison. In a selection of 300 paragraphs (comprising 15,202 words) taken from *Old Curiosity Shop*, Lewis discovers the "coherence" of an "oral style," and if, at times, the sentences can be "diffuse," they are never "obscure." But if Dickens has an ear for the sound of words and a tendency to let his sentences ramble for dramatic effect, Lewis concludes he "has no right feeling for the paragraph as a rhythmic whole."[33] Eliot, on the contrary, does. The 212 paragraphs (16,233 words) sampled from *Daniel Deronda* are similar in size to *Old Curiosity Shop*, but they have an overall "unity" and "logical coherence" that Dickens lacks.[34] And while these stylistic differences may be noticeable for anyone who actually reads what's inside the paragraphs, Lewis attributes them to the way paragraphs are organized, which involves, among other things, the timing and placing of short sentences for rhetorical effect.

There are a few important takeaways from Lewis's book: first, the paragraph as a unit is *measurable*; second, measuring paragraphs, both individually and in aggregate, tells us about how a writer chooses to organize the narrative; third, and most importantly, the English paragraph itself has a history that involves changes not just to size but to the arrangement of the contents. In their analysis of the paragraph a century later, the Stanford Literary Lab gave Lewis's quantitative methodology an update. Instead of counting paragraphs and sentences manually, they rely on topic modeling, using samples of narrative paragraphs, not including dialogue, for their experiments. Their discovery: the paragraph of the nineteenth-century novel prefers polytopicality. Instead of restricting themes to a quantity of one per paragraph, it was more common to find two, three, or four—but what this means, in the bigger picture, is that the paragraph provides access to the novel at a different scale. It is at the scale of the paragraph, they conclude, that we see how *themes in the novel fully exist*.[35]

Ulysses wasn't included in either dataset. Lewis was looking for broad trends across the centuries *before* Ulysses *was even written*, while the lab focused its energies on the internal structure in the nineteenth-century novel. That is not the goal in what follows. Instead of looking to draw broad conclusions about the history of the paragraph, I use the numbers to explore the proportion and design *in this novel*. In particular, I am interested not only in how the paragraph develops across episodes but also in relation to one another as the size of the novel increases. As was true with words and characters, the quantity of paragraphs per episode was never a given. It would change as the writing of *Ulysses* progressed, responding to a whole range of symbolic filters and also experiments with language and narrative that were shaping how the plot was organized.

Joyce knew how to use paragraphs long before *Ulysses*, but one thing, in particular, changed it all: interior monologue. More than a technique for capturing consciousness, interior monologue was also a style of writing defined by distinct limits at the scale of the word, sentence, paragraph, and page. Adrienne Monnier was quick to notice the "short, cut-up, exaggeratedly allusive little sentences" of interior monologue but failed to mention that they were collected in paragraphs, some providing smooth transitions, others more abrupt nonsequiturs.[36] Inside and outside, interior monologue and third person, thought and action: that's the shift that happens between line break and indent. The paragraph is put there to end and begin over and over again, not only interrupting thoughts but also moving the plot forward but not always with a clear connection.

But more than performing a convenient narrative function, the paragraph is, to borrow S. L. Goldberg's phrase, a "dramatic unit of consciousness," a material reminder that no matter how much Stephen or Bloom have their heads in the clouds, there is still a page in the outside world that needs navigating.[37] But what happens when the paragraph becomes a "dramatic unit of consciousness" and is not, strictly speaking, a typographical convention for stacking sentences? What, then, is the paragraph counting, and how might we measure it for ourselves? Here, I want to identify the criticism leveled against *Ulysses* by Wyndham Lewis regarding this new narrative technique: "He had to pretend that we were really surprising the private thought of a real and average human creature, Mr. Bloom. But the fact is that Mr. Bloom was abnormally *wordy*. He *thought in words*, not images, for our benefit, in a fashion as unreal from the point of view of the strictest naturalist dogma as a Hamlet soliloquy."[38] It's the wordiness of interior monologue that irritates Lewis, but the emphasis could just as easily be placed elsewhere: Bloom is abnormally *paragraphy*. If the punctuated words strain the limits of disbelief required for fiction, then so too does the paragraph, which all too often takes more time to read than the experience of the thought itself. And, really, who thinks in paragraphs?

Marcel Proust let his narrator's mind wander extensively, delaying the line break in order to simulate the whimsy of memory movement, but that's not how things work in *Ulysses*. In fact, you could say that Joyce has a tendency to overregulate the paragraph to keep the minds of Bloom and Stephen in check, making them function in the novel much like a word bubble might in the world of comics. The text of his character's thoughts is contained within a structure that has definite limits on the page. So as much as paragraphs organize, arrange, and pace consciousness, they also visualize it. Theodor Adorno identified something similar happening with punctuation marks, but for him it was a process dependent upon resemblance. "An exclamation point," he writes, "looks like an index finger raised in warning; a question mark looks like a flashgun light or the blink of an eye."[39] In *Ulysses*, the paragraphs don't *look like* anything. They are blocks of words in various sizes with line breaks and indents. Once you try to imagine this novel without them, then you also begin to realize just how much they do to begin and end thoughts and provide necessary interruptions to bring in the sounds, smells, and sights of the outside world.

One of the earliest examples of paragraphed interior monologue is found a few pages into the first episode. As Buck Mulligan walks down the stairs into the Martello Tower after shaving, Stephen is left to think in peace:

His [Mulligan] head halted again for a moment at the top of the staircase, level with the roof:

—Don't mope over it all day, he said. I'm inconsequent. Give up the moody brooding.

His head vanished but the drone of his descending voice boomed out of the stairhead:

> *And no more turn aside and brood*
> *Upon love's bitter mystery*
> *For Fergus rules the brazen cars.*

Woodshadows floated silently by through the morning peace from the stairhead seaward where he gazed. Inshore and farther out the mirror of water whitened, spurned by lightshod hurrying feet. White breast of the dim sea. The twining stresses, two by two. A hand plucking the harpstrings, merging their twining chords. Wavewhite wedded words shimmering on the dim tide.

A cloud began to cover the sun slowly, wholly, shadowing the bay in deeper green. It lay behind him, a bowl of bitter waters. Fergus' song: I sang it alone in the house, holding down the long dark chords. Her door was open: she wanted to hear my music. Silent with awe and pity I went to her bedside. She was crying in her wretched bed. For those words, Stephen: love's bitter mystery (*U*, 8).

Indeed, all the trappings you would expect to see in a paragraph are here, and it's pretty easy to follow until the three lines of Yeats pop in, which could either come from Mulligan's mouth or Stephen's brain. They are followed by another indented paragraph beginning in the third person before switching over again to Stephen, the poet, whom we can begin to identify by the alliteration and the focus on rhythm. The cloud—arriving on an indent in the next paragraph—breaks the spell, but then the color on the sea invokes the memory of his mother and we dive right back in again.

Pretty standard stuff when it comes to interior monologue, but consider the role that the paragraph plays in all of this. Here, the indent is a *signal*, a term Wolfgang Iser uses to identify how modernist writers, in particular, can lead readers through "different depths of consciousness" without needing to rely on "extraneous codes."[40] In the example above, the indent is the signal identifying that a switch is being made, which in this instance involves the move from third to first person without the necessity of adding a "he thought," or, more appropriate to Stephen, a "he brooded."

And this move from one paragraph to another, from one mode of narration to another, is more than a signal, it's an image. One thing that happens between *Portrait* and *Ulysses* is the discovery of what prosy thought can look like—not just as an assemblage of free-floating words of different sizes at different angles (what the Italian futurists called *parole in libertà*) but as blocks. Readers, then, don't simply wade through the short, choppy sentences of interior monologue in an unmediated fashion: they see them.[41] The line break, followed by the indent, is there to let everyone know that a change is about to take place. It's a common syntactical feature even in the episodes where there is a lot of shifting back and forth between the narrative registers. Interior monologue had to assume a form on the page, and it is one that will necessarily change the more that Joyce realizes that paragraphs are not just collections of sentences: they have the power to make thought visible.

There are limits, of course, to the shape that these images can take. They are still comprised of words; but just glancing at a few pages, you can see the variations generated by the different positions of line breaks and the quantity of sentences. Monnier, then, may have noticed the choppiness of interior monologue at the level of the word and line, but she failed to mention that they were accompanied from the early stage by the paragraph. Here's a rapid sequence of three, appearing after the pair of long paragraphs with which episode 3 opens:

Rhythm begins, you see. I hear. A catalectic tetrameter of iambs marching. No, agallop: *deline the mare.*

Open your eyes now. I will. One moment. Has all vanished since? If I open and am for ever in the black adiaphane. *Basta!* I will see if I can see.

See now. There all the time without you: and ever shall be, world without end (*U*, 31).

Difficult to pin down what is happening. If we are supposed to be inside Stephen's head, what are the paragraphs doing here? Who is breaking these lines? And why are they so short? If the paragraph is, indeed, an image, it is not mimetic. Thought doesn't really look like that in anyone's head, but it can on the page of a novel. Joyce is clearly experimenting with the rhetorical possibilities of the paragraph as a unit. It does not have to follow the same logic that guides third-person narrators and can serve a semantic function, one that informs how readers process the words. Stephen may think in prose, but his thoughts are clearly guided by the sound and rhythm of poetry.

Even this one early example demonstrates that Joyce is adapting a technique developed by Stéphane Mallarmé, the symbolist who used short paragraphs surrounded by blank space as a display case on the page for his poetic prose. His justification for this practice could just as easily be a description for the three short paragraphs above:

> To mobilize, all around an idea, the lights of the mind, at the proper distance, through sentences: or since, really, these molds of syntax, even expanded, can be summed up by a very small number, each phrase, forming a whole paragraph, gains by isolating a rare type more freely and clearly than if it is lost in a current of volubility. Thousands of very singular requirements appear with use, in this treatment of writing, which I gradually perceive: no doubt there's a way, here, for a poet who doesn't habitually practice free verse, to show, in the form of fragments both comprehensive and brief, eventually, with experience, the immediate rhythms of thought that order a prosody.[42]

Thought in the form of prosody contained in a paragraph: there's no better way to describe what's happening here. But more than marking thought, these paragraphs are also up to something else: they measure time.[43] Each episode lasts an hour, which would mean that the paragraph, like the word, must correspond with the passing seconds and minutes. And if the narration has a clock ticking, with different paragraph lengths, then it would be worth thinking about whether or not quantities of paragraphs conceal quantities of time.

III

If we restrict our analysis for now to episode 3, we are dealing with seventy-five total paragraphs.[44] These seventy-five paragraphs contain all of Stephen's thoughts and are largely organized around three different topics. These include an imaginary visit to his Uncle Richie Goulding; a real, albeit remembered, visit to Kevin Egan in Paris; and a long-distance encounter with the cocklepickers on the beach. The paragraph, though, doesn't just provide the foundation for memory-building: it is part of the visual expression of the performance, with the bigger units, sixty, conveying the bulk of the memories and punctuated now and again by fifteen others made up of two lines or less.

If we want to understand how time is measured, the short paragraphs are a good place to start. While the bigger paragraphs tend to get organized by topic, concept, or event (as happening in present or as remembered in the past), the shorter ones either mark a quick change in topic/concept/idea/event ("What about what? What else were they invented for?"), or they act as the dramatic culmination of a thought or memory ("Weak wasting hand on mine. They have forgotten Kevin Egan, not he them. Remembering thee, O Sion"), or they provide an interruption from the external world ("Passing Now") (*U*, 34, 37, 39). But there's something else going on as well: the words contained in these shorter paragraphs are in step with Stephen. As he walks and thinks, the seconds tick by, and the short paragraphs, distinct on the page, reveal a self-consciousness about this connection between his body and mind in space and time.

Consider, for example, this line: "The Ship, half twelve. By the way go easy with that money like a good young imbecile. Yes I must" (*U*, 32). Here we have a thought about Mulligan, followed immediately in the next paragraph with the information that "His pace slackened." Another longer paragraph culminates with "Ringsend: wigwams of brown steersmen and master mariners. Human shells" with a line break, an indent, and a "He halted." Yet another involving memories of Paris ("You seem to have enjoyed yourself") begin in the next paragraph with "Proudly walking." These examples indicate that the narration, no matter how windy, is keeping track of Stephen. In that way, he is not unlike Dante, whose *passi*, or steps, in the *Inferno*, are both literal (Dante the pilgrim is walking) and figurative (Dante the poet is writing the lines we read). He walks, circle by circle, but no matter how deep he goes, Dante, like Joyce, never forgets the time or the pace.

Long paragraphs, which move away from the external world and physical action, tend to work differently. The hour is still passing in the episode but at a different rate. Instead of real time measured rhythmically and by an awareness of the body in space, the longer paragraph functions more like a *pocket of time*, a place in which the seconds and minutes can expand or slow down. And that's largely because thought is not action, so measuring the time of thought, especially realized as words or in the form of sentences, would end up contradicting the process. Stephen, then, is free to dwell in the realm of abstractions in these long paragraphs so even when remembered or imagined actions enter his mind (talking to his uncle or Kevin Egan, for example), they become part of his network of ideas but do not have to be anchored in time so quickly.

One particular example stands out: it's the one in which Stephen, the poet, finally writes down a line of poetry. In an interesting twist, this action is never actually narrated. It all happens offstage: he looks for paper, thinks about things for twenty-five lines or so, and then crams the paper, which he has scribbled on, back into his pocket. It's that thinking in between where we catch a glimpse of what happens to time when we are deep in the paragraph of his mind: "Darkly they are there behind this light, darkness shining in the brightness, delta of Cassiopeia, worlds. Me sits there with his augur's rod of ash, in borrowed sandals by day beside a livid sea, unbeheld, in violet night walking beneath a reign of uncouth stars" (*U*, 40). Just try pinning these sentences down to the hands of a clock. Stephen's thoughts are what's narrated, but they do not seem to correspond with the passing seconds or minutes.

Or do they? This paragraph is not just a unit of consciousness: it is also a unit of time. It not only contains thoughts, but it also measures seconds and minutes. In the short ones, the process tends to be made more explicit, but the clock never stops ticking even when the paragraphs increase in size. When I did the original breakdown, I mentioned that episode 3 has sixty long paragraphs. Getting to this number requires differentiating them, or their function, from the shorter ones, which add up to fifteen. One could argue that these shorter paragraphs are not really breaks in thought at all: rather, they belong with the paragraphs that come before or after them. In either case, the proportion of that measurement is worth thinking about. Kidd was counting one hundred paragraphs and found Dante's cosmos, but in the sixty, there's something more banal but nevertheless remarkable: a clock. By that standard, sixty paragraphs could be the equivalent of sixty minutes. What's more, these paragraphs, regardless of the variations in length, would count the same: one minute per paragraph.

Sixty paragraphs and sixty minutes is not so surprising. Out of all the possible things to worry about in episode 3, the shape of time, of course, is paramount. An innovation like interior monologue still needs a stopwatch, since the very realism of the novel demanded it. Stephen, after all, is in a real place, with a real body, moving through a fixed distance. So regardless of how oblivious he may be about the passing minutes, the structure itself, the one holding the sentences all together, has a number whose meaning is temporally significant. To measure time by sixty, in this episode and anywhere, is to adopt the sexagesimal numeral system invented by the Sumerians, and it is suspected that this number was selected, in part, because it is the smallest number divisible by the first six counting numbers.[45]

Stephen wouldn't know any of this, of course, but the paragraph, which contains his words and structures his thoughts, has a temporal measurement. In the last section of this chapter, I'll return to this question about numbers, paragraphs, and time; but for now, I want to make a simple point: we don't need intention to make sixty paragraphs legitimate. Joyce may or may not have known that they could be added up in this manner. Regardless, he is still managing proportion, and this episode presents a unique challenge because it was the first but not the last episode that showcased interior monologue exclusively. But if we also bear in mind that this only happens again with Molly's eight paragraphs, which begin in bed and end in eternity, the sixty could represent a different example of mind-time measured in minutes. The minutes of episode 3 may well have been a dress rehearsal for the eternity of episode 18, one that led to the realization not only that a quantity of paragraphs could be symbolic, but they could also be adaptable for experiments with form and temporality.

This is the paragraph measurement for a single episode, but even if Joyce measures all the other ones by the hour, the quantities will vary. Take, for example, the next set of three, which accompany Bloom's arrival in the plot: 107 (episode 4) to 87 (episode 5) to 197 (episode 6). Episode 6 is on the high end, but that makes sense given the increase in the word count (8,388). And for many of the episodes that follow, a similar process unfolds: more words=more paragraphs.[46] That in itself is not very surprising—especially when you acknowledge the return of third-person narrators who not only use longer sentences but also require more paragraphs to fit them in. It's the reverse trend, however, that requires more scrutiny. With its twenty thousand words and sixty-three paragraphs, episode 14 is an obvious exception to the more words/more paragraphs rule. Next to an eight-paragraph episode 18, it has the highest word-to-paragraph ratio in *Ulysses*; so if by word count episode 14 belongs with episodes 16, 17, and 18, by paragraph count it is right next to episode 3.

Kenner was elated by the paragraphs in episode 14. He identified the 11+40+11 combination, but in all the excitement, even he miscounted—or at least pretended to for the sake of numerical symmetry.[47] If you add in the indented song, it's sixty-three paragraphs (which also turns out to be the number of headlines in episode 7), and this matters because episode 14 would then break down into the three *incantations* at the beginning ("Deshil Holles Eamus"/"Send us"/ "Hoopsa!") followed by sixty others mapping out six centuries of the English language, nine months of embryological development, and, according to one critic, tens of thousands of years of geologic time.[48] Prompted by Joyce's own description in a letter, critics have focused largely on the many prose styles that get dispersed throughout. More specifically, they have treated episode 14 as a literary-historical crime scene, using Joyce's own notebooks and sources to identify the fingerprints.[49]

As fascinating as all the archival forensics can be, they've been ignoring the number and function of the paragraphs. The sum of sixty may evoke the mechanical clock of episode 3, but instead of also measuring the time of the mind, the scale has been radically enlarged in order to accommodate passing decades and centuries as strung together by an omniscient narrator. Time gets marked by changes in style, the thirty-one or thirty-two parodies of various authors and works corresponding with different historical periods (figure 1.3).[50] There is never any explicit indication in the episode that a new style has arrived, but that's not necessary. The paragraph is there doing what it always does: providing line breaks and indents. Instead of marking changes in speaker or topic, the paragraph is there to clear the page for the arrival of a new style. So if each one functions like a time capsule, the breaks are where the travel from one decade or century to the other occurs.

Critics have long known about the stringing together of prose styles. What's been missing from the discussion is the function of the paragraph (figure 1.4). Without the paragraph, episode 14 doesn't work. New styles don't just arrive anywhere at any time. They depend upon the line break and indent, so even in those instances when Joyce mixes different authors or even different chronologies, a new period gets marked by the arrival of a new paragraph. In modern terms, the paragraph is a place for transition,

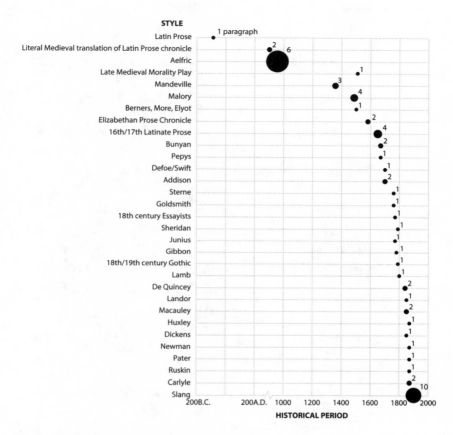

1.3 Quantities of paragraphs across different historical periods.

but that wasn't always the case. In Middle English and Anglo-Saxon, it was an opportunity to break and begin anew, and Joyce would have learned about this from the *History of English Prose Rhythm*, a resource he borrowed from heavily. Though prose style is the main focus, George Saintsbury allows himself one valuable aside on the topic: "Of the paragraph, as such, it may be doubted whether any Anglo-Saxon or Middle English writer had much notion from the purely rhythmical-stylistic point of view. He had done with one subject and took to another: that was all."[51] Line break instead of rhythm and style: you can't have it all.

If you go back and reread the corresponding Anglo-Saxon/Middle English sections from episode 14 (1150–1500), you get to see Saintsbury's point in action. The plot keeps going, but the paragraphs lack transitions.

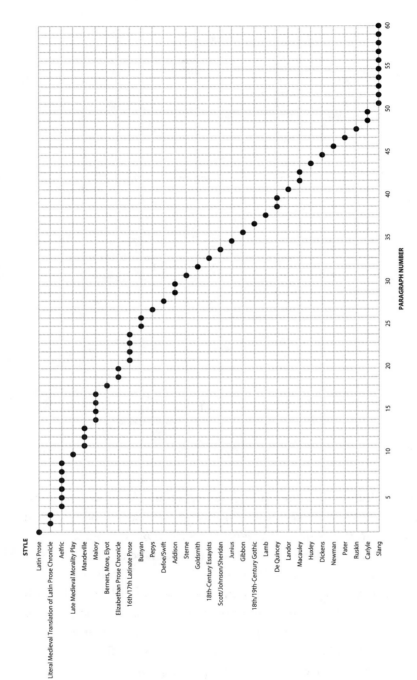

1.4 Distribution of individual paragraphs across different historical periods.

What's most surprising is that they never kick in even after the prose modernizes. In episode 14, *the paragraph is a break*, so even as the events occur, it does not provide links forward or backward. And if you take into account that it all culminates in the broken-down slang that signifies the general collapse of language, then it fits neatly into the critique that evolution (language, biology, history, culture) would signify progress. Like the word, the paragraph was never pure from the start, and no matter how many you assemble over time, there is no cohesion.

IV

Paragraphs break style, they don't make it. At least that's what Saintsbury would argue. Yet, episode 14 proves the opposite point. *Paragraphs do have style*. And what's more, they have this style not only because of their quantity but also because of their function. Paragraphs begin and paragraphs end, and as the various examples I've discussed so far demonstrate, this limit is precisely what makes it possible for *Ulysses* to measure time, consciousness, and narration in the ways that it does. Simply to count the paragraphs is not enough. We also need to compare them, gauging the relative size, while also identifying the form, including its structure, pace, and timing.

Were you to throw *Ulysses* into the samples collected by Lewis or the Stanford Literary Lab, the results would be meaningless. What, for instance, would the paragraph rhythm, length, or number of topics in episodes 3, 14, or 18 mean alongside Dickens, Eliot, and Hardy? They are very much a product of the parameters of the paragraph as set by a novel that includes a symbolic signification system and a ticking clock. Novelists were certainly grappling with the representation of time long before Joyce, but his own discovery that the paragraph could measure time as it passes in someone's head or across the ages was very much his own.

There is a general lesson as well about where style resides in a literary text: the computational methods common to stylometry may be a useful way for parsing paragraphs, breaking them down into smaller units for comparison. But as it stands now, the basis for these investigations continues to be grounded in language—and the word, whether its frequency or position in a sentence, still dominates. The analysis here, however, reveals that there's a lot we can learn by the line break, not what's in the body of the paragraph but what's before, after, and around it. Those breaks, it turns out, were not just the thing that make computation possible. Rather, they are the negative space on the page, there to regulate the transmission of meaning, the stops and starts of time, and the ebbs and flows of thought. Mallarmé transformed that blank space surrounding prose sentences into an art form, but in the process, he exaggerated the presence of something that was there as long as paragraphs have been around. We just had to take notice and, in the process, we begin to see how it manages time and cordons off consciousness.

The results in this chapter are one example of computational close reading. And there's one obvious point to make: you don't always need computers to do the work. The digital files certainly made locating paragraph breaks a lot faster, but it could have been done by hand. In addition, the paragraph counts, once collected, still had to be checked against the 1922 *Ulysses* as much for quantity as for context. Coming back again and again to the paragraphs as they appear on the page, I was reminded of how the materiality must have informed the entire revision process, especially for those episodes with multiple proof stages. The simple fact that the paragraphs can grow is a reminder that the entire creative process is organic, something that happens in time but also over time. The paragraph wasn't just something to fill, it was something to feel. If you read through the episodes with this in mind, you can see what I mean: the paragraph manages our expectations on the page. When too long, it can make our eyes swim; when too short, it grabs our attention; and in between, it moves us along, recalibrating the coordinates of the plot, tracking ideas, and occasionally providing transitions as well as nonsequiturs.

The numbers here and elsewhere can only get you so far. All of the counts were simply a place to begin, not end, the analysis. In the process of providing context, it became possible to try and establish what the numbers mean. There's no general rule that should be applied to all literary works, and I'd even hesitate to recommend that this same method gets applied elsewhere. Not all novels need to have their paragraphs counted. Or, if they do, it may turn out that the results would be more meaningful with an expansive dataset. Still, this chapter was one more opportunity to argue that quantity doesn't precede quality. To the contrary, there is a qualitative value that is already in the numbers before they get counted. That is what makes the paragraph so unique as a unit for measurement: it is an expression of style, and it's as close to intention as the diversity of words or their arrangement in a sentence. No matter how much Joyce may have enjoyed fattening up so many of his paragraphs, all 3,342 of them, there was, finally, a limit, a place where he had to stop.

As it stands now, I'm not making any general conclusions about paragraphs or about novels. I am, however, willing to argue that the paragraphs are not only unique to *Ulysses*, but they are a stylistic unit you could use to prove who wrote *Ulysses*. Sure, other writers have experimented and innovated, but no one managed to combine the symbolic, historical, and temporal together so seamlessly. And what remains powerful about it all is that we can go on reading without taking much notice. The paragraphs will do what they always have, recede into the background, all the while managing our attention, not only letting it stray but also providing an occasional prod or jolt precisely so we can remember why we opened *Ulysses* in the first place.

N° 2
Words in Progress

*And—something of which Homer was innocent—"words" are blocks
delimited by spaces. So we can count them.*

—Hugh Kenner on *Ulysses*

I

Why is Joyce's *Ulysses* as long as it is? Too often we forget that the size
of this book was not somehow written in the stars. It began, modestly
enough, as a sequel to the 85,077-word *A Portrait of the Artist as a Young
Man*, but in the course of seven years, it was transformed from a novel
with modest ambitions into that morphological nightmare made up of
264,448 graphic units (or language tokens); 39,801 different entries; and
25,541 lines of text.[1] What happened? How did it go from being *a book* to
that "fat book" as Vladimir Nabokov once called it?[2] And, in the process
of trying to answer a question about size, we might want to think about
that other unsolved mystery: What formal and material factors may have
actually determined the length of the individual episodes?

That's the subject of this chapter: a quantitative examination of *Ulysses*
that must, by necessity, grapple with a number of genetic issues involving
its evolution through a series of early, middle, and late stages that together
chart the transformation from a more novelistic style mixing interior
monologue and third-person narration to the experimental theatrics

characterized by a series of narrators with a lot of personality. So, as a first step, I need to clarify what version of *Ulysses* I'm talking about. We already know a great deal about the book as it grew from the notes to the notebooks, from handwritten drafts to typescripts, from faircopy manuscripts to proofs. What we don't know much about is the serialization: the thirteen and one-quarter episodes that appeared in the *Little Review* between March 1918 and December 1920 in twenty-three different installments.[3] For decades, critics have largely dismissed the relevance of these versions because of the inaccuracies and excisions, and it's only recently that a publisher even thought it worthwhile to reprint them in a single volume.[4] The regular deadlines, they concede, may have helped Joyce get the episodes written (even if he kept notes to add later on), but the transmission of the text from typists in Trieste and Zurich to Ezra Pound, then to the relay in London (who corrected and sometimes censored them), and on to the compositor in New York (a non-English-speaking Serbian) ended up generating a mutilated version of the novel not worth its weight in pulp.[5]

That, of course, is the problem. Those critics interested only in the accuracy of the text—the ones in search of an ever-elusive authoritative version—have been missing out on what's important about the serial *Ulysses*. Indeed, the *Little Review* may have been responsible, in part, for textual corruption as the novel was appearing, but it remains relevant precisely because it was the medium that first gave this novel a home, and, more important, it shaped the very scale of the episodes and determined the tempo as they came out on a monthly, and later bimonthly and trimonthly, basis.[6] Joyce had been taking notes and drafting versions of various episodes at least three years before the serialization began, but once the clock was ticking and installments were due, he kicked into a regular routine: seven episodes appeared between March and December 1918. That's more than half the total number of episodes published in the *Little Review* before the process was repeatedly delayed by paper costs, meddling censors, and timid printers and then eventually ended by legal battles.

Before moving ahead, it's worth asking what an *episode* is in the first place.[7] The term is common parlance in Joyce circles, one of those words used to show you're in the know. I suspect that the easy adoption had a lot to do with the fact that each installment in the *Little Review* was defined as an episode (without the Homeric titles by which Joyce referred to them) or, in some cases, defined as part of an episode and followed by a roman numeral. The word *episode*, however, does not carry the same meaning as *section* or *chapter*.[8] These are bibliographical terms regularly used to identify the internal structure within a book. And it could be any book: the Bible, the plays of William Shakespeare, the essays of Samuel Johnson, or the poems of John Milton.

But episode as a category for the structural division within a book works differently. The *Oxford English Dictionary* defines it more generally as a digression within a story or poem.[9] Episodes, in other words, are a detachable part of a narrative that can be reintegrated into a larger whole. The serialization of novels, which involved separate installments identified as numbers, ended up benefitting from episodic organization, in part because they could provide places in the plot for installments to break. Episodes within a narrative became a way of thinking about how the novel, which could be long and unwieldy and difficult to remember, was organized. In other words, if readers wanted to identify something they had read in the course of a year or two, the episode in which x, y, or z happened was the best indicator, because it did not rely on a numbering system that very few readers could keep track of.

Episode, then, defines a structural element within the novel that gets associated with a serial mode of novelistic production: episode is not chapter, and, for that reason, it does not depend on the organizational logic of the book for its meaning. The episodic appearance of a novel within a newspaper or little magazine was made possible by serial modes of production with built-in temporal interruptions. Every week, fortnight, or month could bring the continuation of a story, but if you think about it, this passage of time in between would invariably affect how this story was written and received: readers had to keep track of the plots and the characters, which is not an easy task when the serialization process is attenuated. And behind it all, the episodic experience would influence how readers might even imagine the novel itself: Was it the assemblage of fragments released over time in a newspaper or periodical? Do you even need the book for the novel to exist? More to the point, what is the difference between the version housed between two blue covers and the one that appeared serially in the *Little Review*? In asking these questions I'm not in search of an authoritative text; I'm interested in the medium through which that text was transmitted. Thinking about the medium of the little magazine raises some provocative questions about what *Ulysses* is and is not, one of them involving length: *Why are the episodes in the* Little Review *as long as they are* (which gets us to the bigger question I posed at the beginning)?

Measuring the length of the serial *Ulysses*, simple as it sounds, is not such a straightforward exercise. In the process of trying to figure this out, I considered three possibilities: the pages of typescript (sent by Joyce to Ezra Pound and distributed to Margaret Anderson, editor and publisher of the *Little Review*, in the United States), the pages of the faircopy manuscript (drafted by Joyce between 1918 and 1920 and sold to the lawyer and collector John Quinn), and the printed pages of the episodes in the *Little Review* (averaging sixty-four per issue). The typescript isn't reliable because Joyce depended on too many different typists with different habits over the years, too many different typewriters with different spacing, too many different kinds of paper with different line counts, and, on top of it all, there are too many missing pages, episodes, and/or mixed copies. The faircopy manuscript (also known as the Rosenbach manuscript), which Joyce produced by hand (sometimes relying on the generosity of others), does not always correspond directly with the typescript that was used to set the pages of the *Little Review*, and Gabler has suggested that a now lost manuscript was used for many of them.[10] Counting the pages of the *Little Review* might seem like the most viable option, but the page layouts, formatting, line length, and line numbers change too frequently over the years, making it impossible to establish a reliable standard for measurement.[11]

After a lot of searching, I finally realized that I was getting it all wrong. Inspired at first by Gérard Genette's analysis of Proust's *À la recherche*, I was looking for pages to measure when it was really words I was after.[12] Kenner was on to the idea of word counts decades ago when he made the observation in passing that I used as my epigraph. Because words are blocks "delimited by spaces," we can indeed count them. Kenner's own calculations with word blocks led him to a number of conclusions, including the one, mentioned earlier, that the twenty-two words in the first sentence of the novel correspond both with Homer's hexameter (two lines really) and the number of books in Leopold Bloom's library (excluding the one owned by the Capel Street Library that he never returned).[13] But in addition to these more eccentric local correspondences, Kenner also had his eye on the big picture, pointing out that if Joyce had stopped with episode

10, *Ulysses* would have ended up as "a moderately orthodox novel of fewer than 100,000 words, its ten chapters each of *fairly normal length*."[14] Kenner's word count was off by a quarter here (74,720 words is the real total), but the point he wanted to make is still valid: the bulk of *Ulysses* was something that happened gradually, month to month (with occasional lags in between), episode by episode, installment by installment. Joyce was calibrating and recalibrating the size of his novel as he went, and it wasn't just the book that was getting longer, it was the episodes themselves as the book was being written.

After receiving the electronic files generated from Gabler's critical and synoptic edition of *Ulysses*, Kenner was reminded "how deeply our experience of *Ulysses* integrates with a printed text."[15] Counting and reading are possible precisely because there are word terminations still waiting to be measured if we ever want to get into the novel's *numerical unconscious*. And the counting must go on.[16] Of course, I'm not the only one to embark on such an extensive numerical adventure. Long before Kenner brought out his calculator, there was Miles Hanley's legendary word index, first published in 1937 and intended (according to Martin Joos) for the student of "association psychology" tracing image patterns, the Joycean looking for "verbal echoes," and the educators and linguistic scientists decoding the "structure of vocabulary."[17] Almost a half century later, when Gabler and his team assembled the corrected text, an alphabetical index was generated from the "output files." Keen to distinguish his updated "handlist" from the convenience of a concordance or dictionary, Gabler believed that the user might "gain both excitement and insight from exploring on his own the paths of the philologist that often enough lead to discoveries of some moment in the language universe of *Ulysses*."[18] If the word was going to be the philological key to this "language universe," the handlist was there to help pick the locks.

Delivering one of the plenary lectures on the occasion of Gabler's edition of *Ulysses*, even Jacques Derrida got into the spirit of things by tracing the frequency of a single word throughout the entire novel. Strangely enough, he seems to have ignored the handlist altogether, choosing instead to do the counting himself, one *yes* at a time. "I myself computed, a pencil in my hand," he told the audience, "the mechanical figure of yeses legible in the original gives more than 222 in all, of which, more than a quarter, at least 79, are in Molly's so-called monologue(!)."[19] If the image of a pencil-wielding Derrida counting *yeses* one by one is not entertaining enough, it's worth pointing out that he still ended up getting the final number wrong: there are actually 359 "yeses" in *Ulysses* (91 of them in Molly's monologue), and that doesn't even take into account the *yup*s, *yea*s, *si*s, *oui*s, and *ay*s.[20] Which, I suspect, would have been fine with Derrida, since he wanted to demonstrate above all that computer-generated lists, though convenient, are incapable of dealing with the slipperiness of signification for any given word.

Over the decades, the focus on counting has been placed on the book *Ulysses*, and in each case there has been an emphasis on the philological value of tools like word lists, handlists, and indexes. That is not my goal here. Counting words in the serial *Ulysses* is one way we can understand how it was happening in real time over the course of two years. *Ulysses* demands to be read this way. Eliot may have suggested early on that a "mythical method" is what held the various parts of this novel together, but there is, I would argue, an architecture that was necessarily generated by the unit of the word itself. Joyce wasn't just writing month after month in order to meet the deadlines, he was measuring as he wrote, and, even if he would later revise each episode for Darantière in 1921, the early structure for a majority of them was firmly in place. Counting is a way of containing, and the French word for storytelling, *raconter*, is an appropriate reminder here of just how much the two are entwined. To narrate is to count time passing, and, when words are actually inscribed on a page (instead of being uttered by a storyteller), that passage of time, that measurement, is visible to the naked eye. We may like to fashion Joyce as the master raconteur, but when doing so we need to remember that during the serial stage in the evolution of *Ulysses*, he was also a mechanical counter, someone eager to keep track of how many words he was using as the plot itself was unfolding one episode at a time.

II

In what follows, I use the close reading of a single data set to reveal the serial logic of length and rethink the very structure and organization of *Ulysses* in some basic ways. It took me some time to realize that there would be a qualitative payoff for what began as a quantitative exercise. Strange, considering that Pound and Joyce were thinking about numbers as soon as they began talking about the prospect of serializing the novel. In March 1917, Pound approached Joyce with a request: "I don't want, at any price, to interfere with the progress of 'Odysseus', but you must have some stray leaves of paper, with some sort of arabesques on them. Anything you like [*crossout*: And also name your rates, if you can keep within reach attainable limits.] There can't be much at a time, as the format is small. From 500 to 3500 words, is about the limit. Though I [*crossout*: should] could print a story up to 6000 words if you had one. 1000 to 2500 will be about the regular size."[21] At first Pound had a short story in mind, but, after signing on as the foreign correspondent for the *Little Review*, he realized that an entire novel would be even better. Joyce formally accepted Pound's offer in August of that same year, hoping to capitalize on the fact that *Ulysses* could appear in the *Egoist* and the *Little Review* simultaneously: "You suggested that it could appear serially in the *Egoist* and *Little Review* and thus bring me double fees. I am prepared to consign it serially from 1 January next, in installments of about 6,000 words."[22] Once the deal was formalized through Pound, Joyce received a single payment of fifty pounds for the serial rights. *Ulysses*, then, was never paid for by the word, or even by installment, and length subsequently was not going to be motivated by capital.[23]

So, a limit of "6,000 words" per installment: How long is that? If the average word count per page in the *Little Review* is roughly 350, then it would be somewhere around seventeen pages (and, in fact, the first installment was nineteen pages). Pound's limit of "up to 6,000 words" was, for Joyce, an approximate number, "about 6,000," that could be stretched a bit if necessary. When the first episode arrived at Pound's flat in London, these seventeen densely typed pages were made up of 7,001 graphic units, and in the few weeks and then months that followed Pound received four shorter "bundles" of typescript averaging 4,800 words each.[24] Before continuing, I should mention that these numbers were generated from the same files used by TUSTEP (an acronym for Tübingen System of Text Processing Programs) that was specially designed for the critical and synoptic edition of *Ulysses*. Gabler generously passed his master files along to me, and, in preparing what follows, I ran them again through another word-counter program and double-checked them against those of a computational analyst: we both arrived at slightly lower numbers than Gabler's. It turns out that the dashes used to identify bits of dialogue in the *Little Review* files are largely to blame: they were mistakenly counted as tokens along with some of the symbols introduced during the reformatting process to distinguish foreign words.[25] From now on I will use the terms *word/word count*, though I'm referring to tokens, or what you might also call graphic units. The computer counts the spaces between blocks of text to determine a word, so it is the spaces that signal where each unit begins and ends. Initials like J. C., K. M. R. I. A., E. L. Y.'s, and I.O.U.'s will make up a single unit and so too will the hyphenated words, portmanteaus, abbreviations, titles, units of measurement, numbers, abbreviations (*i.e., c/o*), and stand-alone letters.

I want to concentrate now on the length of the first six episodes (figure 2.1). Together they make up Stephen Dedalus's "Telemachia" (episodes 1–3) and the first three episodes of Leopold Bloom's "Odyssey" (episodes 4–6) The episodes in each sequence begin at eight, ten, and eleven in the morning, respectively, and, as David Hayman was the first to notice, they mirror each other structurally and thematically. But there's more going on here: the elements of this pair of three episodes each are actually the same length. Stephen gets, on average, 5,578 words per episode, Bloom gets 5,940. Averaging the episodes in this early stage of *Ulysses* is important because it reminds us that word count does not have to be restricted only to isolated episodes. Therefore, even if the word count of episode 1 is higher than that of the two episodes that follow (which are framed by the higher episode 6 on the other end), the combined average is still just below the

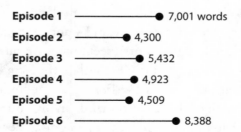

Episode 1 ────────────● 7,001 words
Episode 2 ──────● 4,300
Episode 3 ───────● 5,432
Episode 4 ───────● 4,923
Episode 5 ──────● 4,509
Episode 6 ─────────● 8,388

2.1 Number of words per episode, 1–6.

limit: and with the three episodes of Bloom, the same thing is true. There is episode 6 on the high end preceded by two episodes below 5,000: together that's "up to" or "about" 6,000 words, the number that Joyce and Pound had originally agreed on.[26]

But why 6,000? Where does that number even come from? Dante used between 115 and 157 lines for the *Inferno* (eleven different canto lengths, Joan Ferrante argues, so the chaos of Hell could be properly represented in the poem's form); Shakespeare, writing plays too long to be performed in their entirety, hovered somewhere around 3,000 lines (when his contemporaries stayed closer to 2,430), and Dickens stumbled upon a twenty-part, nineteen-month format, in thirty-two-page installments, that he would use for eight of his major novels. Six thousand words, however, works differently as a unit of measurement: it was identified at first as the necessary length for what was still an undetermined number of episodes.[27] Not only was there no precedent at this moment when 6,000 was decided upon, but there was also no end in sight. Six thousand words multiplied by what? Where, finally, would the accumulation of this number lead? Pound had recommended it at first as an upper limit, and, when he did so, he was asking Joyce for a short story, not the serialized installment from a novel. Once they agreed to bring out *Ulysses* in the *Little Review* (with the possibility that it would appear simultaneously in the *Egoist*), Joyce still latched on to that number, deciding that 6,000 words per episode sounded about right. Was that the average length for a serial installment in little magazines at the time? Was it an average left over by the Victorians?

None of the above: there was no average word count for serialized novels in little magazines because so many of them didn't actually pay in the first place, especially not by the word. And if there were modernists looking to the Victorians for serial guidance, I doubt that length would have been the primary interest. I want to suggest another possible explanation that might, at first, seem preposterous. A total of about 6,000 words is the average episode length in the 1879 Butcher and Lang prose translation of Homer's *Odyssey*, one that Joyce, we know from his friend Frank Budgen, relied on while living and writing in Zurich (figure 2.2).[28] And even if, like Kenner, you disagree with the assertion that this was one of the Homeric sources Joyce relied on, preferring

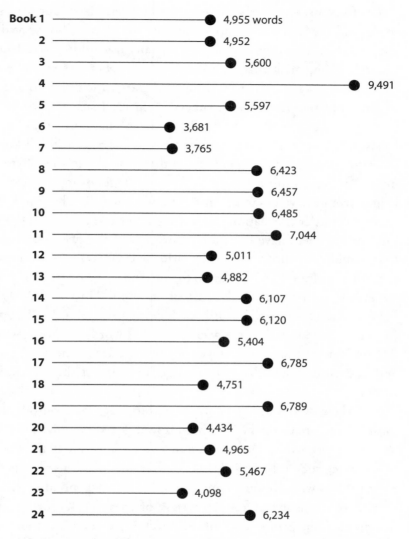

2.2   Number of words per episode in the Butcher and Lang translation of Homer's *Odyssey*.

instead the 1900 Samuel Butler translation that was later recommended by Stanislaus Joyce, then you still get a close word count. It should be added, though, that because Butler is more concerned with the substance of his translation than an ornamental style, the word count in his translation is consistently lower.[29]

I'm fully aware that the *Odyssey* was not serialized, but it was episodic, and the tradition of oral recitation of different books at different times by different poets was, in itself, an early mode of serialization. Henry Fielding made that same point in *Joseph Andrews*, when he joked that Homer "was the first inventor of the art which hath so long lain dormant, of publishing by numbers!"[30] Joyce, I suspect, would have been tickled by the idea: it would have been one more bond between bards. But considering the intense scrutiny Joyce paid to all kinds of esoteric symbols, strange parallels, and tiny details in the *Odyssey*, it's not ridiculous to suspect, even in the early stages of Joyce's work, that length would have come up along the way as well. The Butcher and Lang and Butler translations do not include word counts on the page, but both of them have line counts for each of the twenty-four books that would have made these calculations very easy: roughly 12 words per line multiplied by 444 lines, for instance, make up book 1: that's 5,328 estimated words.[31] The rest of the books in the *Odyssey* vary between 5,000 and 6,500 words each, with a single outlier in book 4 (9,491). Added together, the average is 5,645 words per book, which is 68 words more than the average for the episodes in the "Telemachia" and 295 words fewer than the average for the first three episodes of Bloom's "Odyssey."

Had the episodes in *Ulysses* stayed within that 6,000-word limit, the riddle about length might have been solved. Joyce, we might have been able to suggest, took a Homeric number and ran with it all the way back to Ithaca (episode 17). That, of course, is not how all of this plays out. The length spikes with episode 6 and the following two episodes, when the number of words surges from an average of 5,233 to 8,813 (figure 2.3). At this point in the composition of the novel, Joyce doesn't just exceed the projected word count he and Pound had settled on, he nearly doubles it. At 8,813 is almost twice the average of episodes 2, 3, 4, and 5 (4,791 words). So what's happened here? Why this sudden spike in word count, which effectively, and from that moment forward, changed the terms of Joyce and Pound's serial agreement?

The short answer: Dublin. With episode 6 the space of *Ulysses* suddenly expands, and what Moretti has said elsewhere about the inextricability of adventure plots and novel length applies here as well: an increase in word count is directly related to the widening of space in this novel.[32]

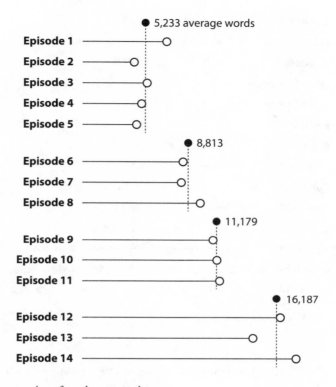

2.3 Average number of words per episode, 1–14.

It's a shift that needs words for the plot to move forward, sideways, backwards, and around. Before episode 6, Bloom's movements are severely restricted: a short walk to the butcher shop in episode 4 followed by a discrete stroll down a few streets in episode 5, but once he gets into the carriage headed to Paddy Dignam's funeral, Dublin suddenly dilates. It is the first extended view of the city (again in episodes 7 and 10), one that officially marks Bloom's headlong leap into the urban fabric. And Bloom is not just in Dublin here as the carriage winds its way through the streets: he is beset on all sides by Dubliners. The restricted social interaction of the earlier episodes, which could easily be condensed into 6,000 words or fewer when he was mostly in his head, gives way to the formation of an expanding network of relationships and new spaces that simply can't fit. And Paddy Dignam's funeral is just the beginning. From that point forward, the cast of characters increases considerably, and the

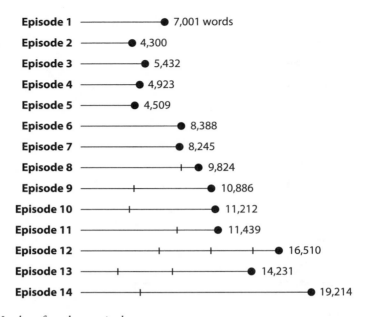

2.4 Number of words per episode, 1–14.

number of different locations proliferates: the newspaper office, Davy Byrne's pub, the library, the Ormond Hotel, the cabman's shelter, all the way back to 7 Eccles Street.

Doubling and Dublin, then: a spike in word count, I'm suggesting here, was generated by the spatial expansion of the plot (figure 2.4). With the publication of episode 6 in the *Little Review* it's as if the artificial constraints first recommended by Pound and seconded by Joyce could no longer contain the scope of the novel as the adventures were developing. And it's worth reiterating here that the serial *Ulysses* was a live event: Joyce may have had a rough plan for the number of episodes and the order in which they were to appear, but once the serialization process kicked in, he was still trying to figure out how to piece it all together month by month both within and between episodes. Even with a general plan, and the notebooks he kept with words, phrases, and fragments of paragraphs, these episodes were taking shape as they were being written with deadlines in mind. By July 1918, when Joyce sends Pound the typescript for episode 6, about 9,000 words was the new limit, and it lasted for two more episodes (episodes 7 and 8).

And then another jump: from episode 9 through episode 11, the average word count rises from 8,813 to 11,179. As was true the first time the word count jumped, this spike is not followed by a sudden jump back to the earlier limit: there's another phase of leveling out for two episodes (and then another jump). It's worth mentioning that in both instances, these moments of leveling out contain three episodes each. It's impossible to say with any certainty why three is the magic number (though I'm sure Kenner would have had a compelling theory), but it seems as if leveling out was a way to normalize the length increase during the serialization process, as if Joyce exceeded the limit originally established and then attempted to justify what he'd done by repeating it twice before doing it again. In the end, that repetition makes the length increase appear to be more of a calculated necessity than a serial aberration.[33]

As evidenced in figure 2.3, episode 4 came in at 4,923 words: six episodes later episode 10 reaches 11,212. But just consider for a moment what it would mean if these numbers were somehow reversed: Could the serial version of episode 10 have been contained in just under 5,000 words? Considering the fact that there are these dramatic increases in series of three episodes, it's worth thinking about. Joyce justified the formal experimentation of his novel on the grounds that each episode "conditioned its own technique," and, looking at the distribution of words on the chart, it's possible to make a similar claim about numbers: *each episode conditioned its own word count.* Joyce may have begun *Ulysses* with some general idea about length, but in the course of writing month-to-month, episode-to-episode, he clearly began to change his mind. The data is compelling for what it tells us about *Ulysses* as the novel was appearing in serial form: some things about proportion, scope, and scale could be anticipated, but word count was not one of them, and, as a result, the rules were bound to be broken again and again.

That, in effect, is the point I want to emphasize. The logic of length is something every writer has to confront. In this case, you could say that there's an internal rhythm to the serial *Ulysses*, but with the production of each installment, Joyce was not just adjusting the size of individual episodes; he was changing the scale of the entire novel. Episode 4, then, to go back to the question just raised, couldn't be the length of episode 10, and vice versa, but that's not because Bloom's kitchen is too small or Dublin and its cast of characters too large. Rather, it's because they both belong to a specific moment in the serial composition of the novel, each one assuming a particular length because of the episodes that precede it, and each one will subsequently help to determine what happens as the process continues (working within the limit of 6,000 words only to break out of it).

Unlike the first spike in word count, however, this second one had serious material consequences: from that moment forward, individual episodes of *Ulysses* had to be broken up into two (and later three and four) different installments. And there was an obvious reason: any single episode published in its entirety would have taken up half the space of the little magazine, which averaged somewhere around 23,000 words per issue. Joyce might not have minded, but it's likely that the other contributors and readers would have taken offense. Looking at the numbers, though, you begin to wonder if that might have been the point: not that Joyce was staging a silent takeover of the *Little Review* but that he finally realized a single episode could be divided between two different issues. After all, this second spike includes another sequence of three episodes that could have been broken down into two installments of between 5,000 and 6,000 words, and the number never dips below 11,000 again.[34]

Is this just a coincidence? Not likely, given the size and consistency of the increase. Joyce, these numbers reveal, wasn't just making his episodes a little longer than before: he was making them big enough to appear as two separate installments of just under 6,000 words. There's no evidence I've found so far to indicate that Joyce explicitly recommended this course of action, and, in their correspondence (at least the portion that has survived), Pound never mentions that he has a plan of this sort up his sleeve, though I suspect that when sending the typescript on to Anderson, he would have made some indication where each of the longer episodes could be divided.[35] Though we will probably never know who, finally, was behind this two-issue solution, it ended up revolutionizing the form of *Ulysses*: once an episode could run beyond the frame of a single issue, who was to say how long it could or should get? It was this act of working within and then moving beyond the material constraints of a little magazine like the *Little Review* that allowed, even enabled, the radical formal experimentation that followed.

I've been talking about the effect of this spike on episode length, but *why does this second one happen where it does*? And what can it mean to the way we think about the episodes that followed (12, 13, 14)? When I first began working through this part of the argument, I hit a snag. The quantitative data was there all right, but I was having a difficult time trying to figure out what, if anything, it could tell us about a qualitative difference in the novel. This is where the genetic component of my argument arrived in full force. I was particularly drawn to an observation made by Groden when he was first piecing together the genetic history of *Ulysses* in the mid-1970s using the available typescripts, manuscripts, and notebooks. Reading through what was available at the time, Groden arrived at the conclusion that the end of episode 9 represented a break with the "initial style," one that Joyce had identified more closely with the technique of interior monologue. As evidence, he used the note that Joyce inscribed at the end of this episode when preparing the faircopy manuscript for John Quinn on New Year's Eve, 1918, which reads: "End of Part I." Critics after Groden have tended to agree that since this end does not correspond with the divisions of the three-part structure of the novel, it must therefore signify the self-conscious departure from the style that was being used up until this point.[36]

After episode 9, Joyce wasn't just moving beyond the "initial style," he was breaking out into the formal experimentation that would go hand in hand with the forceful return of an omniscient narrator who heckles the characters, remembers phrases and events from earlier episodes, and, before long, hijacks the story completely before Molly reasserts control. Groden suspects that this gradual discovery of the need for an omniscient narrator, which forever changed the direction of the novel, was quite unexpected for Joyce, "a result of his episode-by-episode progress on his work, progress that never extended far beyond the immediate episode at hand."[37] Indeed, there are moments of interior monologue after episode 9 that come up in episodes 10, 11, and 13, but in each instance, they are made to accommodate the presence of someone or something who refuses to let any single character cogitate for too long.

Building on Groden's observation, I want to consider in greater detail how word count might fit in. As Joyce moved away from interior monologue and back again toward omniscient narration, the episodes got even longer, and part of the trick would involve figuring out who was wordier: Stephen, Bloom, or these new unnamed narrators. Wyndham Lewis, for one, was convinced that Bloom was the culprit, an "abnormally wordy" character who just didn't know when to shut up. This wordiness, he goes on, ends up making all of his monologues about as convincing "as a Hamlet soliloquy."[38] Rising to Joyce's defense, Stuart Gilbert argued that Lewis was missing the point. There are, he explains, some people who believe that "without language there can be no thought," adding further that even if we don't think in words, "we certainly must *write* in words."[39] What's particularly interesting about this exchange is the way the question of wordiness gets redirected so quickly into the idea that words and thoughts are inextricable from each other: without words, the mind is a blank slate. Gilbert evades Lewis's whole question by emphasizing that length and economy of language are necessary whenever thinking is actually in progress. Joyce, like any other novelist using interior monologue, needed to enter into the minds of his characters but was forced to use words to document what he found there. Even though he knew that brushstrokes and instantaneous impression were not an option, Lewis believed that some of their effects were still reproducible in other media.

I want to take this criticism of Bloom's abnormal wordiness seriously. When, after all, does the gradual accumulation of words in a character's mind make him or her seem longwinded? And is Bloom really any wordier than Stephen or the cheeky narrators that trail the two of them? Any attempt to try to answer these questions requires parsing each of the episodes in order to distinguish, as much as possible, between moments of interior monologue and omniscient third-person narration. In order to do so, I've isolated and counted each of them separately, including the moments of dialogue in the omniscient category, which the narrator would be privy to, along with the sentences that are part of what Kenner calls the "novelistic housekeeping," all "the cames and wents, saids and askeds, stoods and sats, without which nothing could get done at all."[40]

And if we are really just trying to figure out who's the wordiest Dubliner of them all (at least before the blustery episode 12 arrives), then Lewis is right: Bloom wins. Even Stephen's wordiest episode (episode 3) is still two thousand words shy of Bloom's (episode 8). But if we want to document the stylistic shift that Groden first identified, it's necessary to think about the ratio between interior monologue and omniscient narration in all of the serialized episodes. Out of the thirteen that appeared in toto in the *Little Review*, four belong to Stephen (episodes 1, 2, 3, and 9) and seven belong to Bloom (episodes 4, 5, 6, 8, 11, 13, and 12). I've excluded episode 10 from the final tally because of its synoptic view,

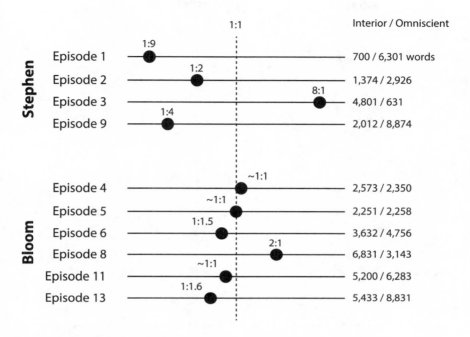

2.5   Ratio of words in interior monologue and omniscient narration, episodes 1–13.

which effectively integrates Stephen and Bloom into the much larger social and urban fabric of Dublin.

Looking at the ratios, a few patterns emerge (figure 2.5). For one thing, Bloom tends to share space equally with the narrator, whereas Stephen gets eclipsed. Even more interesting is the fact that in the later episodes (11 and 13), the narrator, who is beginning to muscle in, continues to give Bloom some time with his thoughts. In fact, the number of Bloom's words in the later episodes is roughly double what it was in earlier episodes (e.g., 4, 5 and 6), and the same is true for the narrator, who had a similar average before Bloom's increase. By way of a provisional conclusion, these numbers suggest that the takeover from episode 9 forward was gradual. Joyce may have begun to make arrangements for the return of authorial omniscience, but he was still thinking in terms of the same ratio. Each of the three episodes is around 11,000 words, which, as I have pointed out, was double the original limit, but shows some sense on Joyce's part that the proportion itself would not be disrupted

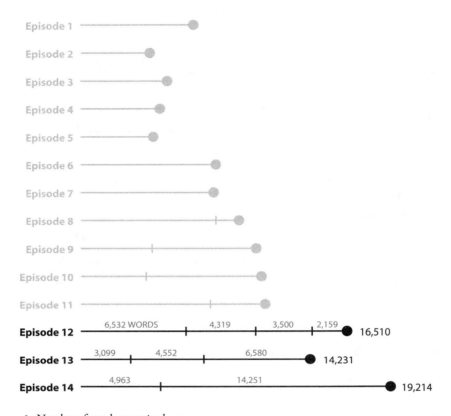

2.6　Number of words per episode, 12–14.

so long as an episode could appear in two or more installments. But once the narrator no longer has to make room for the musings of Bloom or Stephen, the episodes don't get shorter. All of this newly discovered space for more words gets used up and there is even an increase, which, in the end, will make it possible for the stylistic parodies to go on longer, in episodes 12 and 14 especially.

Take a look at what happens when the word count spikes for the third and final time with episode 12, a 16,510-word episode appearing in four different installments of 6,532; 4,319; 3,500; and 2,159 words, respectively. Episode 13 comes in at 14,231 words and appears in three installments of 3,099; 4,552; and 6,580 (figure 2.6). With episode 14, the number jumps back up to 19,214, though only one portion is published before the serialization stops for good. It's clear here from the word counts of these three episodes that the possibility for separate installments radically changed the way Joyce was continuing to think about the length of his episodes. By the time he began drafting episode 12, he was envisioning a much fatter book with even more audacious formal experiments. How else can these proportions be explained? To me they're a sign that Joyce may have known where the ports of call were in the novel he was writing, but he wasn't always sure how long each of the adventures should last: it took the pressure and regularity of serialization to figure that out. And by the time he arrived at episode 12, the same one that marked the "end of the initial style definitively," he had a pretty clear idea of how the technology of the little magazine could be maximized fully for his experiments and spikes.[41]

III

I've been using word count to try to explain why *Ulysses* ended up becoming as long as it did. To do so, I've been arguing that length—and its incremental changes over the course of two years—is intimately connected with the material constraints of serial production, the dilated space of the plot, and the unexpected exigencies of narrative experimentation. Now I'd like to entertain a related question: How long is an hour in *Ulysses*? Is a 5,432-word hour the same as one made up of 11,212 or 16,510 words? "The number of pages and lines in the published work," Paul Ricoeur points out in *Time and Narrative*, are usually the measuring sticks for questions involving novel length and *erzählte Zeit* (chronological time): pages and lines, that is, not words.[42] But with serial novels, where the length per installment was a very real consideration, one that often determined the design and tempo of a novel's plot, word count was a primary, not a secondary, consideration. In Joyce's case, where every episode was made to correspond with one hour of the day (or thereabouts), words on the page were like seconds on the clock, and still we know from the increase of words within and across these episodes that time was not always measured in the same way according to the same rubric.

Here, of course, we're back to narrative, since this question of time and word count is bound up with Joyce's experiments as he was writing. To get started, let's make a baseline calculation using episodes 1 through 5, where, on average, one hour equals 5,233 words. In reading time that's about 87 words per minute if it corresponds exactly with the time of the plot. Too slow. Average readers, capable of consuming between 250 and 300 words per minute, would be able to plow through an episode in about twenty minutes, though we would probably want to adjust for difficulty so that episode 3 and episode 2 would necessarily require different amounts of reading time. At this point, the calculation is pretty simple regardless of the ratio between interior monologue (interior/subjective) and third-person narration (exterior/objective). I say *simple* because the physical action in the external world of the novel and the thought in the interior worlds of Stephen and Bloom are equal in each episode and can be measured in the same way by the same clock. Individual thoughts pile up in the minds of Stephen and Bloom, and they mark the passing seconds as much as the commentary of the narrator does. "Stately, plump Buck Mulligan came from the stairhead": that's about five seconds, and we're not even to the bowl of lather yet. More often than not thought and action are happening at the same time: Stephen walks down the beach *as* he's thinking, he recites lines of William Blake in his head *as* the children are talking, Bloom oogles the woman in the butcher shop *as* he stands and waits in line, he reads the newspaper *as* he defecates, and he spreads the butter on his toast *as* he silently counts ("Another slice of bread and butter: three, four: right" [*U*, 45]).

At this point in the novel, time marches on as the words accumulate one at a time, and the clock ticks as the mind thinks and the body moves. The same thing is true when the third-person narrator observes characters from an external viewpoint. Words pass like seconds and they have the effect of ticking off in the same way so that you can almost hear the buzz chime (or the bell toll as it does in episode 4) when the last word of an episode is reached (*U*, 57):

Heigho! Heigho!
Heigho! Heigho!
Heigho! Heigho!

But what happened to time in *Ulysses* when the word count per episode grew to more than 8,000; 11,000; and 19,000 words? Did the seconds slow down or speed up? Is an hour still an hour if there are more words on the page and in an episode? With the first spike from 5,000 or so words to 8,500, the answer is yes. In episodes 6, 7, and 8, more things happen within the space of an hour—more dialogue, more thoughts from Bloom, more social interaction among characters, more description of the environment—but time does not really change its pace, no slowing down or speeding up. A second, to put it another way, is still a second even if there are more words attached to the passing of each one. In the second spike from 9,000 to 11,500 that is not the case. Once these narrators get reintroduced with such strong personalities, they have a lot more to say. And not only that: it takes them longer to say it because they use more words. When Bloom and Stephen think (even at their wordiest), they can say less, a few words to make their point and on again (and for readers it becomes easier to recognize their thoughts because they revisit many of the same topics over and over again).[43] But narrators need complete sentences that are considerably longer, and, as a result, they have a way of taking up more words while using fewer seconds so that the correlation between word and second is elongated.

More words on the page but fewer seconds passing in the plot: that is a discovery Joyce made while writing *Ulysses*. Time, expressed through words, is malleable, and the narrator is not bound to move it along with the description. That may help to explain why the length of the episodes needs to increase so dramatically during the middle stage when the narrator returns.[44] Episode 9, after all, introduces the playful narrator who gets in the habit of not describing in any linear way: the sentences tend to slow down the action instead of moving it forward. And in episode 10, there is simultaneity, juxtaposition, and backtracking. The narrator in this instance describes different characters in different places, while the minutes of the clock are regularly pushed back to begin again. In addition, Joyce planted an interpolation within each of the nineteen sections marking events that are either happening, have happened, or will happen within that hour. Seen this way, episode 10 is a representation of the serial experience itself, a miniature of the entire novel as it appeared in installments, each one with its own pocket of time and space. Each section had to be consumed in a linear way, but the leaps back and forth across Dublin effectively shatter the assumption that time itself moves forward consistently just because the words are accumulating sentence by sentence.

And from episode 10 forward, time is never the same again. Episodes 12, 13, and 14 are the longest from *Ulysses* to appear in the *Little Review*, and all of them have dominant third-person narrators who describe only to delay the passing hour. There is a lot to say here about how each of them work individually, but for the sake of space (and time), I want to limit my point: Joyce is often credited, along with Virginia Woolf and Marcel Proust, with finding new ways to represent the subjective experience of time in the novel. But it was a discovery not limited to interior monologue alone. What Joyce discovered in the process of writing *Ulysses* was another way to make the time of third-person narration subjective, using the linearity of the sentence to slow down the clock. And none of it would have been possible if he hadn't realized at some point in the composition process that the piling up of words could make time in the novel more elastic. Just think of that early sentence in episode 14 that kicks off the long parody of English prose styles that goes on for sixty-three paragraphs without any divisions between them. There are 118 words in that single sentence, and not one of them gives you the impression that the clock is ticking anywhere except in the room where you might be reading it. Sure, words may be lining up one after the other, but nothing seems to be happening at all, that is, nothing except the language, whose visual appearance on the page becomes the record of time itself. This process first began in episode 6, when Joyce started to move away from the assumption that time had to pass in thought or in action. By episode 14 thought becomes action but narration has become a mode of inaction, which may help to explain why these late episodes require "many more words," as Groden points out, "to say much less."[45]

There's another way to frame all of this: by learning to use more words, Joyce was able to break out from the realm of story into discourse. The plot is happening, events are unfolding over the course of the day, but the meaning of the novel is increasingly bound up with how they happen. Which is to say that once the technique begins to dominate, time becomes less rigid, and, more to the point, there is a way in which the sheer number of words in an episode could effectively make it seem that more time had passed than it had. Is it any surprise, then, to discover that Pound only began to complain about the length of *Ulysses* with the arrival of episode 11? In a letter dated June 10, 1919, Pound informed Joyce that episode 11 was "too long," warning him that it might be a good idea to slow down with the delivery of the other episodes, presumably so they could be shortened.[46] What's so striking here is the fact that Pound put his finger on length in an effort to describe what was bothering him. But length wasn't the problem. In fact, the previous two episodes were only slightly shorter. What Pound's done, however, is elide length with experimentation. The experiment, as he sees it, goes on too long, and unlike the previous episodes, it has a way of making episode 11 seem like the wordiest hour to date. Pound's advice, as we know, went entirely unheeded. Instead of slimming episodes down, Joyce continued to fatten them up so that by the time the typescript for episode 12 arrived at Pound's door, it weighed in at a whopping 16,510 words, and was followed up four months later by a 14,231-word episode 13, with a 19,214-word episode 14 waiting just around the corner.[47]

This frenzy for more words was justified by the formal experiments each episode required. The numbers could not have been anticipated from the start; they had to be discovered gradually, and with that middle stage especially, there was a way in which Joyce stopped caring about any limits, whether defined by words, lines, pages, or single/double/triple installments. And the point, finally, is that the *Little Review* always made the necessary accommodations so that Joyce never had to rein his novel in during the serialization process. What needs to be stressed above all is the idea that no matter how much Joyce used the exigencies of narrative technique as part of his own defense, none of it would have been possible if he had not made the discovery that more words were required. Without them episode 11 is less lyrical, episode 12 less windy, episode 13 less syrupy, and episode 14 less, well, embryonic. An hour may pass in every episode, but the experience of time is different in each, as they variously exercise the power to make the reader feel pulled along, drawn back, blown aside, rolled over, and—why not?—reborn.

IV

Moving ahead, I'd like to focus on words. I'm not talking here about the content of specific words: Molly Bloom's *yesses*, Stephen's *non serviams*, or Bloom's *bloos*. Rather, I have in mind a quantitative approach that might help us better understand certain qualitative differences about word production and distribution during the serialization process. With the publication of Hanley's *Word Index* (compiled manually over the course of two years using index cards), the words of *Ulysses* were systematically counted and alphabetized, and the calculations were revised half a century later by Gabler and his team using the TUSTEP analysis program. All of this data, however, has been organized around the book *Ulysses* as it appeared with eighteen different episodes in 1922: it does not account for the *Ulysses* made up of twenty-three different installments (or thirteen and a quarter episodes) published in a little magazine with 121,864 graphic units. For that reason, these indexes don't provide a very accurate account of what was happening to the words in *Ulysses* as it was appearing in serial form.

Joyce's lexicon was vast, but just how vast was it during the serialization process? More precisely, how were the different (appearing once in an episode) and unique (appearing only once in the entire work) words distributed over the course of two years, and what was the rate of expansion? The chart in figure 2.7 contains the number of different words per episode, showing that in the first five, the average starts somewhere around 1,750; rises to 2,500 in episodes 6 through 8; and jumps up to 3,400 in episodes 9 through 13. While the very idea of an increase in different words might not seem particularly compelling at first (the number of different words, after all, will increase with the number of total words), the percentages are. Word count, as one might expect, increases in these jumps between episodes 8 and 9, and episodes 11 and 12, but the percentage of different words to total words remains the same (29 to 30 percent; 26 percent and 26 percent). Episode 13 is on the lowest end at 22 percent, but the rest of them hover between 26 and 41 percent. As a point of comparison, consider the percentage of total to different words in *Portrait of the Artist as a Young Man*, where the word count for each of the five chapters varies in no particular order between 9,000 and 26,000. The percentage of different to total words in these chapters is, on average, 19 percent; that's about 37 percent lower than *Ulysses*.

What's happened? What does this percentage actually mean? Because there is no data set yet available that could let us compare different to total words on a large scale across thousands or tens of thousands of titles, it's difficult to say with any certainty. However, if we compare Joyce to himself, a few provisional observations can be made. The most obvious is that

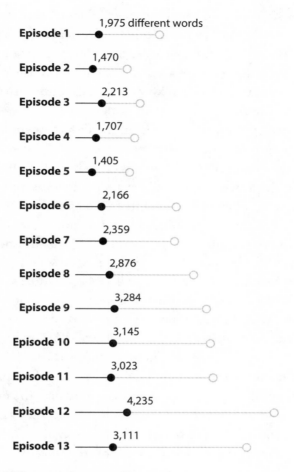

2.7 Number of different words per episode, 1–13.

he used more different words consistently per episode in *Ulysses* than he did per chapter in *Portrait*, where the percentages go from 13 to 22 to 19 to 25 to 18. So even as the number of total words increased, the percentage of different words remained roughly the same. This would mean that even if readers were encountering some of the same different words along the way, each episode would basically have a similar degree of word diversity. But what does that tell us about *Ulysses*? In a broader sense, it gives us a glimpse into the pacing process of the words so we can see what was happening to the language as episodes were coming out month by month.

Joyce, of course, would not have been as conscious of word diversity as he might have been of word count, but that's what makes these percentages all the more compelling: there's a consistency over time, though, I admit, and it is one that still requires further analysis and broader contextualization if we want to understand how exceptional or ordinary it is in the universe of the novel.

The number of unique words within the different words is a better place to examine the lexical diversity of the serial *Ulysses*. It is already known that the number of unique words in the book is high (somewhere around 35,000), but what about the 9,580 unique words that appeared in the serial version? How were they distributed and where (figure 2.8)?[48] Episode 12 has the highest number of unique words (1,730) followed by episode 9 (1,282), episode 10 (941), episode 11 (936), episode 13 (870), episode 8 (720), and so on, all the way down to episode 5 (212). And it's not just that there are more unique words in these middle-stage episodes (since, again, these middle episodes are longer, so an increase is to be expected): it's that the percentage of unique words within the different words is actually higher (unlike the ratio of different words to total words, where the percentage stayed more or less the same): 41 percent for episode 12, 39 percent for episode 9, 31 percent for episode 11, 30 percent for episode 10, and 28 percent for episode 13. The middle-stage episodes average 34 percent, the early ones 24 percent. That difference suggests that the episodes in the middle stage weren't just longer: they were getting filled up with a more expansive vocabulary.

Why? Let's consider, for instance, the different percentages in the "Telemachia" of Stephen and the first three episodes of Bloom's "Odyssey," where the word count is between 16,760 and 17,849. In Stephen's episodes, the average number of unique words to different words is 26 percent; in Bloom's, the percentage drops down to 18 percent. The difference, I suspect, has a lot to do with who these characters are. Stephen's braininess is actually reflected in the number of unique words he uses. And if you don't believe me, take a look at the percentage in episode 9 where he delivers his lecture on *Hamlet*: at 39 percent it's the second highest percentage in the entire list, right below episode 12, which is more than 5,000 words longer (with a unique word count that is higher by 500).

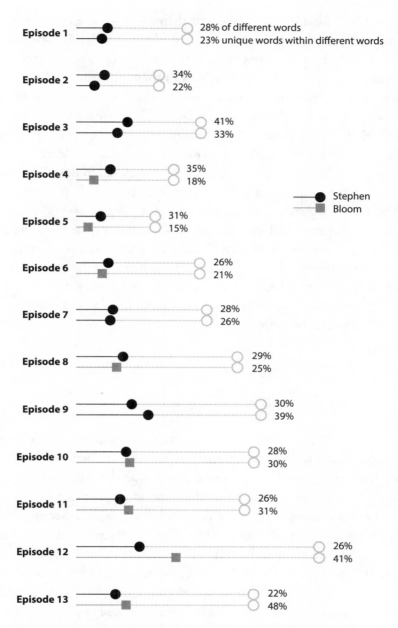

2.8 Ratio of unique within different words for Bloom and Stephen in episodes 1–13.

If Stephen uses more unique words than Bloom in the early episodes, it's the narrator who trumps them both in the middle stage. I speculated earlier that the return of these third-person narrators was connected with the increase in word count, but in light of these percentages, I think it's necessary to refine this statement a bit further: *these narrators are not just using more words than Stephen or Leopold, they are using more unique words.* Had the omniscient narrator never returned to the novel with such force, it is likely that the number of unique words would have stayed somewhere closer to the 22 percent range (as opposed to the 32.5 percent range, which was the average from episode 10 to episode 13). But that's still higher than *Portrait*, which averages 18.4 percent of unique words for its five chapters. And who knows what else is out there waiting to be discovered by comparing Joyce with all of the great serial novelists of the nineteenth century. *Ulysses* is not a universe unto itself. Indeed, there are internal laws at work here, but understanding what they mean requires looking outward, situating this one "fat book" in a larger network that includes many, many more.

V

In the *Poetics*, Aristotle maintains that length is something that emerges organically from within the sequence of events of a particular play and should not be regulated by such things as the *clepsydra*, or "water-clock."[49] *Ulysses* proves to the contrary that the water clock—or in this case the serial installment—was indeed a powerful tool precisely because it set the pace for artistic production and influenced the scope and scale of the entire work of art. Once he heard the clock ticking, Joyce could no longer ignore the fact that the words were accumulating, time was passing, and the novel was growing. Along the way, these episodes were fast becoming part of a sequence, the length of each one determined in part by where it was placed. Indeed, if it was the space of adventure that first necessitated more words in episode 6, it was the potential for multiple installments that made it possible to experiment more fully with time and narration after episode 9. In the act of preparing each episode for the *Little Review*, Joyce found a way to transform story into discourse, making the hours seem longer when they were just getting wordier, and that, in the end, was one way for him to figure out what *Ulysses* could be.

Before closing, I want to make a few observations about the impact of serialization on the physical book published by Shakespeare & Company in February 1922. By the time the final 4,964-word installment appeared in the September–December 1920 issue of the *Little Review*, 121,864 words of *Ulysses* had been printed, and with the addition of four more episodes and a revision of the earlier ones in the next twenty-four months—where words were added and seldom subtracted—that total number more than doubled (figure 2.8).[50] Episode 15 is the most obvious indication of the impact that serialization had on the length of *Ulysses*: in the absence of deadlines and/or any material constraints, Joyce unleashed a 38,020-word monster. At this point in the process, he was writing for book publication, so length was no longer a consideration. But that point alone, one that Groden first made, should make apparent just how much the act of serialization on a monthly basis influenced the overall size of the book: it forced Joyce to figure out how many words per episode would be adequate for the story he wanted to tell and the techniques he eventually wanted to try out.[51] And those word counts were not modified significantly for at least six of the *Little Review* episodes during the great revision of 1921, when Joyce was unifying the book by layering on all kinds of symbols and Homeric correspondences: 375 additional words for episode 1; 107 for episode 2; 261 for episode 3; 1,012 for episode 4; 871 for episode 9; 693 for episode 11; and 1,122 for episode 14.[52] In their eagerness to downplay the relevance of the serial *Ulysses* on the basis of its textual mistakes, that's not a point genetic critics want to make.[53] But it's true. Even though Joyce went back to revise all of the *Little Review* episodes, six of them received only minor additions/substitutions averaging fewer than 1,000 words. And with the exception of episode 7, none of them received structural modifications: the order of the events was the same, the cast of characters all there (no one cut from the final program), the itineraries remained unmodified, and the hours of the day and all of the destinations stayed in place.[54]

There's one more thing to consider: even after serialization stopped, Joyce was still *writing by numbers*. In letter after letter, he bragged to friends about the massive size of episode 15.[55] But even for him, 38,000 words was just too long for the three episodes he still had left to finish,

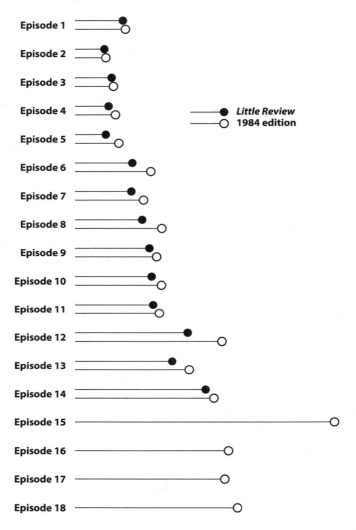

2.9   Comparison of word quantities for episodes in the *Little Review* and in the 1984 Gabler edition.

and, by the time he came to put the finishing touches on episode 18, he was acutely aware of the fact that the first sentence was 2,500 words with seven "sesquipedalian" (literally "long-worded") sentences remaining.[56] Should we really be surprised, then, to discover that episodes 16, 17, and 18 average 23,000 words and make up another sequence of three? Is 23,000 the ideal length for an episode without the burden of serial pressure? Maybe, but it could never have happened without that more modest beginning some-where around 6,000, when the world of the novel was all before him and the rock of Ithaca far away on the horizon. But why 23,000? Well, that's a riddle for someone else to solve, but it's hard to believe that when getting these final episodes ready for the "book" book, which Pound would iden-tify with "the size of four ordinary novels," Joyce wasn't thinking each of them would fit quite neatly in four installments.[57]

Ulysses has been around long enough, but no one has yet tried to figure out something as simple as its word count, including the dimensions of the individual episodes as they were appearing serially. And this quantitative approach, as I have tried to demonstrate throughout this chapter, would have been meaningless had it not been complemented by the genetic back-story we now know so well. Groden's work in the mid-1970s was ground-breaking, and it helped us see how a single novel could undergo so many significant structural changes over the course of a few years. In researching this topic, I was sometimes dazzled by how right Groden turned out to be, reaching his conclusions using so many different notes, notebooks, manu-scripts, typescripts, and proofs. But there are limits here as well, and sifting through the genetic evidence can only tell us so much. In order to try to explain *why* the episodes got as long as they did, it was necessary to read *Ulysses* by numbers. By doing so, it became possible to generate a data set that revealed variations, or spikes, thereby requiring an explanation that could, whenever possible, try to account for them.

There will always be critics who want to assume that Joyce continued to use more words just because he could. The lesson here, however, is that he was much more careful than we have previously given him credit for. Joyce and Pound did set a limit in the beginning, and it was one that Joyce stuck to for a while at least before more words were needed for the episodes to take shape. By exceeding the initial limit, Joyce was not only learning to adapt to the freedom that could be found in the serial format, one that eventually allowed for the breakdown of single episodes across multiple installments, but he was also simultaneously finding a way to elongate an hour and preparing for the arrival of narrators ready to speak in long, meandering sentences replete with unique words. There's still a great deal of work to be done on this subject, and I'm sure there will be other dis-coveries once this data is sifted and, I hope, expanded to include more novels. For now, it's important enough to recognize that Joyce took more from Homer than plotlines, symbols, and characters. Writing by numbers enabled him to merge contemporaneity and antiquity, as Eliot called it, but always with the sense that the words would appear on a page, in an issue, and eventually become part of a big blue book. The point, finally, is that *Ulysses* continue to be read in the future not just as a novel filled with words but as one filled with the possibility for more word counts. Why else would there be so many spaces between them?

Nº 3
One or How Many?

Mais comment rendre intéressant le drame à trois ou quatre mille personnages que présente une Société?

—Honoré de Balzac, preface to *Comédie humaine*

I A COUNTABLE COMMUNITY

How many characters are there in *Ulysses*? This should be a pretty simple question to answer. Yet in the mass of Joyce criticism, none exists. We all identify Bloom, Stephen, Molly, Boylan, Martin Cunningham, and Mrs. Breen as characters, in part, because they speak, walk, talk, think, have bodies and desires. And that's true for so many of the others who pop in and out along the way. But is a character really there if he or she is mentioned only once in passing? And what about the animals with names, or the dead or unborn, or those people who are remembered or simply mentioned even though they are not actually in Dublin on June 16, 1904?

As you can see already, any attempt to count characters immediately raises a much messier question for *Ulysses*: What makes a character count? It was something Joyce had to worry about when preparing episode 15 in the summer of 1920 (figure 3.1).[1] Intended as both an *aide-de-mémoire* for revising some of the earlier episodes still unprinted and a roll call for Leopold Bloom's lengthy hallucination ahead, this list is organized by episode number with references to characters by their first appearances. Once you

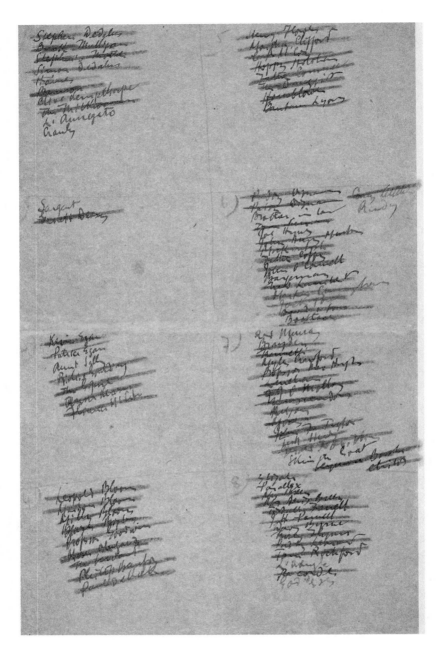

3.1 Joyce's character list for all of episodes 1–14 and part of 15.

Source: Courtesy of the British Library.

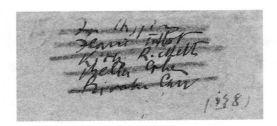

3.2 Joyce miscalculation for total number of characters.

begin sifting through each entry, however, the whole concept of character collapses. Stephen Dedalus, Buck Mulligan, and Haines are present
in the first episode (as would be expected), but so too are four characters
who never actually appear in person (Bannon, Cranly, Clive Kempthorpe,
and the drowned man, referred to as *l'annegato*). Stephen's Mother, May
Dedalus, arrives in a recollected dream from her guilty son, but she's
free to haunt the novel along with Rudy Bloom, Rudolph Virag Bloom,
and Paddy Dignam. Perhaps the presence of ghosts isn't such a surprise
given the fact that Shakespeare, Jesus Christ, the Croppy Boy, Ulysses,
Elijah, Parallax, Goddesses, Moses, Paul de Kock, and even Henry Flower
(Bloom's epistolary nom de plume) make their way in as well.[2]

As eclectic as this crew may be, Joyce wasn't just assembling names here:
he also calculated the sum of 138 characters, putting the number, in pencil,
at the bottom of the list (figure 3.2).[3] And he miscounted: the correct sum
is 140. Still, the slight inaccuracy is not what really makes this document
worth lingering over. Rather, it's the evidence this number provides of
Joyce's desire to calibrate the scale of his character network as *Ulysses* was
still being written. He wanted to know who and how many were already
there. It's a curated selection; not all of the characters that appear in each
episode at this point but most of them.

Unlike the highly symbolic number seven, which I will discuss later in
relation to compositional time, 138 (or the correct count of 140) is not
mystical, but it does signify a quantity that can be known concretely,
even if, in the wider universe of the epic, it turns out to be pretty small.
The Odyssey, for instance, runs to 342 unique characters, *The Iliad* to 716,
and there are more than 500 personnel in the *Commedia*, but even if you
include the big novels by Dickens, Balzac, and Proust or some of the great

masterpieces in China, *Ulysses* is actually on the low end of the scale (at least by Joyce's count).[4]

With *Ulysses* the realism of the crowd is a quantitative problem. Characters can be individualized (or not) and abstract (or concrete), but no matter their importance, they are always part of a greater whole. Joyce did not have a complete list of characters in place before he started writing *Ulysses*. All the genetic evidence proves that he was populating his novel as he went, creating lists along the way to remind himself exactly who went where in each episode. And if such a task was relatively easy in the early stages of the composition process, as his two protagonists more or less kept to themselves, it became particularly difficult once they actually had to move across an entire city bumping into and/or avoiding a cast of characters along the way.

Balzac could have provided at least one reliable model. He was, along with Dickens, one of the few realists who made census-taking a literary practice, and the question he asks in his preface to the *comédie humaine*, one which serves as the epigraph, is particularly relevant here: How does one make the drama of three or four thousand people in a Society interesting? Part of his solution involved writing more than ninety novels and novellas, which he filled with 2,400 different characters (1,400 or so more than Dickens, who, to be fair, wrote fifteen novels with 989 named characters) spanning the Parisian *monde social* at a specific moment in time.[5] "This number of figures, of characters," Balzac explained, " this multitude of existences needed the framework, and, pardon me for the expression, of galleries." [6]

This task of calculating the number of figures, of characters, is one of literary realism's many challenges. If there is the question of who belongs in the novel, which so often falls under the types of characters called for by particular kinds of plots, here we have the *how many*. When comparing the five Bennet sisters in Jane Austen's *Pride and Prejudice* with the fifteen "significant characters" in Balzac's *Lost Illusions*, Moretti points out that this difference is not just a matter of quantity. "It's a qualitative morphological one," he explains. The more characters you have across the social spectrum (and in this case in an expansive urban environment), the greater the potential for conflict, and the more room there is for narrative complexity. But if this quantity of characters, he argues, helps to generate a new form of the novel, it is not just because the space of the plot expands. At a more basic level, it means the quantity is knowable as a quantity. It is, after all, the *five* sisters and the *fifteen* characters that Moretti references, an exact number, there *in the novel*, even if it is never mentioned. These numbers are extracted, and in the process become more abstract units that can shape how we understand what each character means not in isolation but in relation to a larger quantity within a specific setting and narrative structure.[7]

This is one of the reasons that all novels are, in a sense, *countable communities*. I'm modifying Raymond Williams's famous phrase here in order to emphasize that the knowability of characters in communities is a computational problem.[8] These novelistic communities can be big or small, rural or urban, but they all add up to a number that so often gets experienced by characters (and readers) as an abstraction. The community, in other words, is more of a general quantity than an accurate population statistic. There may be a few individuals living in the fictional town of George Eliot's Middlemarch who could assign a number to its inhabitants, for example, but that would not itself be an expression of their inclusion within it. Rather, to know the number of the community, or knowing the inhabitants as numbers, means to exist in some relation outside of it or at a particular distance from it. Part of what's knowable in the communities Williams discusses is a quantity that doubles as a social structure and one that tends to be rooted in vague numerical calculations instead of statistically precise ones.

Character counts, however, can be part of a critical practice used to establish specificity within a given quantity, and historically they help readers manage fictional populations that can often seem unwieldy. Though it has been particularly popular for those interested in compiling taxonomies, the simple question about why computational reading would be necessary in the first place gets ignored. No matter how sprawling they may be, novels are definitely *not* as crowded as real cities, and I'm willing to bet that a comprehensive study across tens of thousands of titles will one day prove that the number per novel rarely exceeds one hundred.

In the age of big data one hundred is a small number, but in the world of the novel it is still at the upper end of the scale especially when character networks are under discussion. Novelists don't just need characters for their plots, they need specific numbers of them, and the history of the genre has moved far beyond one man stuck on a faraway island with his goats. We also should not forget that there are limits to numerical cognition. In fact, the history of numbers across cultures has itself been shaped by the simple fact that "the natural human ability to perceive number does not exceed four." This human limit has radically defined various modes of number notation around the globe for millennia even if, for the novel, the impact of this limit of four has been less obvious.[9]

Since novels are not strictly speaking visual, involving as they do events over time, then perception happens sequentially. Readers may not be inclined to think of individual characters as numbers in the plot (Lizzy 1, Kitty 2, Lydia 3, and so on), but when pressed to identify who's who, they would, at some point, be forced to calculate once the number exceeded four (1+1+1+1+1). "Beyond four, quantities are vague," Georges Ifrah explains, and the counting in *Ulysses* begins once readers want to know who appears in Barney Kiernan's pub?[10] How many Dubliners made it to Paddy Dignam's funeral? Who's there to witness Stephen's lecture in the library?

These should be easy questions to answer were it not for the fact that the "who" and "how many" requires figuring out the what. What, to return to my original question, counts as a character? If we use Joyce's list as a point of reference, then a character can be a person (real, historical, fictional, living, or dead), a thing, or even a concept. One doesn't need a body or a heartbeat, never has to speak, and he/she/it doesn't have to be present in the actual episode. And take the lineup for episode 1 as a representative example: Stephen Dedalus, Buck Mulligan, Stephen's Mother, Simon Dedalus, Haines, Bannon, Clive Kempthorpe, the Milkwoman, L'annegato, and Cranly (figure 3.3). Out of ten total names, only four are present in bodily form *in the actual episode*. One is a ghost, the other a missing person, two are remembered by Stephen, and one is mentioned in conversation. Based on this sample, we might conclude, albeit provisionally, that a character can count as a character in *Ulysses* even when he or she is located elsewhere in time or space. That is one of the reasons why episode 3 can have seven people listed, none of them actually present except in Stephen's head, and why in episode 4, Paul de Kock, Philip Beaufoy, and Blazes Boylan get identified, even though they are all mentioned in passing.

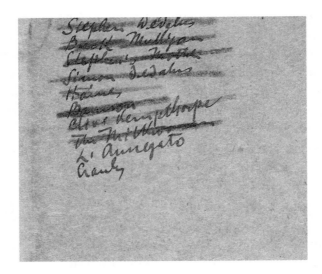

3.3   Characters from episode 1 in Joyce's character list.

Joyce may have been the first one to try and count characters in his own novel, but other empirically-minded readers have followed suite. In his biographical dictionary, first compiled in 1947, Richard Kain even claimed to have arrived at a definitive answer: 150, with the qualification that 122 of them "appear in person or in vision" leaving twenty-eight who were technically *there* even though no one else could see them. Kain also estimated that the "total number of cross references is over 900," which is entirely possible based on his initial character count, but he provides no documentation to support it.[11]

Kain's character count fits in to a subtradition of empirical research on the novel, but it is seriously flawed. For one thing, he was only interested in numbering the named characters, completely ignoring not only the nameless but also the cast of inanimate objects, animals, and ghosts who speak in episode 15, and the lengthy lists of historical personages that clutter episode 14 and episode 12. Assuming the role of census-taker in 1980, Bernard and Shari Benstock set out to assemble a definitive who's who for the novel even if they were less interested in establishing an actual number.[12] Along with an alphabetized directory of names, they included a section of anonymous listings that brings in everyone from the twenty-two unnamed wives to the "dullbrained yokel" who won Gerty MacDowell's "favors."[13] You'd be hard pressed to find any reader, present or past, who would be able to name and number all of these characters, but for the Benstocks this list was an affirmation that even the most minor characters are still *there* in *Ulysses*, as much a part of the fabric of the novel as the Blooms and Dedaluses. In fact, even Whodoyoucallhim, Strangeface, Fellowthatslike, and Sawhimbefore earn entries (*U*, 478), and that's simply for being part of the chaotic crowd that chases Bloom through Nighttown.[14]

Some critics will privilege the named character over the unnamed one, the animate human or animal over the animated object, the ones who speak over the ones who keep quiet, but *Ulysses* remains, among other things, an elaborate and incredibly diverse character system where all of these categories are up for grabs.[15] Is the single reference to a name of someone or something who never appears in bodily form enough to make them count as a character? And what about the characters who lack a proper name, an identifiable address, a physical trait, or even a discernible heartbeat—Does that exclude them from the character system?

If we follow Joyce's lead, the short answer is no: characters without bodies, names, heartbeats, or fixed addresses do count. But for the sake of clarity in the computational work that follows, we can break them down further into four different categories, which, for the sake of convenience, I've labelled major, major minor, minor, and minor minor (figure 3.4). Major characters, as you might expect, are the three protagonists: Stephen Dedalus, Leopold Bloom, and Molly Bloom (represented as triangles in figure 3.5). Major minor characters are the ones who appear in more than one episode: they don't require a proper name, but they do have to speak. Minor characters may appear in more than one episode, but they do not

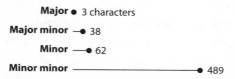

3.4   Major, major minor, minor, and minor minor characters in *Ulysses*.

have to speak in a conversation. Minor minor characters only appear in a single episode, they do not have proper names, and they do not speak (exception here would be the inanimate objects who chime in throughout episode 15).[16] These minor minor characters are the most abundant, the ones that we barely notice, and along with servants from so many nineteenth-century novels, they are, as Alex Woloch explains, "so completely reduced as characters that they hardly make an impact on the semantic or the *thematic* register of the novel, functioning on the more superficial register of plot." But even if they are less significant semantically, narratively, or thematically, these minor minor characters are there in the novel to "create a structure of characterization," and the implications are vast. Most notably, the proliferation of this "multitude of human figures at the perimeter of the narrative" helps to foreground the singularity of major characters, making them part of "one unified, although asymmetric field."[17]

Superficial, yet significant, on the very perimeter of the plot but still central to the structure: that's exactly what's happening with the various minor subcategories in *Ulysses*. There are, by my count, 489 minor minor characters present in the entire novel; so many that it can become all too easy to ignore not just Whatdoyoucallhim but also the old tramp. But approaching them, along with characters in the other categories, as a computational problem, puts us in a better position to understand the dimensionality of the entire character network, one that takes shape gradually with specific proportions and limits established over a sequence of episodes. It's a system, sure, but one that can be measured.

And just consider, for instance, that in the 1920s, at a moment when Vladimir Propp was busy decoding the thirty-one narrative functions of the seven *dramatis personae* in one hundred folk tales and E. M. Forster was dividing the universe of novelistic characters into two types, the flat and the round, Joyce had proven by example that this illusion of dimensionality within a fictional world was not always something that came from the individual characters whatever their social type or narrative function. In fact, it was an effect that could be generated by the number of total characters in the network. They may or may not fit into any clearly defined category, but what mattered above all was the fact that the *sum of the network was always greater*, and it gave individual characters depth not because of who or what they were but because of *how many they were among*. That is the focus of this chapter: the character

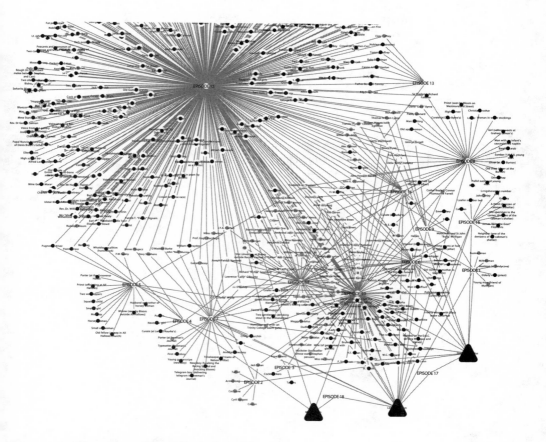

3.5 Character network of all episodes in *Ulysses*.

network in *Ulysses* as a quantity that can be calculated to understand what characters are and how they function.

And here's what happens when you visualize that character network (figure 3.5).[18] It's a far cry from the rows and columns of Joyce's handwritten list, one, we should remember, that he needed at a specific moment in time so that he could see *Ulysses*, the novel, as a set of character quantities. Here instead we have all eighteen episodes reimagined as a series of clusters, each one of them organized around a specific episode, or node, with edges that identify those characters who move between several different episodes. It is a network diagram that focuses more on the relationship between character quantities and less on degrees of familiarity between social types or groups.

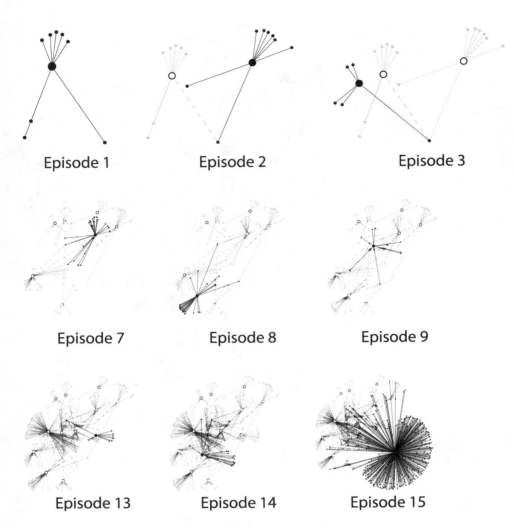

3.6   Character network of *Ulysses*, episode by episode.

This arrangement of characters in a network provides an immediate spatial perspective of what is otherwise experienced over an attenuated period of time. What's radically different, however, is the sense of scale. Without even parsing the information, we immediately see the "asymmetry" that Alex Woloch first identified in "the character system" of novels: some of these clusters are significantly larger with more edges than others, the distribution skewed by episode 15, the squid-cluster that dominates the top half. But instead of taking us out of *Ulysses*, network visualizations such as this one

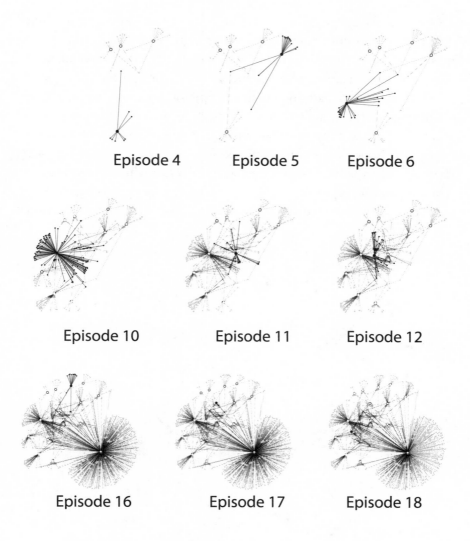

have the potential to throw us right back in by providing an estranged perspective on the scale of a literary work so often obscured by the bibliographical accoutrements and semantic units of sentences, paragraphs, and pages.

And this particular example of the network we call *Ulysses* is itself a starting point for analysis. We may not need a visualization to know that episode 15 has more characters than all of the other episodes combined, but that's not really the point. Network visualizations are at the beginning and not the end of interpretation. They don't just tell us which characters appeared where or how often or in what order (figure 3.6).

They also make us see the organization of the system by foregrounding where characters cluster and to what degree they overlap or disappear, making the entire novel less like a compendium of static details and more like a dynamic organism whose shape changes from episode to episode.

Here's one particularly poignant example of what was happening at a late stage in the creative process. Episode 15 arrived with more than 445 total characters, 349 of them unique. If you remove the nodes and edges of episode 15 from the network, *Ulysses* gets a whole lot simpler (figure 3.7). That unwieldy cluster of 592 total nodes whittles down to 235 (counting through episode 14). Not only is a *Ulysses* stripped of episode 15 significantly smaller: it corresponds with a radically different conception

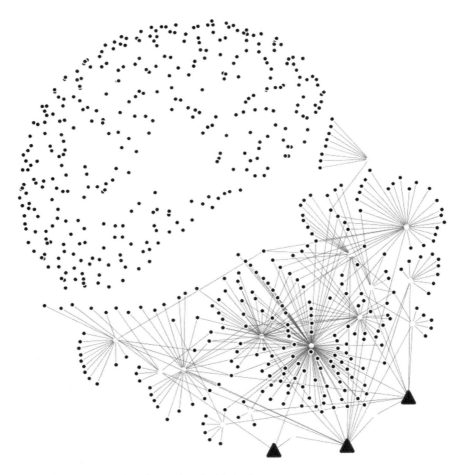

3.7 Character network with episode 15 highlighted.

of character for the novel as a whole. Even though different numbers of characters appear and disappear episode to episode, the novel itself is an aggregate and the *meaning of each one depends upon the presence of the many scattered throughout.* Once episode 15 arrives in the sequence, there's no going back. These characters are there in the novel even if more than half of them never appeared before and never would again. Whether you want to think of this accumulation of characters as generating a universe, a world, a city, a system, a community, or a network, they are a number that no reader ever counts even if every reader is made to wonder at some point if it even matters.

Which brings me back to Joyce's list. By his own erroneous count, the unfinished *Ulysses* had 138 characters after fourteen episodes (with the principal living cast from episode 15 included), but for someone with epic ambitions (and with four episodes left to write), that was definitely not to scale. *Joyce needed more.* With the events (and episodes) that remained, however, including a brief respite at the cabman's shelter (episode 16), followed by cocoa for two at 7 Eccles Street (episode 17), and a monologue by Molly (episode 18), the options for random encounters were extremely limited. And in many ways that didn't matter. In the course of writing the previous episodes, he had realized that the consciousness of a single individual could also contribute to the total number of the crowd. If episode 15 is the most crowded episode of all that's because the narration stops relying on the fictional reality of a concrete world outside. *Consciousness doesn't need the city to be crowded, and characters can still count by being there in mind only.*

II THE NUMBER OF THE CROWD

Before I get into questions involving the crowded mind, I need to backtrack a bit in order to establish what makes a crowd in *Ulysses* seem so crowded in the first place. To do that, I'll consider another question: How many characters are present in each episode? And does the number and its variation tell us anything? Episode 6 is the best place to start because it represents the first social outing in the novel, one that ends up setting the scale for the others that follow.

Are we all here now? That's the question Martin Cunningham asks at the beginning of episode 6 as the mourners prepare to go to Paddy Dignam's funeral. Given the fact that Bloom is still outside of the carriage, they are not, in fact, *all there*. Bloom is the one that's missing. What this episode prepares us for, then, is the experience of finding a place to fit in, and it plays out during an uncomfortable carriage ride in which the other characters find different ways to offend Bloom, some more malicious than others. Cunningham's question is more complicated than it might seem, for what we discover in this episode is the fact that being *here now* can mean many different things. Bloom was not there at first, but he fills a "vacant place," which means someone else was there earlier. The same is true for the old woman staring at him from the "lowered blinds." "Thanking her stars she was passed over," Bloom observes (*U*, 72). The old woman is *here now* but that means someone else has taken her place (at least for the time being).

Fitting in, or being *all there*, is an existential, metaphysical, and social problem, but it also connects with a practical numerical conundrum. How many characters can Leopold Bloom realistically cross paths with as he travels by carriage to and from Glasnevin cemetery? The previous five episodes have had, on average, eight characters, with a leap to eighteen during his stroll in episode 5, but this one jumps to thirty (figure 3.8). The dramatic increase makes sense, given the fact that members of the community

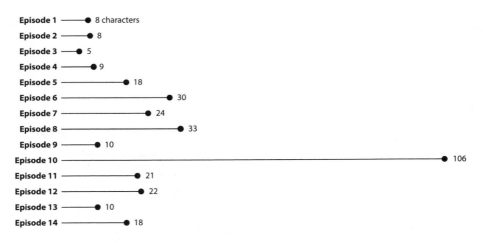

Episode 1 ——————● 8 characters
Episode 2 ——————● 8
Episode 3 ————● 5
Episode 4 ——————● 9
Episode 5 ——————————● 18
Episode 6 ————————————● 30
Episode 7 ——————————● 24
Episode 8 ———————————————● 33
Episode 9 —————● 10
Episode 10 ———————————————————————————————————————● 106
Episode 11 ——————————● 21
Episode 12 ——————————● 22
Episode 13 —————● 10
Episode 14 ——————————● 18

3.8 Number of characters for episodes 1 to 14.

are there to pay their respects, but packing thirty characters into a single episode requires significant orchestration, grouping and regrouping them as they make their way from the carriage to the grave and back. These thirty characters in episode 6 do not just represent an erratic quantitative leap, however. It is the first in a cluster of episodes in *Ulysses* that vary between eighteen and thirty-three (episodes 7, 8, 11, 12, 14), each one corresponding with a different public outing. I'll discuss the full significance of this number later on, but for now I want to make a simple observation. For this moment in the plot, Joyce needed to come up with a number for the crowd, and thirty was it. This number is big enough to make us feel as if Bloom is in the presence of mixed company during the course of an hour and still small enough to keep him from getting lost.[19]

And this question about the number of the crowd actually plays out in the episode itself, when Bloom gets distracted by the mysterious man in the mackintosh just as he's trying to count his fellow attendees. "Mr Bloom stood far back, his hat in his hand, counting the bared heads. Twelve. I'm thirteen. No. The chap in the macintosh is thirteen. Death's number" (*U*, 90).[20] Each of these "bared heads" have names, but at this moment they have been transformed into numbers. In the process of counting, Bloom even tries to manipulate the sequence, partly for the sake of accuracy but also because he wants to avoid getting stuck with the unlucky number by pinning it on someone else. As we come to find out later, none of the other characters know if the "man in the macintosh," as Bloom calls him, was ever really there, so this number in episode 6 remains unknowable, plus or minus one depending on who you choose to count.[21]

Is it entirely a coincidence that the first crowded episode prompts the very question about character that circulates throughout the entire novel: Who counts? Bloom isn't so sure, so why should we be? There's the "man in the macintosh," of course, but what about Paddy Dignam, the "finest purest character" Bob Doran ever knew (*U*, 249). He is definitely in the plot, so to speak, but, pure or not, he's also dead (potted, as the pun in the Plumtree's ad goes, not plotted).[22] Technically, then, Dignam is present during the service when Bloom's counting bared heads, but in body only and not in mind. That certainly didn't stop Joyce from putting Dignam on his own character list—an issue I'll get back to—but for now I want to remain focused on the characters who are *present and alive*.

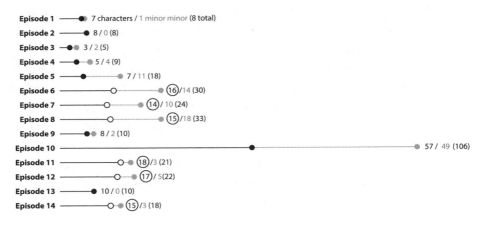

3.9 Number of minor minor characters for episodes 1 to 14.

In *Ulysses*, there are different degrees of being there, which I've broken down earlier into the four categories (major, major minor, minor, and minor minor). Out of thirty total, sixteen characters in episode 6 fall into that minor minor category, and curious to see if this ratio was unique, I then compared the crowd in episode 6 with the other episodes. What I found was surprising (figure 3.9). If you remove the minor minor characters from the final count, they all added up to between fourteen and eighteen. So even when there was some variation in the final crowd size (eighteen to thirty-three with a twenty-five average), the quantity of the crowd remained consistent.

Novelistic crowd control, perhaps? That's one way we might think about it. There is a limit, in other words, to the number of characters who can appear in each episode. Dante's *Inferno* was no exception. He carefully followed the numerological symbolism for each canticle, but just imagine if he tried to pack in more than two or three encounters between Dante and the damned per canto. The balance of setting, action, pacing, and character would have been lost. I'm not recommending here that the actual number of sinners corresponds with the "cosmic *ordo*," as Curtius calls it, but it is certainly part of the proportionality of an "aesthetic organism" (Gunnar Qvarnström's phrase).[23] Like Dante, Joyce had to figure out how many characters could fit given the constraints with time and space in the plot.

That's one reason why episode 12 is such an important example. It belongs to that middle stage in the compositional process that marks the departure from a more solitary interior monologue and into, what Groden calls, "expansion and encyclopedism."[24] What interests me most here is the way that these new forms of experimentation do not disrupt the character counts (with episode 15 as the exception). Critics have unpacked the strong thematic parallels with earlier episodes, but character count has not been identified as a significant factor in the overall design.[25] But it should be because the numbers of, for example, twenty-two for episode 12 and twenty-four for episode 7, reveal that there was a measurement getting used to frame the encounter between Bloom and the Citizen. Instead of going mano a mano without an audience, there are fifteen other characters sitting in or walking by the pub, all of them appearing in previous episodes (J. T. A. Crofton gets mentioned).[26] Aside from the Citizen and his dog, these other characters function either to humor the Citizen or provoke him, an effect, David Hayman argues, that makes none of them "guilty of outrage" even though they still contribute to the "chaos."[27] These characters also give Bloom some much-needed external dimensionality, providing details about who he is, some of it flattering, some of it specious. "By their number and power," Hayman concludes, "they gradually tip the scale in Bloom's favor."[28] This is the formula of the one and the many that Woloch identifies: the minor characters moving about the plot precisely so that the protagonist can emerge.

When writing episode 12 in late June 1919, Joyce even prepared another character list with sixteen different names. Only eleven of them would appear in the final version, but that's half the total. Groden suspects that Joyce made this list early on in the process to "fill in the gaps in character-ization in the existing draft," but, he admits, there's the added difficulty of figuring out what to do with those characters who are not "really present" (in the final version and the list) including Mr. and Mrs. Breen (identified as "Dennis Breen" and "Mrs Breen b. Powell" on Joyce's list) and Corny Kelleher, who quickly pass by the window.[29] It may not be surprising to find characters who count even if they're simply strolling by, but what's so surprising about this reshuffling of characters between the early list and the final version is the fact that the crowd ratio remains the same in the end. Out of twenty-two characters in the final version, five of them are minor minor (Helmsman, slut, loafer with a patch, nymphs, and Garryowen).

But there's one more fascinating genetic detail: on the last page of an early copybook for episode 12, Joyce made another list that introduces characters by their first appearance.

Arrival Alf Bergan: Breens pass
Arrival Bloom
Arrival John Wyse Nolan
Arrival J.J. O'Molloy, Ned Lambert
Arrival Cunningham, Power
Finale[30]

It is at once a sequence of arrivals and a character list. Unlike the other examples, this one corresponds with the structure of the plot. These characters are not just following one after the other: *they are the episode*. Episode 12 is as much a technic (gigantism), an hour of the day, organ of the body as it is a sum total of those characters who appear in it. And no matter how exaggerated or overblown the style may become, the crowd ratio remains consistent, providing an anchor for the chaos that ensues.

III THE NUMBER OF THE CITY

But if there is, as I've been arguing so far, a number to the crowd in *Ulysses*, what about the city? According to the Census of Ireland conducted in 1901, Dublin had 290,638 official inhabitants, but how many characters would you need to make the fictional representation a few years later seem expansive enough?[31] *Ulysses*, as we know, is not just a collection of discrete episodes with isolated character sets. It is also the sum total of characters in a specific urban environment so that even the nobodies have a number and are part of a larger quantity that evolves over a period of time. This point, would significantly influence the population sample as the plot moves across a variety of mostly public places. As readers, we don't have to wait until the last episode for a wide-angle view of Dublin. It is placed smack in the middle of the novel, providing a snapshot of the city as it has never been seen before and recycling many of the characters who have already appeared.

The most precise documentation on the timing and spacing of episode 10 is contained in Clive Hart and Ian Gunn's *Topographical Guide*, which includes, among other things, a table identifying who is where when down to the minute.[32] What often gets lost in all of their intricate detective work is the fact that the nineteen locations across Dublin are organized around thirty characters, almost half of them arranged in pairs or small groups (counting cavalcade, for example, as one). Thirty, as you'll remember from episode 6, is not a random number. It is the average quantity of characters whenever the plot moves into a public space.

But what are we to do with the seventy-six others who pass by on the streets of Dublin? If thirty is the number of the crowd, does that make 106 the number of the city (at least as imagined within the constraints of a single episode)?[33] Maybe, but then we also would need to determine who, and perhaps what, is getting counted here. Critics have often noted that episode 10 recycles characters from previous episodes, thereby making it possible to stage some memorable cameos, but none of them have yet asked *how many characters only appear here and nowhere else* or *how many of them appear here for the first time* and reappear in the second half of the novel.

This is how it all breaks down: thirty-five characters appeared before and in episode 10, twenty-two appeared for the first time in episode 10 and after, and forty-nine appear only once (figure 3.10). This breakdown reveals that the network of 106 characters is proportional. Too many of them in any one of these categories would disrupt the balance between the new and old, the seen before and the never-to-be-seen-again, and this point is particularly significant given the fact that this episode, number 10 out of 18, divides the novel in half. And what makes these proportions all the more revealing is that episode 10 (with its eighteen different sections and one crescendo) is a microcosm for *Ulysses*, reaching backward into the past, ahead into the future, all the while incorporating half of the population that would never be seen or heard from again.

Here's where things get interesting. In the course of compiling this data, I began to suspect that getting to one hundred characters in a single episode would have been particularly meaningful for Joyce because of his numerological superstitions, which involve his belief in all kinds of allegorical correspondences that can be arrived at through the addition, subtraction, division, and multiplication of numbers. Other critics have demonstrated that episode 10 is the tenth episode of *Ulysses* and ten, which can be symbolized by the Christian Cross (an X).[34] If you map out the routes of Father Conmee and the Viceregal procession, symbols for the Catholic church and the British Empire, that X appears with Bloom smack in the middle browsing at a book stall.

Dublin is a maze, with the hearts and souls of its inhabitants under the control of foreign powers, but it is also a numerical equation with proportions that can be measured. And if the measurement had added up exactly to one hundred, then that would be God's number, 10 squared or 3 to the third power plus 1. One hundred is the number employed, most famously,

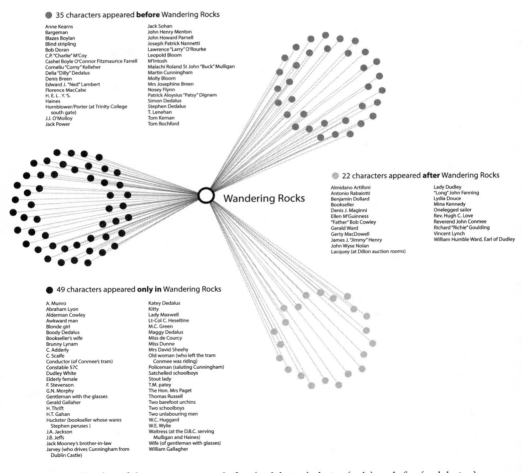

● 35 characters appeared **before** Wandering Rocks

Anne Kearns
Bargeman
Blazes Boylan
Blind stripling
Bob Doran
C.P. "Charlie" M'Coy
Cashel Boyle O'Connor Fitzmaurice Farrell
Corneliu "Corny" Kelleher
Delia "Dilly" Dedalus
Denis Breen
Edward J. "Ned" Lambert
Florence MacCabe
H. E. L. Y. 'S.
Haines
Hornblower/Porter (at Trinity College south gate)
J.J. O'Molloy
Jack Power
Jack Sohan
John Henry Menton
John Howard Parnell
Joseph Patrick Nannetti
Lawrence "Larry" O'Rourke
Leopold Bloom
M'Intosh
Malachi Roland St John "Buck" Mulligan
Martin Cunningham
Molly Bloom
Mrs Josephine Breen
Nosey Flynn
Patrick Aloysius "Patsy" Dignam
Simon Dedalus
Stephen Dedalus
T. Lenehan
Tom Kernan
Tom Rochford

Wandering Rocks

● 22 characters appeared **after** Wandering Rocks

Almidano Artifoni
Antonio Rabaiotti
Benjamin Dollard
Bookseller
Denis J. Maginni
Ellen M'Guinness
"Father" Bob Cowley
Gerald Ward
Gerty MacDowell
James J. "Jimmy" Henry
John Wyse Nolan
Lacquey (at Dillon auction rooms)
Lady Dudley
"Long" John Fanning
Lydia Douce
Mina Kennedy
Onelegged sailor
Rev. Hugh C. Love
Reverend John Conmee
Richard "Richie" Goulding
Vincent Lynch
William Humble Ward, Earl of Dudley

● 49 characters appeared **only in** Wandering Rocks

A. Munro
Abraham Lyon
Alderman Cowley
Awkward man
Blonde girl
Boody Dedalus
Bookseller's wife
Brunny Lynam
C. Adderly
C. Scaife
Conductor (of Conmee's tram)
Constable 57C
Dudley White
Elderly female
F. Stevenson
G.N. Morphy
Gentleman with the glasses
Gerald Gallaher
H. Thrift
H.T. Gahan
Huckster (bookseller whose wares Stephen peruses)
J.A. Jackson
J.B. Jeffs
Jack Mooney's brother-in-law
Jarvey (who drives Cunningham from Dublin Castle)
Katey Dedalus
Kitty
Lady Maxwell
Lt-Col C. Heseltine
M.C. Green
Maggy Dedalus
Miss de Courcy
Miss Dunne
Mrs David Sheehy
Old woman (who left the tram Conmee was riding)
Policeman (saluting Cunningham)
Satchelled schoolboys
Stout lady
T.M. patey
The Hon. Mrs Paget
Thomas Russell
Two barefoot urchins
Two schoolboys
Two unlabouring men
W.C. Huggard
W.E. Wylie
Waitress (at the D.B.C. serving Mulligan and Haines)
Wife (of gentleman with glasses)
William Gallagher

3.10   Number of characters appearing before (and during), during (only), and after (and during) episode 10.

by Dante, who was at the end of a long tradition of numerically-minded writers. *Numerical composition*, Curtius argues, has a long and rich history, intended, above all to prove that "God's disposition was arithmetical!" The presence of *numero disposuisti* in Roman poetry, medieval Latin, and vernacular literature, leads Curtius to ask the more general question: "Must not the writer likewise allow himself to be guided by numbers in his disposition?"[35]

In Joyce's case, yes: he was guided by all kinds of numerical systems, but as critics sifting through and comparing them, we're left to ask: Which one is it? Did he want 100 and end up with 106 (another miscount perhaps)? Was 106 the plan all along (and if so, why the extra six characters)? Given the presence of so many other numerical symbols in the novel, 100 characters, though wrong, would have Kenner's "ring of rightness" about it, and if we begin to weed out the awkward man, the satchelled schoolboys, the Gentleman with the glass, and that mysterious M'intosh, it is a number that would be attainable. But if we begin to ignore the number that is there, focusing instead on *the one that could be there*, aren't we also in danger of delegitimizing the quantitative method, making computational close reading more an exercise in critical desire than an opportunity for data-minded empiricism?

IV RECOUNTING THE COMMUNITY

Computational close reading can work well when measuring those characters who are present in bodily form, the same ones wandering around the city in episode 10, but things get complicated once characters are no longer just themselves. Consider, for example, Bloom's escape from the Citizen at the end of episode 12 in the guise of ben Bloom Elijah. Up until this point in the novel, characters have either been named or nameless, animate or inanimate, nobodies or somebodies, but this is the first time when we've had a major character transform into someone else right before our eyes. This apotheosis sets us up for a computational problem in the episodes that follow. If Leopold Bloom can also be the prophet Elijah during his escape, then does that make him one or two characters? And would the same hold true for the correspondences of Deasy with Nestor,

Pisistratus with Sargent, Kevin Egan with Menelaus, Eumaeus with Skin the Goat, and Father Coffey with Cerberus. Put simply: Can one character be many?

Stanislaus Joyce certainly thought so when he observed that "Whoever studies [*Ulysses*] in detail will find that a number of generations of Irish history have been superimposed on one another."[36] A number of generations, certainly, but not all of them Irish. From the very first page of a novel with a borrowed title, each character is already someone else. The difference at the end of episode 12 and after, however, is that this process has been externalized, not something that happens allusively or behind the scenes, but actually as a part of the plot, and it anticipates some of the most outlandish character swaps in literary history, including the genealogical developments of language and the human fetus in episode 14, the hallucinatory performances involving inanimate objects in episode 15, the interstellar transmutations of Stephen and Bloom at the end of episode 17, and the climactic metamorphosis of Molly into Gaia, the earth mother, in episode 18.

Once we begin to think that one character can be many, though, *it's time for a recount*. But doing so requires that we jump into their heads to see who else is there. That, I think, was one of the more remarkable, if overlooked, freedoms enabled by the invention of interior monologue. As much as this narrative device made it possible to register sense impressions and memories of fictional characters, it also allowed for the introduction of other populations far from the time and space of the present, thereby creating the conditions for an entirely new understanding of character networks. You are who you think about, remember, and repress.

Gilles Deleuze and Félix Guattari's essay "One or Several Wolves?" is particularly useful here when thinking through the connection between characters, their networks, and multiplicity. In their critique of Sigmund Freud's case history of the Wolf Man, and of psychoanalytic paradigms more generally, they focus their attention on the misnumbering of the wolves. Freud's patient, they observe, identifies six or seven wolves in his verbal recollection of a dream he once had as a boy, but he draws a picture with five. In his analysis, Freud chooses to ignore the mistaken number of wolves sitting on the tree branches in the image, choosing instead to spin out his analysis of the six or seven so that he can work through his narrative about the primal scene that will eventually lead all the way back to the boy's castration anxiety thereby reinforcing the connection with one wolf, the father. That reduction of six or seven to one is precisely the problem for Deleuze and Guattari for it reveals that Freud, in his desire for unity, forgot, remained ignorant of, or chose to ignore the fact that wolves travel in packs—thereby missing the point that a wolf is always many even when it is one. The larger implication of Freud's mistake, then, was that "he did not see that the unconscious itself was fundamentally a crowd."[37]

If interior monologue makes it possible for readers to enter into the minds of other characters, wouldn't this same principle of the crowd apply? Stephen, Bloom, and Molly are not just impersonal nodes in the social network that is Dublin. Their minds contain networks, making it possible for the first time in the history of the novel to have so many characters packed into the mind of one. But what makes this discovery of a crowded mind so revolutionary is the fact that these characters don't even have to inhabit the same time or place. That's one reason that the morphological nightmare we know as episode 15 becomes possible. It is a hallucination filled with living and dead individuals, objects, concepts, past and future selves, all of them filtering through Bloom's head in less than an hour, none of them *really there*.

Getting to this point of the *one as many*, however, is a gradual process, one that begins in earnest with episode 3 when we first find a solitary Stephen walking down the strand. Up until this episode, Stephen has thought about others, mostly literal or historical personages, but this is one where he interiorizes those who exist externally. Here's what the narration tells us: "They came down the steps from Leahy's terrace prudently, *Frauenzimmer*: and down the shelving shore flabbily, their splayed feet sinking in the silted sand. Like me, like Algy, coming down to our mighty mother" (*U*, 31). The *Frauenzimmer* are objectively there in the episode, but they are quickly brought into the vortex of Stephen's own subjective associations (and lyrical fantasies), which, in this instance, involve mothers (symbolized by the sea) and the writers (including Algernon Charles Swinburne) who write about it. When a similar intrusion with other characters takes place later on, they quickly become part of the crowd in Stephen's mind, which is punctuated again by his desires, memories, and whimsy: "A woman and a man. I see her skirties. Pinned up, I bet.

Their dog ambled about a bank of dwindling sand, trotting, sniffing on all sides. Looking for something lost in a past life" (*U*, 38).

A *Frauenzimmer* [Florence MacCabe] with a friend [possibly Anne Kearns], a woman/a man [cocklepickers], and a dog [Tatters]: that's the complete list of characters who are actually present in episode 3 (and independently of Stephen's mind). Now, if you include those who pass through Stephen's mind during this episode (including Lantern Jaws, Queen Victoria, and Moses), the number jumps to one hundred, and this includes the whole range of real and fictional personages, a majority of them reappearing in later episodes. As readers, we get caught up in the flotsam and jetsam of Stephen's thoughts, making it difficult to appreciate that the character-system continues to expand exponentially. This early peek into an internalized network is a model for what's to come. Episode 4, for instance, has eight characters present excluding Bloom (though including the Pussens) but there are really seventy-two if you also include those who are mentioned, and it is immediately followed by episode 5 with eighteen characters present, 111 if you add in all the rest.

With minds this crowded, it turns out that our two protagonists are never really alone. And there are times when that's a problem. Consider the moment when Bloom begrudgingly meets M'Coy on the street. The entire exchange is preceded by the incomplete phrase: "Hate company when you" (*U*, 60) *want to be alone* are the words that would naturally follow. Even with M'Coy right in front of him, Bloom retreats inside his own head, and what he finds there are more characters. What makes the distracted exchange between the two even more poignant, and hilarious, is the presence of the dead Paddy Dignam. He appears, ironically enough, when M'coy recounts his own surprise at finding out the news, and it comes just as Bloom strains to watch the woman enter the carriage across the street: "*Is it Paddy Dignam*? I said. I couldn't believe it when I heard it. I was with him no later than Friday last or Thursday was it in the Arch. *Yes*, he said. *He's gone. He died on Monday, poor fellow.* Watch! Watch! Silk flash rich stockings white. Watch!" (*U*, 61).

Is it Paddy Dignam, indeed? Bloom's desire for the fleeting woman in front of him blocked by talk of the man who's irrevocably gone.[38] The humor of this whole exchange comes from the inability to keep the networks of the living, the dead, and the missing separate. M'Coy and Bloom are out on the street: M'Coy remembers finding out Paddy was no longer among the living; M'Coy announces his absence from the funeral in order to be present for the arrival of a body of someone that has not yet been found. Bloom, not wanting to think about Dignam, tries to concentrate on the woman in front of him; left on his own, shortly after, he ends up remembering his father.

Like Freud, Bloom seems to have forgotten that wolves travel in packs. His unconscious is crowded, but just when he's trying to keep the focus on the living characters outside his head, the inner network refuses to keep quiet, and out of his repression, the more painful memory of the father surfaces shortly thereafter. It's tempting to conclude that M'Coy is there but Paddy and Virag are not. But the technique of interior monologue provides another variation. Paddy is there along with M'Coy but so too is Virag, who only appears after the conversation has ended. Interior monologue is the narrative technique that allows for this kind of multiplicity.[39] It was also a powerful reminder that the more realistic representation of human psychology can foreground the magical and at times unsettling truth about character networks. As long as our minds have the capacity to remember, we can always evoke the presence of others who are not there. And the novel itself as Woolf, Joyce, Faulkner, and Proust demonstrated so effectively is one genre that can effectively grapple with a crowded, conscious mind.

A crowded conscious mind is one thing: a crowded unconscious mind quite another. When Bloom or Stephen think about other characters in the first fourteen episodes, they are in a conscious state. With episode 15, however, that is no longer the case, especially once we enter Bella Cohen's brothel. Characters can be *there* on the page but there's no clear sense that they are either in a physical place, the brothel, or in a conscious mind, Bloom's or Stephen's. This inability to locate them, however, should not keep us from counting. I suggested at the beginning of the chapter that Joyce's erroneous calculation of 138 characters was a wake-up call that he need to enlarge the network. Episode 15, as I see it, is the pointed response. This sequence of hallucinations is an opportunity to push the boundaries of character representation further, doing so, in part, by asking who's there and who's not.

And why would Joyce want to rely any longer on real characters when even objects can speak? Critics have examined what this raucous population means to our understanding of Bloom's psyche, but I want to keep the emphasis here on number. If we count all the characters present, animate and inanimate, living and dead, human and animal in *Ulysses*, the number is 592, 349 of them from episode 15 (figure). That number of unique characters present in episode 15 is not only significantly larger than the other episodes, it makes up 59 percent of all characters present in the entire novel, radically modifying the scale. One could argue that these characters really don't matter, they are just playful distortions in the troubled minds of Bloom and Stephen, but in doing so, we would then have to reconsider the significance, or status, of all the other minor minor characters that pass through the novel as well.

Put another way, we might ask if the Murray girls (episode 18) or Lizzie Twigg (episode 8) count as much, say, as the Blushing waitress (episode 15). All of them appear once in *Ulysses*, none of them utter a word, which means that in the larger narrative economy they don't do much of anything. But to place the emphasis only on function or frequency is to miss the point. No matter how minor individual characters may be, the network is the sum of them all, the accumulation of the many, some more significant to the plot than others, some with stronger interpersonal ties than others, all of them central to the scope and scale of this fictional world. If Joyce had kept the number down with episode 15 so that there was relative parity among episodes, our experience as readers would have been significantly different. Dublin would have become smaller, sure, but the number of its inhabitants would have seemed significantly reduced, making it even more likely that his Dubliners could not only be counted, they could be counted correctly and with relative ease.

Episode 15, though, is a world unto itself, a single episode strong enough, as Groden once pointed out, to make the entire novel a "character."[40] That's a tantalizing idea, one I would stretch in my formulation to mean that if episode 15 is the unconscious of *Ulysses*, all of the episodes before, and even after it, provide material for the crowd. In this recount, the numbers are revealing. Critics have long suspected that episode 15 is, like episode 10, one more character reunion even if a whole range of inanimate objects and anonymous others show up to speak. No one, however, has actually done the math. It turns out that ninety-six different characters from the previous fourteen episodes reappear here, and they're not often the ones you would expect.[41] There's the Bent Hag, Moses Dlugacz, and Larry O'Rourke from episode 4; the Pugnosed Driver and Postmistress from episode 5; and the Blind Stripling from episodes 8, 10, and 11.

100, as I said before, might not be large enough for those working with big data, but in the world of this novel it is. There was that character list of 138, the city of Dublin at 106, and now the world of episode 15 at 96. These are all approximations for a character concept Joyce was working through repeatedly as his novel kept growing. Yet, even when he assembles all 445 characters in episode 15, that basic quantity remains the same. Indeed, there could have been versions of episode 15 with different ratios—one, in fact, with even more unique characters—but that's not what happens. *Ulysses* explodes with this episode, pushing his experiment with character ever further, but the numbers leave us with an important lesson: even the unconscious has a limit. He can fill the minds of Bloom and Stephen during this extended sequence all he wants, but thirty-eight thousand words later, and the core character quantity is the same.

In an effort to complicate things further, I want to work through Molly Bloom's network, which functions as the dramatic counterpoint to Bloom's internal pantomime not just in episode 15 but throughout the entire day. How many characters new and old do we find in episode 18? With Molly wide awake in bed and a husband soon snoring by her side that's two characters, right? No. If we've learned anything at all from the previous episodes, that bedroom in 7 Eccles Street turns out to be pretty crowded, and it doesn't help that her capacity to remember names is so awful. After a long day offstage, Molly finally gets the chance to be many instead of one, a single character who loops in more than 284 others, 186 of them unique. And to get a sense of the scale of that number, consider that even in his most introverted state, Stephen maxes out at 96 during his stroll on the beach in episode 3, and Bloom, a more social creature, hits 206 during episode 8.

The large size of Molly's crowd can be attributed, in part, to the fact that she gets to think in peace, her mind free to wander through memories of the past and the characters who have populated it. Many of the unique references are generic (Fellow opposite, Guard on Belfast Train), impossible to pin down (Delapaz, Jamesy) or fictional (the Odd Priest disturbing a nun's sleep), but they are still part of a long list of names and types passing through her mind. Molly's present life is the sum of the characters who have passed through it, not only the more immediate ones (Boylan, of course, and Stephen), but also the generic (including little bitch, man with curly hair) and the remote (including Conny Connolly who once wrote her "in white ink on black paper sealed with sealingwax") (*U*, 631).

We can divide characters into categories based on degrees of impor-tance, but these complex networks in *Ulysses* also reveal a truth about life and living common to everyone: our minds are filled with characters we can't always keep at bay or separate into clearly defined hierarchies of importance. And that's also what makes us unique: the very composition of our networks distinguishes us from one another. Leopold and Molly are no exception (figure 3.11). They share a large number of acquaintances, 97 of them to be exact, but that leaves 186 others, who don't appear any-where else.[42] There are certainly some names that Leopold Bloom would recognize if given the chance to go through Molly's mental list, but the arrangement at this particular moment belongs to her, generic types she admires and despises, names from her childhood she barely remembers, others from adulthood she can't keep track of, and still others she prefers not to think too much about.

If you want to capture the autonomy of two human beings, the forma-tion of differentiated social networks is certainly one way to do it. Unless you live your entire life together as a couple from birth, and work, travel, and live every day in each other's company, it's inevitable that your networks will be different. That was certainly true with the hallucinations from epi-sode 15, but here we discover just how commonplace the experience of such an expansive network can be. We get to know Molly so intimately at this moment because she conjures up a past organized around a network of peo-ple from the various stages of her life. Molly is many precisely because she contains a multiplicity of characters both named and nameless, and all of them countable even if no one else will ever know or, perhaps, care.

V MISCOUNTING THE COMMUNITY

A year after *Ulysses* appeared, Joyce was surprised to discover he was not included in a popular "Irish 'Who's Who.' "[43] "It contains 2500 names," he complained to Weaver, "but not mine."[44] Even with a number this high (including eight other Joyces no less), there was still not room enough for the author of *Ulysses*. The novel he left behind, however, has ended up as a particularly powerful antidote to the collective forgetting of his countrymen (in his native city no less), a list of characters, it turns out,

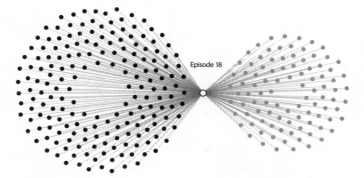

Episode 18

186 UNIQUE characters

A. Brierly
Abrines (R. and J.)
Absentminded beggar (from Kipling's poem)
Adultress (in Wife of Scarli)
Alexander Findlater
Alfonso XIII
Alicia Lambe
American
Aunt Mary (song)
Bill Baily
Bishop
Blackguardlooking fellow
Blazes Boylan's sisters
Boatmen (who rented a boat to Bloom doesn't like)
Briggs (hypothetical name Molly doesn't like)
Burglar
Butcher
Cameron highlander
Capt. Grove(s)
Captain Rubio
Catherine Opisso
Charles Gounod
Christopher Friery
Coalman
Common workman
Conny Connolly
Dean or bishop
Delapaz (name Molly remembers from Gibraltar)
Delgracia (name Molly remembers from Gibraltar)
Don Miguel de la Flora (Molly's pretended Gibraltar novio)
Dr J.R. Collins
Edward Bulwer-Lytton
Eugene Aram
Fast widow
Father Corrigan
Fellow (guitarist Molly remembers)
Fellow opposite
Fellow that was something in the four courts
Fernando Gomez
First man
Floey Dillon's husband
Florence E.C. Maybrick
Fr Vial Plana
François Rabelais
Freddy Mayers
General Charles George Gordon
George Edward Skerry & Co.
George Simpson
German Emperor
Girl (assumed by Molly to have married Mulvey)
Girl (object of a man's pursuit in Molly's conjectures)
Girl (waitress at D.B.C.)
Governor
Guard (on Belfast train)
Hardened criminal
Harry Devan
Henry Dunbar
Hester Stanhope
Horatio Jones Sprague
Hornblower/Porter (at Trinity College south gate)
Husband (cuckolded without recourse, according to Molly)
Idiot in the gallery
Ines
James Maybrick
Jamesy
Jealous old husband
Johannes Paulus Kruger
John Lewis Sprague
Juan Valera
K.C.
Kathleen Kearney
Kitty O'Shea
Lady (the queen in Molly's fortune cards)
Larby Sharon
Lillie Langtry
Little bitch
Little Italian boy
Lord Robert Cornelius Napier
Lover (of Spanish girl in window in Ronda, imagined by Molly)
Lt Stanley G. Gardner
Lucie Manette
Luigi
Lunita Laredo (Molly's mother)
Man (yearned for by Molly)
Man at the corner
Man with the curly hair
Mandola
Manning Ltd
Margaret Hungerford
Married woman (whom Molly views as an easy prey for men)
Mary Ann (name for overdressed female)
Mary Driscoll's aunt
Mary Elizabeth Braddon
Masetto
Medical (at Holles Street hospital, remembered by Molly)
Messengerboy
Miss Gillespie
Miss Stack
Miss Theother (from Molly's mock list of patriotic sopranos)
Miss This (from Molly's mock list of patriotic sopranos)
Moll Flanders
Molly Bawn
Mordejai Benady
Mother (of hardened criminal seen by Molly in newspaper)
Mr Riordan
Mr Stanhope
Mrs Dwenn
Mrs Galbraith
Mrs Henry Wood
Mrs Joe Gallaher
Mrs Ramsbottom (type of name deplored by Molly)
Mrs Rubio
Murderer (in Molly's fantasy)
Murray girls
Nancy Blake
Nicelooking boy
Night woman
Nurse (to whom Bloom would play up to if hospitalized, according to Molly)
Nurse (whom Molly remembers pursued the medical in Holles Street)
O Sweetheart May (song)
Odd priest
Old Arab
Old beggar
Old bishop
Old Cohen
Old woman (who was murdered by the hardened criminal)
One in the cream muslin
Onelegged sailor
Other woman (whom Molly considers inviting to a picnic for Bloom)
Phoebe (song)
Pisimbo
Poor child
Poor man
Priest (for whom Molly assumes dying atheists go howling)
Priest (remembered by Molly in Gibraltar)
Proper servant
Prostitute (seen by Molly with K.C.)
Protestant clergyman
R.G. Lewers
Robber of a woman
Rosales y O'Reilly
Sailor (whom Molly contemplates picking up)
Samuel Benady
Scarli
Sentry (from Molly's recollections of Gibraltar)
Sentry (from Molly's recollections of the governor's house in Gibraltar)
She (prostitute Molly supposes Bloom had been with)
Shop girl (in Grafton Street)
Shopgirl (at Lewer's)
Sir Garnet Joseph Wolseley
Sir Herbert Beerbohm Tree
Some woman (subject for a poet's writings, according to Molly)
Some woman (typically vicious, according to Molly)
Somebody (object of Molly's desires)
Somebody (who always comes to the door at the most inconvenient time, much to Molly's annoyance)
Switzer and Co.
Sydney Carton
Tall old chap
Tom Devan
Tom Devan's two sons
Tom the Devil (Molly's contemptuous name of one of Bloom's clients)
Trilby
Two gentlemen (remembered by Molly from railroad journey)
Two stylish dressed ladies
Ulysses S. Grant
Uncle John (from song)
Walter (on train to Marlborough)
Walpole Bros.
Warden (remembered by Molly)
Warden Daly
Watchman (sereno in Algeciras remembered by Molly)
Wife (in Fair Tyrants)
Wife (of hardened criminal seen by Molly in newspaper)
Wife (of the K.C.)
Wife of J. Citron
Wife of Julius Mastiansky/P. Maslansky
Wildlooking gipsy
Wilkie Collins
William Hunter Kendal
Williams and Woods
Woman in the next lane
Woman...with the watercress
Wretch with the red hair
Young girl

98 NON-UNIQUE characters

Adam
Alexander Keyes
Alexander Thom
Alice Dignam
Andrew Burke
Aristotle
Arthur Griffith
Atty Dillon
author (of Sweets of Sin)
Baby Dignam
Bartell D'Arcy
Baruch Spinoza
Benjamin Dollard
Blazes Boylan
Boody Dedalus
C.P. "Charlie" M'Coy
Caroline Doyle
Charles Wisdom Hely
Charles-Paul de Kock
David Drimmie and Sons
Denis Breen
Dirty Dan Boylan
Dr Francis Brady
Edward VII
Ellen Bloom
Epps
Fanny M'Coy
Female religious
Floey Dillon
Freddy Dignam
Gautama Buddha
Georgina Simpson
Harry Mulvey
Henry Doyle
J. Citron
Jack Power
Jack Power's mistress
Jack Power's wife
Jesus Christ
John Buckley
John Henry Menton
John Jameson and Son
Joseph Cuffe
Joseph M'Carthy "Joe" Hynes
Julius Caesar
Julius Mastiansky/P. Maslansky
Katey Dedalus
Katti Lanner
Lawrence "Larry" O'Rourke
Leopold Bloom
Lipoti Virag
Lord Frederick Sleigh Roberts
Lord George Gordon Byron
Luke Doyle
Maimy Dillon
Major Brian Cooper Tweedy
Martha Clifford
Martin Cunningham
Mary Dedalus
Mary Driscoll
Mathew "Mat" Dillon
Michael Gunn
Milly Bloom
Moses Dlugacz
Mr M. Comerford
Mrs Fleming
Mrs Josephine Breen
Mrs M. Comerford
Mrs Riordan
Narcissus
Nosey Flynn
Nude señorita
Nymph (from Titbits on Blooms' bedroom wall)
Patrick Aloysius "Patsy" Dignam
Patrick T. "Paddy" Dignam
Penrose
Professor Goodwin
Queen Victoria
Ruby
Rudolph Bloom
Rudy Bloom
Simon Dedalus
Sir John Martin-Harvey
Sir Thomas Lipton
Stephen Dedalus
Susy Dignam
T. Lenehan
Theodore Purefoy
Throwaway
Todd, Burns and Co.
Tom Kernan
Unknown gentleman
Valentine Blake Dillon
Victoria Frances "Budgy" Purefoy
Virgin Mary
Wilhelmina "Mina" Purefoy
William T.C. Prescott
Wynn (hotel)

3.11 Number of unique and non-unique characters in episode 18.

that have been remembered when so many of those listed in the "Who's Who" have not. What makes Joyce's achievement all the more remarkable is the fact that his characters, many of them based on real people, are assembled together in a fictional plot generating a series of imagined networks, internal and external, conscious and unconscious, that still reveal something fundamental about life and living in the modern world. What will continue to distinguish readers from now on are the computational tools and digitized formats so readily available to sift through these and so many other novelistic networks, making it possible to visualize the data in order to see what the words, paragraphs, and plots conceal.

For those readers who still want to know the answer to the question with which I began this chapter, it's 2,896, more characters in one novel than Balzac put into ninety (figure 3.12). That number includes all the characters present and mentioned, real and imagined, animate and inanimate, human and animal, living and dead, major to minor minor, all of them assembled together to create the Dublin of *Ulysses*. I'm willing to bet that the final tally would be even higher if we were also able to count all of the ones that Joyce forgot.

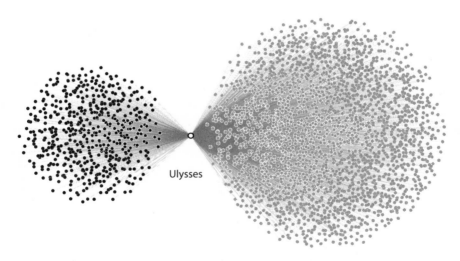

592 UNIQUE characters present   2,304 UNIQUE characters mentioned

3.12 Number of characters present and mentioned in *Ulysses*.

N° 4
GIS Joyce

I suppose he wants readers, but he is perfectly prepared to do without readers.

—Sisley Huddleston, review of *Ulysses* (March 1922)

No ten men or women out of a hundred can read Ulysses through, and of the ten who succeed in doing so, five of them will do it as a tour de force.

—Joseph Collins, review of *Ulysses* (May 1922)

I

Who read *Ulysses*? Or, to be more precise, who read *Ulysses* after the first batch of copies was printed and bound between February 1 and 16 March 1922, the day when an exhausted Maurice Darantière could proudly declare, "The binding of *Ulysses* is complete" ["Le brochage de *Ulysses* est achevé"].[1] If two of the earliest reviews excerpted above are to be trusted, then the answer could have been anywhere between zero and one hundred (10 percent of the total first printed), but everyone would have had to agree that the original readership could not exceed one thousand.[2] By mid-April of the previous year, the total number of copies was already a known quantity (even if the people who would buy them were not), and for the subscription forms and other promotional material that circulated soon thereafter, it was broken down further by price to attract different kinds of readers (100 copies at 350 francs, 150 at 250 francs, and 750 at 150 francs).[3] Some committed early, and in hard cash, others sent back subscription forms and later changed their minds, and still others subscribed, paid, and then waited to see if their copies would arrive (and with the exception of a few in New York City, they did).[4] Eager to trace the genetic evolution of *Ulysses* or map out its itineraries in further editions, impressions, and translations, critics interested in the reception don't dwell very long on the nine months that passed between February 2, when copies first began to trickle in, and October 12 when a second numbered edition of two thousand copies appeared from the same plates allegedly selling out in four days.[5] It's easy to see why: after all the travails involving censors, typists, customs officers, and publishers, *Ulysses* was finally in print, its readers were beginning to receive copies, the reviewers were slowly beginning to assess the contents, and the rest, as they say, is literary history.

It's the second step in the process that deserves much more of our attention. These first subscribers, visualized on a map here, are *what happens* (figure 4.1).[6] Often lumped together as the group lucky enough

United Kingdom	442	Canada	4	Netherlands	2
France	275	Switzerland	3	Spain	2
United States	153	Belgium	2	Luxembourg	2
Ireland	42	Austria	2	Australia	1
Italy	11	Germany	2	Yugoslavia	1
Argentina	11	Sweden	2		

4.1 World map documenting distribution of subscriber copies in 1922.

to be in the right place at the right time, or treated as a cohort of oppor-
tunistic investors, they are the reason that *Ulysses* exists at all, important
enough, in fact, to be the subject of Beach's earliest essay dealing, in part,
with her fascination about "How They Grew."[7] Without this batch of
subscribers, Darantière's bill of 42,492.55 francs would have been impossible for Beach to cover on her own, especially when you consider that she
was only generating 100 francs or so a day from her bookshop (though
I should add that three-quarters, maybe more, of the payments arrived
after the publication).[8] But more than simply crowdsourcing production
costs, the so-called *Ulysses* subscribers were also helping to define what
this novel meant at a time when it was more of a curious object getting
measured than it was a literary work getting read.[9] And while for Beach,
each paid subscription translated into badly needed francs, for Joyce, it
was an opportunity to *watch his readership grow* while episodes of the
novel were still being written and revised.

If the difficulty of *Ulysses* would soon end up alienating or shocking
the common reader, this was a time when author and publisher could
capitalize on the convenience of *the subscribed reader*, which in this case
included private individuals, booksellers, critics, export agents, collectors, and curiosity seekers who had to pay up in advance to receive a copy
(or copies) of the book through the mail once it was published.[10] Indeed,
the kind of reader who could purchase "legally obscene texts" through
private subscription lists dates back several decades, and at this moment
in time there was no other option if *Ulysses* was going to circulate at all
in the United States or the United Kingdom.[11] These subscribed readers
were knowingly supporting the production and distribution of a banned
book, one that was not intended originally for purchase in bookstores
or to be borrowed from libraries.[12] Paris was the perfect city for such an
enterprise because the French authorities, Rachel Potter explains, "were
not interested in prosecuting publishers of English-language material
that was being transported off French soil."[13] If trouble was to be found, it
would be upon the attempted entry into the English-speaking countries
where *Ulysses* was banned.

Subscribed readers were part of an exclusive group, each one of them
corresponding with a unique number.[14] A few of the copy numbers were
carefully assigned (#1 for Harriet Shaw Weaver, Joyce's patron, #1,000 for
Nora, his spouse), but for the most part, they were dashed off to readers

as soon as the small batches arrived.[15] Readers would have had little, if any, knowledge of who else was out there, but not so for Beach. As the hands-on publisher involved with packaging each one (and sometimes with the author's assistance), she was in a position to identify most if not all of the subscribers by name, address, and copy number.[16] And unlike the "implied reader," which Wayne Booth defined as the imagined recipient of an author, the *subscribed reader* is "real." In fact, the entire transaction between subscriber, publisher, and author depended upon the reality of that readership if the novel was expected to circulate at all. Finding them, however, turned out to be more time consuming than Joyce expected. Instead of having a batch of printed books up for sale, the subscription process required a lot of back and forth. Along the way, he seems to have forgotten Pound's advice from 1917 about the potential readers of *Portrait*. "How many intelligent people," Pound asked him then, "do you think that there are in England and America? If *you will* write for the intelligent, how THE HELL do you expect your books to sell by the 100,000 ? ? ? ? ? ?"[17]

Tracking the subscribers of *Ulysses* is one way to gather important empirical data about its first readers, who they were and where they were located. More than that, it lets us access a foundational moment in literary history not on the scale of years or decades or even centuries but in the days, weeks, and months as the novel started moving out into the world. This is the compressed time span that critics skip over in order to get to the livelier parts of the novel's life as it moved toward canonical legitimacy. But no matter how many editions continue to get printed or digitized now and in the future, *Ulysses* will always be a book that first appeared in a print run of one thousand, even if Joyce first recommended printing a "dozen or so," lamenting to Beach at a later stage, "you won't sell a copy of it."[18]

Lawrence Rainey first argued that this limited quantity was a tactical maneuver from the start intended to attract collectors and investors, but he plays down the fact that one thousand was at the upper limit of what author, publisher, and printer could imagine at the time (ten months before publication), and that wasn't just because of the production costs. It had just as much to do with the process by which the readerly desire of the subscribers gets measured, and it involved trying to calculate, at a particular moment in time, just how many readers would want to buy a copy.

So even though *Ulysses* ended up having three different prices, they were all worth one thousand copies. It was a quantity common enough in the late 1400s, when the printing press was first invented, and still five hundred years later, it was a respectable size for a coterie audience more patient with literary experiments than a commercial one.[19] One thousand is as much a concrete number for this print run as it is a symbolic one, precise yet rounded off to identify the symmetry of a closed system, or perhaps, of a creative process that had a beginning, middle, and end. One thousand was more than the sixty or one hundred that Pound believed he needed to accommodate the readers of his *XVI Cantos*, but definitely not large enough to match the critical appraisal that would appear at different points in the 1920s and 1930s when *Ulysses* was getting established as, what Morris Ernst would call, a highly popularized "modern classic."[20]

Looking back a century later, it might seem odd that such a small number of copies was printed, but why would it be otherwise given the circumstances? Publishers in the United States and the United Kingdom were deterred for legal and economic reasons, the little magazine where it first appeared had stopped the serialization two years earlier, and there is no evidence to suggest that Beach, Darantière, or Joyce ever thought the first print run should be higher.[21] "The publication of *Ulysses* was arranged here in a couple of days," Joyce told John Quinn matter-of-factly, and without further ado, that was that.[22] One thousand copies wasn't unnecessarily low for any of the parties involved: it was a sufficient projection based on the amount of readerly desire that could be imagined at a specific moment in the novel's history. And if Dante the poet used one thousand to signify an endless quantity of sinners shown to Dante the pilgrim by Vergil, and in the Bible, as the number assigned to the sum of wives and concubines of King Solomon showing his splendor, in the publication history of *Ulysses*, it was just high enough, and just expensive enough, for Joyce to wonder if enough readers could be found.[23]

The act of measuring this readerly desire played a role in the reception of *Ulysses* not only in late 1922—when the rapid release of a second English edition prompted Joyce to declare, "No bibliophile has the right to tell me how many copies of my book are to be inflicted on a tolerant world" (the number was 2,000; 499 burned by Customs officials in Folkestone, England)—but also in 1927 when he claimed to have lost royalties on 250,000 copies in the United States because of Samuel Roth's pirated edition.[24] In a mathematical calculation worthy of that pseudo-scientific narrator in episode 17, Joyce informed the defense, "that the sales of the book in the United States, published at a minimum price of ten dollars a copy with a royalty to me of fifteen or twenty per cent, with an English-reading population of a hundred and twenty million as contrasted with the small English-reading public in France, would have brought me at least six or seven times as much, viz., five hundred thousand dollars."[25]

Joyce's calculation of a lost readership is not based on actual data. But it is revealing both for what it tells us about his wish to punish the book-pirate Roth as it is with his estimation about how many there may have been in the first place. Out of 120 million inhabitants, 250,000 might not seem such a large percentage, but Joyce is basing the size of a lost audience against the population of the entire United States as presented in the 1920 Census, one that did not take into account the rates of literacy of its "English-reading population."[26] As part of his argument, it's also worth noting the quick reference to "the small-English reading public in France," by which he means his first readers. One thousand has become a small public, but he also pretends as if the first readers belonged only to France. When Random House was finally able to publish the first U.S. edition in 1934, Bennett Cerf and his team arrived at a much lower projection of ten thousand. With advanced orders, it turned out too modest to meet the initial demand of twelve thousand, but at least it was based on actual data that his team compiled by directly contacting hundreds of libraries and bookstores.[27]

Getting that distribution number calculated when the obscenity ban lifted was one thing but finding actual subscribers for that first edition when it was firmly in place was quite another. By the time two copies arrived via express train from Dijon on February 2, 1922, only ten thousand francs (from fifty different subscribers) had actually been paid.[28] Subscribers may have been eager to return their forms, but very few were willing to pay up until the book was actually in print (figure 4.2). That delay in payment also has something to do with the time-consuming nature of this process, one that began ten months earlier when Joyce and Beach began assembling an audience: subscription forms, designed by Adrienne Monnier, were printed by Darantière in Dijon, sent to Beach in

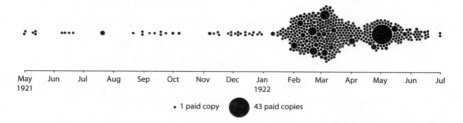

4.2   Number of copies paid between May and July 1921.

Paris, then shipped off to potential subscribers in twenty-three different countries who, in turn, would fill them out, send them back, and wait "a long, long time."[29] When the printing was near completion, another form was dispatched by Beach asking subscribers for payment before copies would be wrapped and sent. Though expedient, given the circumstances, subscriptions were still far from efficient, and the book-keeping was chaotic and inconsistent.

At an early stage, one that likely coincided with the arrival of the first subscription forms, Joyce compiled a two-page wish list of his own containing sixty-seven names and addresses, which can be divided further into eleven different countries (one principality, Monaco) with the greatest number of potential subscribers in England (thirteen) followed by the United States (twelve), Italy (eleven), France (eleven), Switzerland (seven), and Ireland (five). It's a snapshot of readers Joyce expected to rely on, a majority of them personal acquaintances from his years in Dublin, Trieste, and Zurich mixed in with a few of his more recently discovered counterparts and patrons scattered across Europe.[30] Out of sixty-seven potential subscribers, twenty-seven of them received copies with at least five of them taken from the unnumbered press pile. In another list intended for potential reviewers, librarians, and general influencers, the results did not turn out very promising either. Out of seventy-eight names, only thirteen ended up with copies. A 28 percent return on his wish list and, assuming each subscriber took a single copy, more than 958 copies left to sell: if nothing more, these numbers prove that Joyce was better suited at writing his novel than he was at finding readers for it.

Thankfully for him, there were others to help out with the promotion, but it still proved challenging. There was a grass-roots campaign taking place with local admirers from Paris, but there were also two thousand "prospectuses" dispatched around the world in mid-May followed up by another one thousand in early July and another one thousand in late September.[31] The number of sold and promised subscribers was not easy to keep track of because bookstores often changed their orders by letter; Beach kept payment and copy number information on subscription slips (presumably when sending them out), payment logs, and three different address books. There was also the added problem of having subscribers change their minds, which helps to explain why, when writing a limerick in Beach's honor, Joyce decided on the following lines: *Throngs about her rant and rave/ To subscribe for Ulysses/ But, having signed, they ponder grave.*[32]

Others have tried to balance Beach's books in search of lost or damaged copies and missing subscribers, but even now, individual copy owners cannot be identified, and that's in addition to the pile of four hundred or so distributed through the bulk orders of individual bookstores. So, 1,022 copies were printed (counting the two copies Darantière retained), but not according to the original plan, and we have complete information [name, address, and copy numbers] on 324 subscribers, 786 copy numbers, and with incomplete information can account for 957 copies to 416 different subscribers.[33]

In her memoir, Beach describes Joyce waiting around the bookstore for orders to arrive, while Richard Ellmann colorfully adds that he could also be found "fondling the subscription lists."[34] From Joyce's letters at the time, it's evident that what may looked like absent-minded fondling was actually something more deliberate: counting. "About 400 subscriptions are made," Joyce told Harriet Shaw Weaver on November 1, 1921 (made, mind you, not paid).[35] A month after the first English review of *Ulysses* appeared, Robert McAlmon and Ezra Pound would find out that there were "136 orders," while Weaver was informed the same day that there were "145 letters asking for prospectuses" and his brother Stanislaus that "148 copies were ordered" with the added information that "only fifty of the deluxe and about eighty of the 250 franc [were left], so the bowsies had better hurry up."[36] One hundred and thirty-six, 145, 148, 50, and 80: these are not approximate numbers. In fact, their exactness betrays an anxiety that the extraordinary efforts in composing the novel may not be appreciated by the public. Success, in other words, was measurable not by the total number of sales, since that was already a known quantity, but by the fact that each and every copy within that known quantity could be accounted for.

And with all this waiting around, the absences were notable as well. Among the more contentious was the one involving George Bernard Shaw, who received Beach's prospectus but refused to commit. He responded to Pound's angry denunciations by sending along a postcard of Jusepe de Ribera's *The Lamentation over the Dead Christ*, which he recaptioned: "Miss Shakespeare consoling James Joyce, who has fainted on hearing of the refusal of his countryman to subscribe for *Ulysses*. Isn't it like him?"[37] Joyce blamed Shaw's refusal on the steep price tag, telling Weaver (two years later) that "he ought to be informed that there is now a special cheap edition 565,423 words=8 × 70,877 ⅞ = 8 novel lengths, slightly shopsoiled, a genuine bargain going for 60 francs = 60/68 = 30/43 = about ¾ ×20 / − = 15/− ÷ 8 about 1/11 ¼ per normal novel suitlength real continental style—you can't beat it for the money."[38] Unwilling to accept the fact that Shaw would remain a "missing subscriber" forever, Joyce bet his friend Frank Budgen "4.75 francs" that he would order a copy anonymously through a bookshop.[39] Joyce lost, but it's highly unlikely Budgen ever got paid.[40]

II

Joyce's knowledge about the readers of *Ulysses*, both present and absent, was unique during these months. He knew who and where they were in a way he never would again. But that is one of the reasons why that final sign-off on the last page of his novel is so significant. In the most basic terms, he provided the coordinates of his own location during and after the composition of the novel. By doing so he had also, quite literally, provided an *address to the reader*, one that we can imagine as a response to the ones he kept finding on the subscription forms from those same individuals who promised to "pay on receipt of notice announcing that the volume has appeared."[41] And while it is an address that may be less

shocking, say, than Jane Eyre's (*Reader, I married him!*), it still provides
a jarring exit from the fictional world set in Dublin some eighteen years
earlier. *Reader, I am here, in Paris, now!* is the message inscribed on that
last page, and it works precisely by asking each member of his audience to
consider another question: *And where are you?* The answers will change as
the generations do but never the question. This exchange between sender
and receiver is part of the pact that all readers make with *Ulysses*. To arrive
at the end of the novel means to confront where you are but always with
the knowledge of where *Ulysses* once was.

Using the address notebooks and lists she first compiled in 1921, Beach
was one of the first to try and reconstruct where it all happened. Her
answer: "all over the globe."[42] First, there was the "list of *Egoist* readers"
in England (probably including the 150 orders from Weaver's abandoned
first edition), followed by a "good many French subscribers" mostly in
Paris. In addition, there were American subscribers, including the "Little
Review crowd" (saving her "a great deal of postage by coming over to Paris
and subscribing in person") and last but not least were the more exotic
ones from "far-off places like Sarawak, the Straits Settlements, China,
Borneo, etc." It's no surprise to find the *Egoist* readers, French subscribers,
and the *Little Review* crowd in the mix, but in Beach's account the news
about *Ulysses* spread far beyond her "little bookshop" and who knows,
really, how many destinations that "etc." covers.[43]

Looking back on it all from the distance of more than three decades,
Beach remembers *Ulysses* as an instantaneous *global success*, a novel that
conquered the world in one thousand copies almost as soon as it appeared.
The problem with this version of events, however, is that it's wildly untrue.
Not just the timing, as I mentioned before, but also the spacing. Indeed,
a majority of the copies arrived in France, England, and the United States
(over the course of the next ten months), but if we follow the paper trail
there were no subscribers from the "far-off places" of China, Borneo, Sarawak, and the Straits Settlements.[44] Beach's mistake, or convenient distor-
tion of the facts, is significant since it reveals a much bigger problem about
the way the reception history of *Ulysses* has often been treated over the
past century. She sees, or thinks she sees, a global audience at a time when
copies of the book were incredibly scarce. It was this scarcity that ended
up increasing the desire for copies, which would not be freely available
for another decade after the ban was lifted in the United States. In 1922

and for much of the decade, however, *Ulysses* was still a book more talked about than read, prompting Kenner's astute observation that "All the early discussions have this curious property, that readers who had never seen a copy were required to assume Joyce's book was what the protagonist of the moment said it was."[45]

Given its canonical status in world literary history, it might be comforting to think that *Ulysses* has always been there as if Joyce anticipated Homer and not the other way around. In fact, efforts to measure its impact all too easily conflate literary value with global reach. But when did it become possible, or even desirable, to measure the value of this or any other literary work on a global scale shortly after its publication? This is a complex question but one that comes to bear on the way we think about reception more generally as something measurable not just for *Ulysses* in 1922 but throughout the twentieth century and into the twenty-first as bans were lifted and copyrights expired. Is the number of copies printed the best place to measure reception? How about the number of copies sold or the ones actually read (if that is even measurable)? We live in an age in which an instantaneous global blockbuster is common enough, and that's due, in large part, to the arrival of the internet and the formation of conglomerates such as Amazon. In addition, there's the rapid circulation of electronic texts and reliable publishing metrics keeping track of how many copies are sold, where, and to whom.

At the beginning of the twentieth century, however, none of this infrastructure existed: the distribution channels, technologies, and publishing platforms were still very much shaped by a book industry as it emerged at the end of the previous century. Publishers and booksellers were able to establish international networks for commercial distribution, but in England, at least, they were engineered for a market made up of university presses and commercial publishers catering to emerging markets while still capitalizing on the more established transnational, transatlantic, and European ones. *Ulysses*, then, might have had some geographical diversity with its small run, but it was not exceptional by any means. In fact, you could say it was *global on a small scale*, nowhere near as expansive as the most popular novelists from the previous century (including the market for republished classics).

As a useful counterpoint, consider the global literary reception model described by Pascale Casanova in *The World Republic of Letters*, one anchored in Paris, the same city from which the copies of *Ulysses* began their journey. In order to receive international *consecration*, literary works, she argues, need to be vetted by critics, translators, and editors in this Western metropolitan center before moving outward into the world. Though published by a bookseller in Paris, *Ulysses* complicates this model. The distribution itinerary, for instance, was determined by private subscription lists, so there was never any need to move through the official channels involving critics, editors, and translators in Paris before circulating internationally. And what's more, translation was not an issue since it was a novel written in English, intended for export and therefore less objectionable to the French authorities. With the first edition we have a distribution model involving a novel intended for destinations elsewhere. In that way, it's easy to see how fantasies about the global reach of *Ulysses* are so attractive. By not belonging to the country of its print origins, *Ulysses* was made to seem as if it was at home everywhere, even Borneo.

The United States, where it quickly became a "bootleg classic," was a glaring exception.[46] Copies of the first edition and the subsequent editions and impressions would get past customs officials until 1933, but the demand, which no one had a number for at the time, always exceeded the supply.[47] But even with the contraband copies, this question about the number of readers became particularly valuable as the pressure to publish an American edition mounted. Given that the book was banned for more than a decade, how many readers were still interested? And if you can't rely on the size of previous quantities for an audience made up largely of expats and English speakers in Paris, Europe, and the United Kingdom, then how do you go about measuring the desire that remains?

Crazy as it might sound, those are precisely the questions that Morris Ernst, an American attorney, and Bennett Cerf, the president of Random House, discussed when preparing their case against the United States in 1933. They knew that future readers were going to be found scattered across the country, but where? And how do you go about finding them? In search of answers, Ernst and Cerf sent out questionnaires to a pool of more than nine hundred university and public librarians, the very people on the front line of book distribution, who could provide some sense of the public's opinion.[48] "Has there been *any demand* in your library for it [*Ulysses*]?" they wanted to know, following up with the redundant question: "*Much demand* in your library for it?"[49]Turns out from the "several hundred" librarians who responded (285 total), there was, indeed, *some demand*, but it was by no means unanimous, and contrary to Ernst's summary of the results in the brief prepared for the court, there were a lot of dissenting voices: 9 YESES and 3 NOS in California, 1 YES and 3 NOS in Colorado, 8 YESES and 9 NOS in Illinois, 1 YES and 1 NO in Vermont and Nebraska, and so on.[50] The greatest demand came from the students (much more so than the public), but a majority of the librarians sampled still acknowledged that there was general value in its publication.

Based on the data collected from these questionnaires, Ernst and his legal team created a "Map of the United States Showing the Location of Libraries That Have Expressed a Desire to Circulate *Ulysses*."[51] The title pretty much sums up the contents: it's a generic black and white map with fifty or so red dots indicating the states desirous of a copy (figure 4.3). There is no variation in the dot size that would indicate the differences in the number of responses per state, but it's hard to miss the blank states in the middle of the continent juxtaposed against those clustered together on both coasts.[52] This divide between the country and the city is not what Ernst wanted the court to notice. Instead, as he explains in a brief description, "The purpose of this map is to show that *Ulysses* has won nation-wide recognition and acclaim, and that it is not being championed by radical or ultrasophisticated literary cliques located in large metropolitan centres."[53]

It turns out that the demand of libraries is not the only thing getting mapped out here. It is also Ernst's desire to control who and where the future readers would be and what they might mean as a nationally defined public. In an effort to generate the illusion of nation-wide consensus, Ernst was hoping to reduce the impact of intellectual communities in the various metropolises so *Ulysses* would seem less like an avant-garde import and more like a book made in America for honest, book-loving Americans. Readers, in this fantasy, are not simply urban dwellers: they are also country-folk, the kind usually snubbed by the literary elites. And if this is a map of readers that don't yet exist, it is also one organized paradoxically around the idea that the novel they will read had already achieved nationwide recognition. Once copies become widely available, the public, then, does not need to judge for itself: *Ulysses* was deemed a modern classic while circulating illegally.

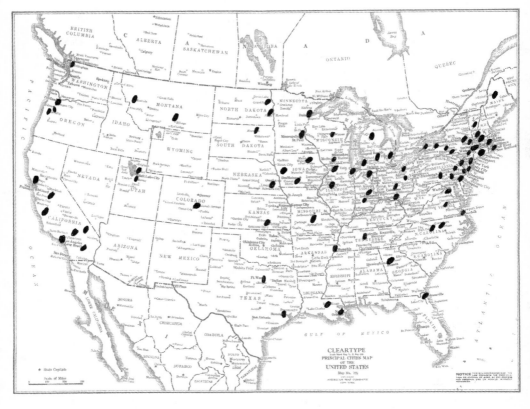

4.3   Morris Ernst, "Map of Librarians and Booksellers Interested in Copies of *Ulysses*."

Source: Reproduced courtesy of the Harry Ransom Center, University of Texas at Austin.

In the act of mapping desire to make their case, Ernst and his team ended up generating a fascinating document about the reception history of *Ulysses*, one that imagines the geographical distribution of future readers and circumvents any need for critical judgement since it has already happened. As the lawyer representing a publisher keen to remove an obscenity ban, Ernst was not interested in the veracity of the literary historical record. He needed to convince United States District Court Judge Woolsey that Random House could publish a novel that would not corrupt an innocent American public. In order to make a convincing case, *Ulysses* needed to seem like a book written for an *American everyman*, the type as much at home in the streets of New York City as in the fields of Lincoln, Nebraska. By doing so, however, Ernst played down the fact that he was inadvertently creating the conditions for a global readership that had been impossible before. Though tried in a United States court, the effects of the decision itself would be felt across the English-speaking world. And if this is a map of America's desire for *Ulysses*, it is one that introduces the possibility of an entirely new population of readers that had been missing from the global tally since 1922.

Ernst never had an exact number of readers in mind for his legal brief, but that was something Random House needed to establish when preparing its first edition. By the time printed copies started to appear and bookstore orders poured in, Random House could barely keep up with the demand. By April 1934, less than three months after copies were printed, thirty-three thousand had been sold.[54] That was more than the total number Shakespeare and Company sold in the eleven editions that appeared between 1922 and 1930 (twenty-eight thousand copies).[55] Fast forward to the fiftieth anniversary of the first edition and that number from Random House would rise to 880,000 copies, and if you add the other 630,000 from the John Lane/ Bodley Head edition in the United Kingdom, *Ulysses* far exceeded the million copy mark in the United States and United Kingdom alone.[56]

It is impossible to know whether or not that same number of copies would have sold in the early 1930s if access to *Ulysses* had not been blocked for more than a decade, but there's nothing like an attenuated delay—and one caused by an obscenity charge no less—to entice potential readers. And though it was unable to receive a homecoming worthy of the hero after which it was named, *Ulysses* never disappeared entirely from public view: there was the piracy case against Samuel Roth, the arrival of a prominent French translation in 1929, Stuart Gilbert's *Study* in 1930, and the Odyssey Press edition of 1932.

The increase from one thousand copies to 1.6 million copies took fifty years. But consider once again where it all started: zero to one thousand copies printed over the course of six weeks and distributed over a period of at least six months (figure 4.4).[57] Adding the number of copies from the second edition published in 1922, even Herbert Gorman paused in his obsequious account of the "first year of its life" to remark: "This fact is amazing when we consider the tremendous amount of publicity concerning the book that was appearing in England, France, and America, and already spreading into several other countries."[58] For Gorman, as for Beach, the measure of

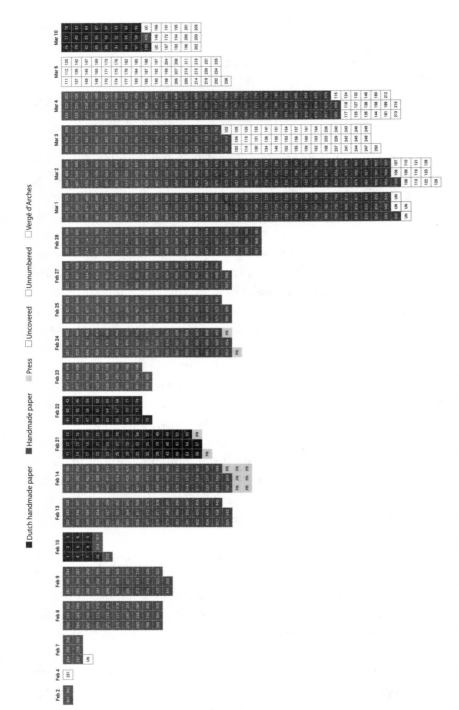

4.4   Number of copies printed by Daràntiere between February 2 to March 10, 1922.

Ulysses's success was not to be found in the number of copies printed or sold: it belonged to the publicity, giving readers an account of the book when copies were hard to come by. As soon as it appeared, *Ulysses* managed to attract more readers than there were copies available and it did so, according to a hyperbolic Gorman, more than "any prohibited work had done before or since."[59]

In this continued drive to give *Ulysses* immediate global recognition, the impact of that original number has been lost and with it an opportunity to examine a moment in the history of its reception when nothing extraordinary happened except the fact that it was finally in print. But instead of a reception history focused on critical responses, public reactions, and the biographical pedigree of readers, what if we instead took this number seriously, treating it as evidence of what many would consider a *nonevent in literary history*, the kind that lets us examine the complex relationship between the low numbers and a major shift in scale (reception, value, and computation)?[60]

In their "deep history" of human civilization, Andrew Shyrock and Daniel Lord Small argue that these smaller-scale shifts can be just as significant as the larger ones. "A leap from human communities numbering in the tens of people to those numbering in the thousands," they argue, "may be just as momentous for social relations as the leap from millions to hundreds of millions. Indeed, the smaller shift probably required more complicated and durable alterations in human interactive styles."[61] The publication of *Ulysses* may not be comparable to a population explosion in a Paleolithic society, but this kind of insight about deep history can help us think about the reception history of a single literary work more broadly. In this shift from zero to one thousand, *Ulysses* underwent a scalar leap that would subsequently shape literary relations throughout the twentieth century, but at this moment these effects were barely, if at all, discernible, and, as is true with so many other literary works across the millennia, they can't be traced in the responses of critics or readers.

Instead, as I'll argue, the effects are there in the geography, the scalar leap expressed in the circulation of copies outward from Paris to destinations worldwide. If the number of possible readers was a known quantity as early as April 1921, the locations where the copies would eventually arrive was not. And in the subsequent months as the supply decreased, Beach kept sales open to all, never limiting the number by city, country, or continent, or the bulk orders from bookstores on behalf of their anonymous clients.

Even with the ban in the United States, *Ulysses* was still free to move around the world, and copies were being sold on a first-come-first-serve basis. That original pool of subscribers may have been precipitated in part by the prospectuses and word of mouth, but it generated a reading population for *Ulysses* as it existed at a specific time. Demand certainly exceeded supply, but at this early stage, as I mentioned before, we also need to remember that the subscriptions were trickling in slowly with a few promotional spikes. The readers who did not get copies of the first edition in early 1922 either didn't know, didn't care, or couldn't afford it.

Measuring the geography of literary reception has long been the provenance of book historians, one of the most notable examples belonging to Lucien Febvre in *L'apparition du livre* in which he maps out the spread of printing presses to document the emergence of a European print culture between 1450 and 1800.[62] Other critics have used similar cartographic methods to measure literary historical events and sociological processes, of which Pierre Bourdieu's *Les règles de l'art* and Moretti's *The Atlas of the European Novel, 1800–1900* are prominent examples, but they also include the "Mapping the Enlightenment" project at Stanford University, which uses the epistolary correspondence between leading Enlightenment figures to generate dynamic visualizations of the intellectual networks they created.

Mapping first subscribers, however, works a bit differently. It is first and foremost a way to access a reception history anchored in the geographical distribution of readers who received copies of a first edition. As interested as I am in visualizing the location of readers and copies by city, country, and continent, I do so in order to recuperate some of the concreteness of the experience of this novel at a particularly formative, if quiet, moment in its history. I say *experience*, which, of course, would imply that I am interested in events of the past that have already been digested, but equally urgent is the way this experience involved the expectation of a future whose meaning had not yet been revealed. Experience and expectation are at odds in that way largely because, as Reinhardt Koselleck explains, "past and future never coincide." He continues: "Experience once made is as complete as its occasions are past; that which is to be done in the future, which is anticipated in terms of an expectation, is scattered among an infinity of temporal extensions."[63]

The maps that follow are one way to imagine the expectation of readers in 1922. Better yet, they provide an opportunity to think about a "horizon of expectations," as Hans Robert Jauss called it, one that places the emphasis less on the readers' imagined connection with the novel and instead forces us to think about the readerly network of which it was a part. Though uninterested in the geography of reception history, Jauss was aware that there are "empirical means which had never been thought of before—literary data which give each work a specific attitude of the audience."[64] The geographical information about subscribers is such a dataset, but what's more, it provides a unique perspective on the *attitude of an audience* whose coordinates have never been mapped before.

III

With the exception of Beach, no one else would have really known how far the distribution of *Ulysses* extended, but thanks to her notebooks, this information is part of an incomplete, occasionally inaccurate, but nevertheless valuable, geographical dataset that lets us do to the readers of 1922 what Ernst and his legal team did a decade later: map desire. By mapping desire, we are able to identify the routes of circulation, locations with the greatest density, and the inevitable dead spots, but in doing so, we can establish how this particular publication event had a rhythm, structure, and design that was very particular, bound as it was by a wide range of material and legal constraints but also whimsy, chance, and preference. Unable to go everywhere all at once, *Ulysses* was forced to move along specific channels, and it was a process shaped as much by the institutions involving bookdealers, agents, critics, and media outlets as it was by word of mouth and personal connections.

Mapping the desire for *Ulysses*, then, is not just an attempt to demystify what the first readers wanted when they wanted it (investment, knowledge, entertainment). Rather, it is part of a critical practice that lets us examine the degrees to which this desire was communicated across such a vast geographical expanse. Subscribing to *Ulysses* was as much about eventually getting a copy of the book as it was in becoming part of a community of readers and institutions that wanted the same thing at the same time in different places. *Ulysses* never made its own exclusivity a secret. In fact, that was what motivated enough readers to pay up sight unseen. By breaking this geographical information down even further it becomes possible to measure the desire at different scales and in doing so compare the effects of not only proximity and distance but also the nationally defined formations of country, city, and region across different continents. The goal is not just to identify who did and did not read *Ulysses*. It is to locate that desire not only across Paris, London, and New York but also the United States, the United Kingdom, and Europe and, in doing so, make explicit a dynamic process involving the desire for something that was as much symbolic as it was real, the words in *Ulysses* still unknown and the deluge of critical interpretations so familiar to us today not yet unleashed.

Paris, the hub of the entire enterprise, is the most logical place to start. As copies arrived in February and March, they were being shipped out from Beach's bookshop on 12 rue de l'Odéon, but they were also getting picked up or delivered locally to 118 documented subscribers (totaling 254 copies), some of them reserved for the wandering expats and holiday travelers passing through. The "good many" Parisian subscribers praised by Beach were later singled out by Monnier for their intense loyalty and support, but neither of them could have known that these subscribers actually comprised one-quarter of the total number, with London coming in at ninety-two, before dropping off precipitously to the twenty-nine in New York City (figure 4.5).[65]

One hundred and eighteen is the number of Parisian subscribers that can be positively identified, but it was certainly higher. Monnier, for instance, was also distributing an unknown number of copies at an increased price in Paris through La Maison des Amis des Livres.[66] In addition, there were the local expats, mostly American and British, who were buying copies to deliver elsewhere—some but not all filling out subscription forms once actual copies started arriving in Beach's shop. And we can't forget the case of a single subscription that came in from the group of "poor artists from Montparnasse" (three total) who saved what few francs they could by staying in bed to consume less food.[67] The identities of these starving artists remain unknown, but their presence somewhere in the list reminds us that one private copy could, in fact, sustain many through a pass-along readership.

London had fewer subscribers than Paris, but it actually purchased significantly more copies: 341 (including the thirty-six of Weaver) to 254 (figure 4.6). This discrepancy between the quantity of readers and copies reveals the degree to which mediated subscriptions dominated the

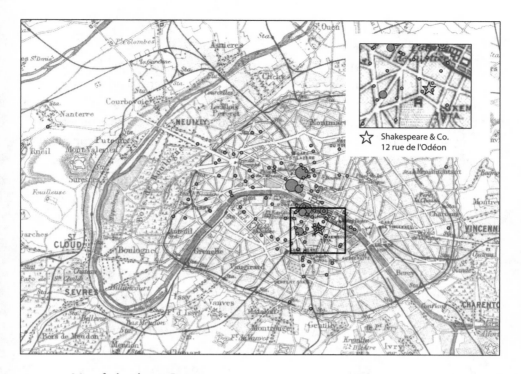

4.5 Map of subscribers in Paris.

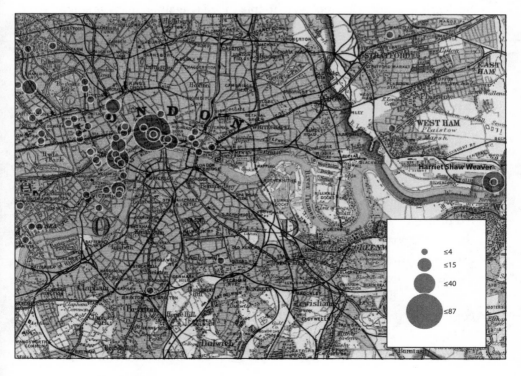

4.6 Map of subscribers in London.

reception process. Out of 786 or so trackable copies, 436 went to booksellers around the world (494 if we include publishers, agents, and libraries).
In London alone, more than 220 of them went to twenty-two different
bookstores (if we include the copies without complete information), the
largest single order belonging to William Jackson (eighty-seven copies),
but the average bulk order was closer to ten.[68] The dominance of bookstore subscriptions over private ones indicates that there was more specu-
lation in this city than anywhere else. Indeed, a percentage of the London
booksellers would complete the transaction for clients, but they were also
generating stock for future customers who had not yet subscribed.

Lawrence Rainey claims that Beach and Weaver had very different ideas
about the role that would be played by these London booksellers (and
English readers in general), the former catering to a market of limited editions, the latter to the general public. It is largely with the participation of
these booksellers that Rainey locates a modernist divide, the one separating
general readers from a group of newly emerging patron-investors interested
in experimental literature. "The reason to buy a book published by Weaver,"
Rainey argues, "was to read it; the reason for buying the edition proposed
by Beach was quite different—to be able to sell it again perhaps at a significant profit if all went well."[69] There were certainly booksellers and agents
ready to capitalize on the scarcity, but as Edward Bishop argues, Rainey's
conclusions are blown way out of proportion and not supported by auction records or the fact that cheaper editions sold out long before the more
expensive, but certainly more collectible, signed ones. Beach, he claims to
the contrary, wanted a readers' edition even if she was caught up in a publishing strategy that treated books as investments.[70] A *Ulysses* printed for
readers, then, but one in which the transaction itself was also executed by
agents and booksellers. If we exclude those eighty-seven copies that went
to William Jackson, the London orders were modest, which also reveals
the degree to which the desire to invest was limited. But even if we assume
that a large portion were advanced orders, that means the number itself was
extremely low—a few copies here and there, and definitely nothing that
would indicate any single bookseller was expecting a windfall (certainly
not the kind described by Beach when she had to remove one of the first
copies from the window fearing that it would be stolen).[71]

More subscribers in Paris, more copies going to London, and then
there's New York City (figure 4.7).[72] When it was serialized, Margaret

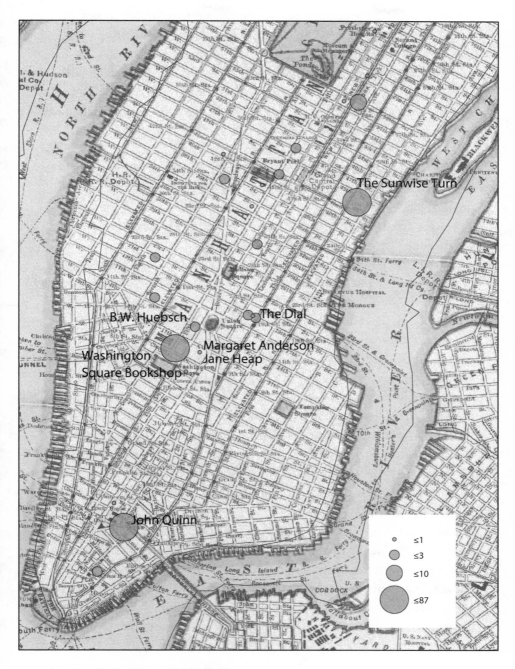

4.7 Map of subscribers in New York City.

Anderson claimed that the appreciation came from the "far west" but noticed that "New York was particularly cold."[73] Not much had changed once the book was out. Twenty-nine readers purchased 107 copies, half of them went to three different individuals, three of them for booksellers (fifteen to John Quinn, eighteen to Marion Peter, twenty-five to Egmont Arens). This isn't the first time that the numbers in New York City were lower than expected. Remember the 250,000 readers Joyce thought he lost by 1927 as a result of Roth's pirated edition followed by the 12,000 actual copies printed by Random House in 1934? The American audience, in general, may have been difficult to gauge, but the one in New York City proved to be even more so.

Ernst's numbers from the New York State librarians and booksellers are useful in this regard: seventeen out of twenty four librarians indicated that there was "some demand" for *Ulysses*, but only two were willing to concede "much demand."[74] If these librarians are to be trusted at all, then the demand for *Ulysses* in New York State was fairly modest. A number of different factors would have influenced the public's opinion in 1922, but it's worth considering the possibility that *Ulysses* just wasn't as widely desirable as the literary histories, many of them motivated by anecdotal evidence and fantasies about a cataclysmic literary event, might want us to imagine. The wider circulation of excerpts in the *Little Review* could have been one reason (followed by a two-year delay when serialization stopped), but there's the added fact that the intellectual orbit, the same one that advertised and promoted the novel in Paris and London, was not as substantial on the other side of the Atlantic, and it didn't help that so many of American expats were still located overseas.

But if New York City is surprisingly low, Dublin is high (figure 4.8).[75] Beach recalls that Joyce was particularly keen to have "all Irish notices" sent out as soon as the copies were available. The result was sixteen different subscribers making up the forty-two copies, not so far off, in fact, from Richard Rowan's calculation of his own book sales in *Exiles*. "Thirty-seven copies have now been sold in Dublin."[76] In this case, one donated (National Library of Ireland), ten sold (or gifted) to private individuals, and the rest to bookstores (thirty-one copies divided between four of them).[77] Given such a high number of bookseller copies, it is possible that many of Joyce's countrymen preferred to keep their identities hidden (as he suspected),

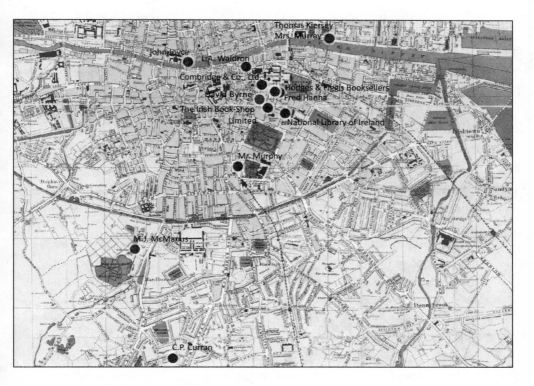

4.8 Map of subscribers in Dublin.

but we should also not lose sight of the fact that Dublin was still higher on the list than the more than thirty other towns and cities, including Trieste and Zurich, the other two places he included in his address to the reader on the last page. Unable to identify any of the actual names could only have fueled his sense of betrayal, and it was no doubt corroborated by the first Irish review labeling *Ulysses* "the most infamously obscene book in ancient or modern literature."[78] It seems fitting that Oliver St. John Gogarty, one of the few Dubliners Joyce actually included on his original wish list, failed to buy a copy. But why, it's worth asking, would he need to become a reader *of the novel* given the fact that he was already immortalized *in the novel*?

The reception history of *Ulysses* is really a tale of three cities. London, Paris, and New York purchased 699 copies while the rest were distributed in quantities of one or two to lone subscribers in all the others.

But while this data may reveal the exclusively metropolitan nature of Joyce's readership, it also confirms the importance of the local place and population on its original reception. Had *Ulysses* been published in an English-speaking country, Paris would not have been as prominent on the list. But that simple fact tells us something about the way the bookshop, the promotional events, the newspaper blasts, the locals, and even the tourists, all contributed to the configuration of that first audience in fundamental ways. *Ulysses*, then, was set in Dublin and directed to an audience of English speakers in London and New York City, but the support of a Parisian readership helped ensure that the printing bill got paid, especially in those early months when the novel was still unprinted and unreviewed.

But what can these numbers tell us at the scale of the country? If we move outward from New York City across the United States, for instance, the distribution gets incredibly sparse—most of the subscription activity was concentrated in the Northeast, and with the exception of two copies shipped to Los Angeles and New Mexico (Yvor Winters), pretty much stopping at Chicago with Sherwood Anderson (to the West) and Virginia (to the South). If you combine the rest of the U.S. subscriptions with the ones I've already mentioned for New York City, that makes 153 total, which is still half of the number of copies in London (figure 4.9). Granted, of course, that more copies were entering the United States from citizens traveling abroad (and through export agents such as William Jackson, based in the UK), but this approximate quantity is still on the low end given the size of the country and its population. There is always the possibility of a general lack of interest, readerly apathy, and the absence of promotional material, but it's also very likely that the subscription forms were just not easy to obtain, especially for those living far from urban centers.

The four thousand prospectuses Darantière printed for the first edition were not enough to blanket any city, country, or region. So even at this early stage in the process, the rules for gauging readerly interest were not only highly personalized (depending on who you knew), they were also incredibly random (McAlmon getting people to sign up on the streets of Paris, for instance). As a point of reference, consider how many U.S. readers on Beach's original wish list actually ended

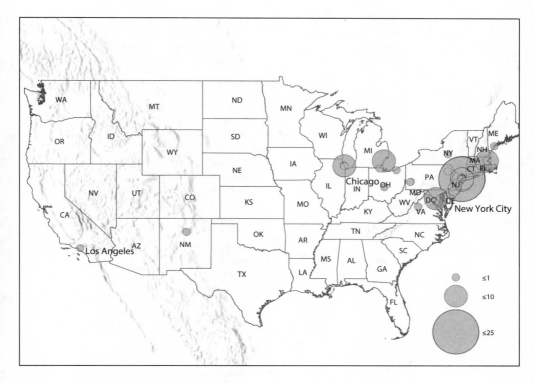

4.9 Map of subscribers in the United States.

up subscribing (44 out of 199).[79] Again, French readers took the lead with the total number of copies (103 out of 218), most of them in Paris. Still, she managed to enlist 213 subscribers, at least following the names on this list, which is roughly 20 percent of the total number of copies printed (figure 4.10).

The evidence here proves that this was not a random group of book lovers where access was open to everyone. Rather, it was a more close-knit network made up largely of individuals with personal connections either to the publisher or her coterie of local supporters. *Ulysses* may have generated some attention in the American Press but it was *after the publication*, and news about procuring copies beforehand was difficult to come by. The absence of randomness in this reception history, in fact, is not a minor point. It is part of the structural logic behind the formation of this

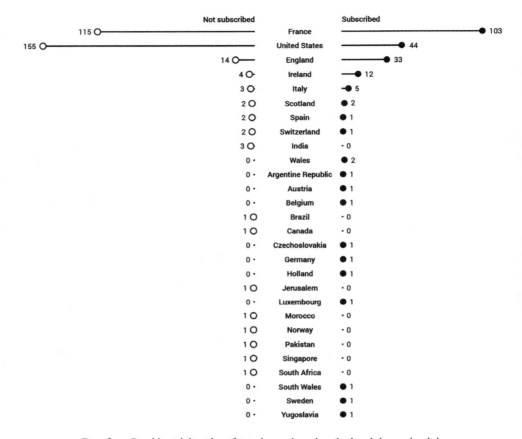

4.10   Data from Beach's wish list identifying those who subscribed and those who did not.

first audience. Readers were not accidentally found: they were designated either by word of mouth or through the more deliberate circulation of promotional material. And at this particular moment in the history of publishing, that meant large portions of the public would simply not have had any access to the consumption process.

Which, of course, takes us back to the question with which I began this chapter: Who read *Ulysses*? It's not something we can answer by compiling lively biographical sketches of individual subscribers and publishing statistics or developing sociological or economic theories regarding the production/consumption of literary works. Rather, it also requires thinking about *reception as a quantitative problem*, one that gets reflected in the geographical distribution at a particular moment in time. In this case, the geography of subscribers in the United States tells us how *Ulysses* was and was not moving in the world. This movement is not just one isolated factor in its reception: it lets us access the readerships at different scales (city, country, globe) to identify, as much as possible, why the routes of circulation were open in some directions and not others. Finding a large majority of U.S. readers congregating in the Northeastern part of the United States, then, might come as no surprise, but it should inform how we understand the numbers later not just with a document such as Ernst's map but also with the first American print run. In 1922, *Ulysses* belonged to an elite, urban cluster, one whose exclusivity, no doubt increased the longer copies were kept out of America.

A separate ban on *Ulysses* was issued in the United Kingdom as well, but that didn't stop England, Scotland, Wales, and one bookshop in Northern Ireland from assembling the greatest concentration of copies: 441. That may come as no surprise when you already know in advance that London had the highest number of subscriptions (341) but that leaves one hundred more, twenty-one of them going to bookstores and the rest to private individuals (figure 4.11). If we can't attribute the increase to the ban (just as we can't blame the decrease on the ban in the United States), then what's to account for the significant difference between the number of subscribers in the U.S. and UK?

There are a few factors to bear in mind: with the exception of four incomplete episodes in the *Egoist*, the serialization of *Ulysses* in England had failed; there was publicity already generated by Weaver for an edition through the Egoist Press before she stepped aside to let Beach take over; news about the arrival of *Ulysses* was appearing in the British Press, including the review by Sisley Huddleston, which resulted in the largest subscription spike on a single day (136, see figure 4.2); and there was a long-established network of 30 booksellers working across the English Channel, the same ones who purchased roughly 246 copies for distribution to private individuals. Booksellers were not willing to lose money in this transaction, so in mediating between Beach and these unknown readers, they provided a pretty accurate account of the demand that existed during that period.

SCOTLAND

Glasgow Edinburg

UNITED
KINGDOM

Newcastle
upon Tyne

Belfast

Douglas

*Irish
Sea*

Leeds
Manchester
Manchester

Dublin
Dublin

IRELAND

Nottingham

ENGLAND
Birmingham

WALES

London
London Engl
chan

Cardiff

*Celtic
Sea*

*English
Channel*

St Helier

Sources: Esri, HERE, Garmin, FAO, NOAA, USGS, © OpenStreetMap contributors, and the GIS User Community

4.11 Map of subscribers in the United Kingdom.

4.12 Map of subscribers in France.

In Paris, *Ulysses* was very local affair tracked by "the daily bulletins in the press," but the enthusiasm did not spread across France.[80] Only twenty copies were intended for destinations outside of Paris (figure 4.12). When read against the results of the other countries, this data make it hard to ignore that the *actual location of its publication actively shaped the geographical diversity of its audience*. The Parisian pedigree of *Ulysses* was one of the reasons it was so prominently on display there in the press, in the various intellectual circles, through Beach and Monnier, by chatter among fellow writers, etc. And if before I asked how many *Ulysses* subscribers in Paris would have been had it been published in America or England, now it's just as fitting to ask where it might have gone.

There is no doubt that proximity of the publisher affected the degree of interest in the audience, but, in this case, it also proves just how the scope and scale of the geography was very much in and of its time. Looking at *Ulysses* as a geographic information system (GIS) reveals that it could only have been published from Paris during these months in 1922. It's one of the great ironies (or insults) that the 1934 Random House edition failed to include this place and date on its copyright notice, effectively suggesting *Ulysses* was in the public domain since it had not been printed in the United States six months after publication in Paris. However, doing so promoted the book's status as a "modern classic" with no obvious origin, unintentionally making it as timeless and placeless as the epic upon which it is based.[81]

But what about the rest of the world? Forty-five copies of *Ulysses* went to thirteen other countries, and that quantity, which made up less than 5 percent of the total published, was enough for Beach to imagine that *Ulysses* was a global phenomenon. The numbers, however, just don't add up. The presence of a single copy in two different countries or two copies each in seven more may establish that a subscriber was present, but just as the missing subscription of Shaw does not extend to all of Ireland, the reverse is also true: a single subscription does not a country or city, or continent of readers make.

These singular subscriptions are outliers in a distribution system organized around three central nodes, but Beach's wish list, which included the addresses where she would send prospectuses, reveal that it was largely her doing. She was the one who stirred up interest in these far-off places. In the process of locating readers, she didn't just meet the quota, she also generated a degree of geographical diversity that the reception history of *Ulysses* would have otherwise lacked. These outliers belong to a highly personalized network that would, of course, include the recommendations of others, but is not, as I mentioned before, open to a process of random selection for subscribers.

Which is one of the reasons that even now, GIS Joyce is as much about generating data involved with the geographical distribution as it is about accessing an imaginative construction heavily influenced by the one person responsible for getting it out into the world in the first place. In 1922, the process of finding a local audience of the fit and few may have been hard but getting it to the fit and even fewer in countries so far away was even harder. If *Ulysses* became global on a small scale at this moment it was because *Beach made it so*. Looking at these numbers, it can be tempting to launch into general conclusions about modernist book history or the use of computational methods in literary reception but only if we are also willing to account for the ineffable desire of publishers, authors, readers, and even critics for an object they didn't have in their possession.

They wanted *Ulysses* without realizing it was *Ulysses* who wanted them. None of this would have worked if subscribers weren't around waiting to be counted. As much as they were acquiring an object for consumption, invest-ment, or edification (or all of the above), they were making the number of that first audience concrete. One thousand was an embodied quantity, something that started out as the more abstract expression of an audience that could be imagined while also anticipating one that would be unimag-inable in the future. That process of naming, knowing, and counting sub-scribers is not only what made this entire experience unique in 1922 but also unrepeatable as the history of this novel's reception unfolded. Never again would novelist, publisher, and audience be triangulated in this way, each angle representing a complex exchange of wanting but also of being wanted.

After the first printing, Joyce never needed to know if copies sold or where they went. But the same is true for all the readers left to buy later editions: from that point forward, they were less numbers and names corresponding with copies than they were the percentages on the prof-its from copies sold. And it was this subsequent acceleration that made *Ulysses* a bestseller in the 1930s, proving, finally, that this first number was as much symbolic as it was concrete, the 1 and 3 zeros representing not the final quantity of copies sold but the quantity that could be sold once *Ulysses* was allowed to wander freely across the world.

IV

"Where?" It's the final question in episode 17 followed by the last "word," which takes the form of an enlarged em dash. Richard Ellmann has sug-gested that this isn't just any piece of punctuation: it represents planet

Earth as seen from "interstellar space" signaling to readers that Stephen and Bloom have been transformed into heavenly bodies.[82] But what Joyce did to his characters at the end of his novel is what we can continue to do as critics when we ask the same question about his first readers: Where? The pursuit of an answer, however, will not lead us to eternity and the stars above even if the final number of copies, approximately 1,022, recalls the 1,022 fixed stars of Ptolemy (adapted from the star catalogue of Hipparchus) that Dante references in *Il Convivio*.[83] In fact, as the maps scattered throughout this chapter attest, it is a process that requires throwing ourselves back into the presentness of the past as much as possible to recuperate some of the complexity of this fleeting interaction between author, publisher, reader, and world that was very much *in and of its time* but also *in and of its number*. For the briefest of moments, Joyce knew his readers, they were part of a countable community that could be known, and it didn't matter what any of them actually thought of the novel or if they even read it at all.

By counting subscribers, we arrive at the realization that readerly desire can have an address and a number. It is a desire as evident in the wish lists and questionnaires as it is in the notebooks, address books, ledgers, prospectuses, legal briefs, maps, and even on the last page of the novel itself. As with all of the other chapters in this book, though, the numbers alone are not the answer. In fact, it is the precise and approximate quantities that help us to generate new questions not only about where it went but also what it is made of. This quantity of one thousand will seem small for data-minded distant readers. Yet, working at such a reduced scale expands the significance of a number that has lost its potential to generate any sense of wonder. But for those who don't think the numbers mean anything, remember it was copy one thousand that Joyce inscribed to Nora, even if she was never actually part of that first group of "ten men or women out of a hundred" who actually read it through.[84] Still, the act of giving this particular copy was a symbolic affirmation between husband and wife, similar, in fact, to Molly Bloom's "Yes," but it also signified the end of a cycle that began so many years earlier. A century later and *Ulysses* seems as if it's everywhere, the copies now printed innumerable. But this was the edition from which all the others derived, and it was part of a publishing event that generated a unique assemblage of reader/subscribers who would discover in the front matter that the novel was "LIMITED TO 1000 COPIES" pages even before reading the first line.

Any attempt to number, name, and locate these readers now, to trace the outlines of that horizon of expectations, brings us face to face with our own position on an ever-expanding list. "For the literary historian must first become a reader again himself," Jauss once claimed, "before he can understand and classify a work."[85] This task of becoming a reader again was as true in 1972 for Jauss as it is in 2022 with the centennial of the novel's publication as it will be again in 2222, the perfect year for *Ulysses* if there ever was one. And while critics can keep adding zeros to that original tally over time, they won't ever change the number of its first reception. One thousand was there from the start and looking at it distributed across a map of the cities, countries, and continents makes it impossible to ignore that *Ulysses* was never separate from the geography of its first readers. They were as encoded in the order and design as the 732 pages, the 264,448 words, the 3,342 paragraphs, the 592 characters present, and the 7 years of composition, which I will address in the next chapter. The trick, as always, involves knowing where to look for the numbers and then figuring out how to count them and why.

N° 5
Dating *Ulysses*

For it is a difficult business—this time keeping.
—Virginia Woolf, *Orlando*

I DATES OR DATA?

The previous chapters consider questions involving who wrote *Ulysses*, why it is as long as it is, how many characters there are, and who read the first edition, but there's one more that needs answering: When did Joyce write *Ulysses*? Anyone who finishes the novel will claim that the answer can be found on the last page: 1914–1921 (figure 5.1). Though certainly the quickest answer, it's not the most accurate, and that's because this process of beginning, middling and ending was much less straightforward than Joyce is letting on here. By dating *Ulysses*, it's as if Joyce needed to reaffirm the whole thing happened at all and that he was more like the wandering hero moving through the world than the "God of creation" hovering above it.[1] But what Ezra Pound first said when coming across the dates appended to the last page of *A Portrait of the Artist as a Young Man* applies here as well: "It is the [time] spent on the book . . . *that counts*. No man can dictate a novel, though there are a lot who try."[2]

Any hope of determining what the dates in *Ulysses* actually count means sifting through, and at times arguing against, a century's worth of critical assumptions about where these numbers even came from, and

732

girls laughing in their shawls and their tall combs and the auctions in the
morning the Greeks and the jews and the Arabs and the devil knows who
else from all the ends of Europe and Duke street and the fowl market all
clucking outside Larby Sharons and the poor donkeys slipping half asleep
and the vague fellows in the cloaks asleep in the shade on the steps and the
big wheels of the carts of the bulls and the old castle thousands of years old
yes and those handsome Moors all in white and turbans like kings asking you
to sit down in their little bit of a shop and Ronda with the old windows
of the posadas glancing eyes a lattice hid for her lover to kiss the iron and
the wineshops half open at night and the castanets and the night we missed
the boat at Algeciras the watchman going about serene with his lamp and O
that awful deepdown torrent O and the sea the sea crimson sometimes like
fire and the glorious sunsets and the figtrees in the Alameda gardens yes
and all the queer little streets and pink and blue and yellow houses and
the rosegardens and the jessamine and geraniums and cactuses and Gibraltar
as a girl where I was a Flower of the mountain yes when I put the rose in
my hair like the Andalusian girls used or shall I wear a red yes and how he
kissed me under the Moorish wall and I thought well as well him as another
and then I asked him with my eyes to ask again yes and then he asked me
would I yes to say yes my mountain flower and first I put my arms around
him yes and drew him down to me so he could feel my breasts all perfume
yes and his heart was going like mad and yes I said yes I will Yes.

Trieste-Zurich-Paris,
1914-1921.

5.1 Dateline for *Ulysses*.

it requires working with biographical hearsay, anecdotal invention, and
evidence from the manuscripts, typescripts, and proofs. If to begin and
end means to write the first and last word, page, or sentence, then these
dates are certainly wrong, but any effort to correct them by moving the
years forward or backward would inevitably disrupt the symbolic duration of seven.[3]

Getting that timeline adjusted to grapple with this ambiguity is not my only objective in this chapter. I also want to use it to examine, in more general terms, how compositional time can be measured, and in doing so think more broadly about the strategies used to access and visualize the creation and reception of this or any other literary work using numbers. In what follows, I'll be considering Joyce's dates both as an attempt to quantify time and challenge the idea that time can be quantified at all. Joyce may have left this timestamp behind for others to see, but it was one that foregrounds the complexity of seeing time as a line. And in this he is not alone. Joseph Priestley, the eighteenth-century polymath who revolutionized the design of timelines, summarizes just how strange the whole enterprise can be, writing in the introduction to his *Chart of Biography*:

> Thus the abstract idea of time, though it be not the object of any of our senses, and no image can properly be made of it, yet because it has real quantity, and we can say a greater or less space of time, it admits of a natural and easy representation in our minds by the idea of a measurable space, and particularly that of a line; which, like time, may be extended in length, without giving any idea of breadth or thickness. And thus a longer or a shorter space of time may be most commodiously and advantageously represented by a longer or a shorter line.[4]

Timeline, time as a line, a line of time: in every case, it's an image invented so that an abstraction can seem concrete. No one can actually see time passing in an instant, but that line, which can transform time into space, makes the process of imagining duration at different scales possible.

But 1914–1921 doesn't belong to the life of a man, or an empire, or a period: it is a *literary timeline*. This device is still getting used to organize writers, works, and movements across decades and centuries, mixing together biography, world history, with moments of creative invention. *Frankenstein* would be one example: the origin of the novel pinned down to a single evening on June 16, 1816 when Mary Shelley got her inspiration for the story whilst staring at the moonlight from her window.[5] On a timeline, Shelley's moment of creative inspiration could also be linked up with a more expansive set of circumstances involving the Enlightenment and the rise of Romanticism. In the process, *Frankenstein* becomes not only a point in time on the line, highlighting forces, ideas, and events converging at a specific moment, but it is also used comparatively to trace an evolutionary narrative at different scales (years, decades, centuries).

As pervasive as they may be, and whether as images on paper or in our heads, no one is ever entirely satisfied with literary timelines. They are either too general or too specific, too arbitrary or too deterministic, too schematic or too simplistic. But whatever the reason, the timeline is not something that most of us would want to stake literary history on. It's too messy, too much overlap, too many belated events or writers, works that are forgotten and recovered later, and too many writers and works outside of their own time. To think of literature on a timeline would mean to think of literary history as a sequence. That's where that timeline from *Ulysses* comes in. Instead of waiting for the professors, Joyce took the liberty of doing it himself. It was a willful act done to control the time of the novel in history. But let's not forget it was done by someone who had just experimented with narrative temporality, using one novel to show how easily it can get manipulated. Yet, still he plants a timeline on the last page and critics take him at his word, many of them using "1914–1921" either to celebrate Joyce's heroic resilience (as if he were the only novelist to take so long!) or to establish correspondences between the timing of the novel with the beginning of World War I and the founding of the Irish Republic.

But Margaret McBride is right to remind us that the "critical event . . . could be the novel's composition."[6] Eventful as it may seem, Joyce was not the first or last one to put a date at the end of a novel.[7] In fact, he may have come across an example in *Lord Jim*, though with a few telling differences: the dates in Joseph Conrad's novel, which include the month and the year ("September 1899–July 1900"), appear awkwardly after the last sentence and before "The End." In all of Joyce's novels, there is a marked difference: the *dates are the end*, even though the temporal measurement is left more ambiguous. Joyce decides to insert a year and never a day or a month or an hour, as if the time of composition was not, unlike the plot of the novel itself, something that needed to be pinned down.[8] The absence of such precise information is revealing, especially when you consider that in the course of writing Joyce actually did have exact months and days in his mind. And this attention to numbers would often lead him to find more cosmic correspondences between the publication dates of his books and the birthdays of him, his friends, and figures from the past whom he admired.

Conrad's *Lord Jim* may be a convenient point of comparison, but it's also necessary to establish from the start that the practice of dating books was not a convention at the Imprimerie Darantière. Between 1922 and 1925, William Carlos Williams's *Spring and All*, Gertrude Stein's *The Making of Americans*, John Rodker's *Montagnes Russes*, and Adrienne Monnier's *La Figure* all appear without dates on the final page, indicating that it was more of a personal choice than anything else. Joyce, unlike so many novelists before and after him, didn't just want to have some vague "sense of a beginning" (Edward Said) or "sense of an ending" (Frank Kermode):[9] he needed to leave behind a very public timeline and it was one that appears, ironically enough, after the end of an episode (18) with "no beginning, middle, or end."[10] But no matter how mystical, cyclical, abstract, or elastic time becomes in the plot of *Ulysses*, there was no getting around the fact that on the page everything had to begin and end somewhere. And since the time in the novel would eventually expire, the act of anchoring *Ulysses* in time was one way to anticipate what it might come to mean to literary history and, perhaps a more dramatic a claim, to world history.

By dating *Ulysses*, Joyce left behind a temporal measurement that would not have been discernible anywhere else in or on the book, and the significance of this gesture is far from obvious. Dates, of course, anchor *Ulysses* in time, thereby corresponding with Alain Robbe-Grillet's suggestion that "the writer must proudly consent to bear his own date, knowing that there are no masterpieces in eternity, but only works in history."[11] But as much as "1914–1921" may have been a note in a novel (like a message in a bottle) left behind for the future, it is also backward looking—there to signal that a significant event had already passed. These numbers are there as evidence that *Ulysses* is very much *in and of its time*, but like Petrarch with the dates attached to his imaginary letters to Cicero and Vergil, they also establish a distance from predecessors both ancient and modern and emphasize that even if he is in his time, he is not entirely of it.[12]

Joyce needed that autobiographical detail instead of a fictional *finis*, but what does it mean to think of *Ulysses* in this final moment not as a novel with words to be read but as a collection of numbers to be counted?[13] Indeed, 1914–1921 is a date with a duration, but we might also think of it as a mathematical equation: $1914 + x = 1921$ or, by reversing it, $1921 - 1914 = x$. In both variations, x is the unknown quantity. It is the variable you need or the sum you get when adding or subtracting these numbers. And as simple as the equation might be, *the act of counting*, in fact, proves critical to the success or failure of this moment. Readers need to do the math, and what they discover is an unwritten seven.[14] By leaving this number suspended on the final page, Joyce ensured that every copy would be numbered in perpetuity, each one counting the same no matter how many different editions appeared or copies sold.

Consider another possibility. What if the numbers of *Ulysses* existed before they were counted by Joyce or anyone else? This computational paradox is reminiscent of the one identified by William James when he explained how the very act of counting the known planets—seven of them, no less, when his argument was made—can make a manufactured truth seem as if it was always already there. In this "quasi-paradox," as he calls it, "something comes by the counting that was not there before. And yet that something was ALWAYS TRUE. In one sense you create it, and in another sense you FIND it."[15] With *Ulysses*, something similar is happening. Seven years is a manufactured truth waiting to be found by readers, but it is also something already there. Joyce is not creating ex nihilo. Rather, he developed a strategy to reveal a truth about the time of composition that would have otherwise remained unknown.

And what's more, that seven has a mystical correspondence with the six days of creation and one day of rest, but so too does the sum of numbers containing it. $1 + 9 + 1 + 4 + 1 + 9 + 2 + 1 = 28$: it's a perfect number built from the sum of its positive proper divisors ($1 + 2 + 4 + 7 + 14 = 28$), one that Pythagoras, Euclid, Philo of Alexandria, Nicomachus, St. Augustine, and others associated with the cycle of the moon. This presence of seven and twenty-eight, then, is one more signal that *Ulysses* exists beyond the limits of any mortal creation, thereby becoming part of a numerical system that organizes the universe while also fitting into the chronology of a much longer literary historical timeline reaching back as far as Homer and ahead to whoever might arrive in the future.

Dates, like so many of the other types of numbers I've already discussed in this book, can have a mystical charge that infuses the object or event with meaning. But let's face it, they are also the data of literary history; the two terms sharing the same Latin root, *dare* (to give), but also *dactylus*, or "finger," which is there to point. The dates in *Ulysses* are a given, but they've become signposts marking a significant shift not just in the history of the novel but of art more generally. To say that dates are data is to recommend that we consider what and how they are marking time, making it not only legible but also coming to influence how we continue to organize the past for the present.

To understand what is really at stake in dating *Ulysses*, we can learn a lot from two different timelines Joyce compiled himself—one involving the life and works of William Shakespeare and the other Leopold Bloom. Though one figure is historical and the other fictional, both of their lives are made to fit within diagrammatic structures that can be used to represent a period of time. Joyce's Shakespeare timeline for his 1912 lectures in Trieste is about as basic as you can get. In a notebook otherwise filled with biographical details and historical events is a list of works organized chronologically:

> *Julius Caesar* 1601
> *Hamlet* 1602 (38 years old)
> *Measure for Measure* 1603
> *Othello* 1604
> *King Lear* 1605
> *Macbeth* 1606[16]

I said this timeline is basic, but that's in format only. All of the temporal data about the literary works is actually much more complex than it might seem. Of the eighteen (or nineteen) plays Shakespeare wrote, there is a discrepancy in every case among the composition, the performance, and publication (if they are even known at all). So, the 1595 of *King John*, the 1602 of *Hamlet*, and the 1606 of *Macbeth* are all misleading, since the first one is based largely on stylistic evidence (lacking external evidence and internal topical allusions), the second corresponds with the performance, and the third to a revision by Thomas Middleton and not corroborated by evidence from an original, and likely shorter, prompt book.

"Shakespeare Dates" is the title Joyce added to another notebook he used in 1917 when preparing the Hamlet chapter (episode 9) for serialization. Each year is given a separate page, and this time around he identifies whether the plays were recorded, revised, produced, staged, or begun. In addition, he intermittently includes a running log on the right hand side tracking the relative ages of Shakespeare and his family members (1593, 1596, 1601, 1613). In 1593, at twenty-nine years of age, Shakespeare publishes *Venus and Adonis* and "probably" begins his *Sonnets*. He returns to Stratford in 1596 at the age of thirty-two (after eleven years), turns thirty-seven in 1601 when his father dies, followed in 1613 by the death of his brother Richard when he is forty-nine.

As with the first example, the Shakespeare dates do not resemble a classic timeline laid out on a single page. And still, the sequential distribution across pages performs the same function: it quantifies time. Laying out the life and work numerically is one way to imagine what is otherwise intangible about literary time and literary creation. Instead of asking how Shakespeare became Shakespeare, the emphasis is on the when, and if the sequence makes the stages of his career legible, it was never something he could have known himself for the simple reason that the future was always before him. Not so for us or for anyone who chooses to look back on literary history. We already know in advance what was done in these years, so the laying out of the works in sequence functions much like the planets in James's "quasi-paradox." Counting time creates time, making visible what is already there.

But this timeline also emphasizes that the growth was gradual, part of an organic process with the life and works arriving together. To see that *Hamlet* was staged in 1602 is one thing. But to see it was staged in 1602 when Shakespeare was thirty-eight years old is quite another. This is biographical time informing compositional time. *Hamlet* didn't just happen at that particular moment. It could only have happened at that moment in Shakespeare's life and career, and as singular as this event may be in 1602, it is also relational, requiring the recognition that time moves on with other works getting produced as Shakespeare ages.

The timeline Joyce made for Bloom in late 1921 works differently (figure 5.2).[17] A sequence of years runs down the left hand side of a single page from 1866 to 1904, half of them containing facts about Bloom's personal and professional life, most of them confined to the years after 1886 when he's reached the age of twenty. The birthdates of Molly, Milly, and Rudy are included, along with the streets where the Bloom family lived, and the timeline ends with an entry that Milly Bloom is in Mullingar in 1904. Jotted in pencil on the right-hand side, are a series of running calculations comparing the respective ages of the Blooms in different years, the same kind he did for Shakespeare. He needed these calculations during the revision process as he went back to add memories to earlier episodes and implant others in the later ones. All of these numerical details were a way

5.2 Joyce's incomplete chronology for the Blooms.

Source: Courtesy of the National Library of Ireland.

5.3 Close-up of Molly Bloom's fiftieth birthday (8/9/921).

to give the Blooms a more substantial past, and John Henry Raleigh has pointed out that many of them were tweaked along the way proving that the timeline was made to be modified.[18]

Which gets us to one of the more puzzling entries: Molly Bloom's birthday. The year 1871 includes a note reading: "M.B n [nata]," or, Molly Bloom born. It is one of the calendrical mysteries that have kept the critics busy, in part, because there is so much conflicting evidence in the novel, the notes, the letters, and the timeline.[19] One thing everyone can agree on is the day: Molly's birthday takes place on September 8. Eight is a number (vertically) and an infinity sign (horizontally) packed into one. But it's the day/month/year that Joyce added in pencil next to Molly's birthday that requires more scrutiny: 8/9/[1]921 marks Molly's birthday all right, but that's seventeen years *after* the plot ends, which should make us all wonder what this time-warped detail might be here (figure 5.3).

Here's one possibility: Joyce, as he was finishing the final pages of episode 18 in early September 1921, realized that he was writing about Molly on what would have been her fiftieth birthday.[20] That note, in other words, is there to mark the writing event itself. But there's more. What if we also consider that 8/9/[1]921 represents the complete fusion of the biographical time of the character and the compositional time of the author: on September 8, 1921, Molly Bloom finally has a complete birthday because her episode is written. And though it may be true that Joyce shared the real year of Molly's birthday with his friend Frank Budgen a few weeks earlier, this is the moment when the creation of

Molly is complete. By seeing her birthday as if it was fifty years later is
the surest sign that the fictional clock ticks in tandem with real time. His
novel may have an end, but the characters still live on long enough to see
their own story written down.

If Molly has a birthday without a definite year, the reverse is true for
Leopold: he has a *birthyear* without a day.[21] Thirty-eight years old when
the novel opens, his age coincides with Joyce's during the composition of
Ulysses, but it's also the age of Shakespeare when he wrote *Hamlet*.[22] If,
based on other evidence, we can deduce that the month for Bloom's birth
takes place in May, we will also want to remember it's the name of Joyce's
mother: May Joyce is to James Joyce, then, as James Joyce is to Leopold
Bloom. Try as we might, though, the month and the mother still don't
bring us any closer to pinning down an exact day.

And why should it? The year is all that matters when measuring
Bloom's life. I just mentioned that his age has an autobiographical correspondence, but in *Ulysses*, the mystery of his birthday is given one more
twist. We never know *a day* but there is a *period* of time marked by the
arrival of a star, one of "similar origin" to that appearing at the birth
of William Shakespeare, another figure whose exact birthday remains
unknown:

> the appearance of a star (1st magnitude) of exceeding brilliancy dominating
> by night and day . . . about the period of the birth of William Shakespeare
> over delta in the recumbent neversetting constellation of Cassiopeia and of
> a star (2nd magnitude) of similar origin but of lesser brilliancy which had
> appeared in and disappeared from the constellation of the Corona Septen-
> trionalis about the period of the birth of Leopold Bloom and of other stars
> of (presumably) similar origin which had (effectively or presumably) ap-
> peared in and disappeared from the constellation of Andromeda about the
> period of the birth of Stephen Dedalus, and in and from the constellation
> of Auriga some years after the birth and death of Rudolph Bloom, junior . . .
> (*U*, 575).

As with all the other answers in episodee 17, this one is scientific in
sound and imprecise in sense. There is some astrological information that
makes it possible to calculate the season, month of year—but try as everyone might, the day proves elusive. Even with the guidance of the stars,

Bloom's day remains unidentifiable. Bloom is an age instead of aged. Like the stars, his beginning happens at a different scale, one that resists any human desire for the precision of minutes, seconds, hours, and days.

What is the point of all this? An unreliable narrator in the novel using the same kind of fuzzy temporal accounting that we find in Joyce's timeline for the Blooms. Consider how this fuzziness should inform our understanding of 1914–1921, a date that was written down on the last page of episode 18 at the same time that Joyce was finishing the fair copy for episode 17 and revisiting his character chronology (late August-mid-October 1921). It may seem as if these are three unrelated examples, but they share in common the same problem: What does it mean to measure time? Or, put another way, what does the measurement of time actually count? Putting a day or year to Molly or Leopold's life could determine their fate or describe their character, but when it comes to the novel in which they appear that same logic is at work. It's not when is *Ulysses* born, or when does it begin, but rather, what might the day of its birth say about what it is and is not. To pin the beginning and end of *Ulysses* on a month or a day would necessarily restrict the possibilities for its significance. It is the novel of 1914 and 1921, but, in another way, the presence of a specific day or month would also reduce the time scale, making the creation too specific—shrinking what's otherwise reflected in the annual (vs. diurnal or monthly) measurement.

1914–1921 is a timeline. Accessing it fully means that we need to accommodate all the different temporal registers: biographical, autobiographical, fictional, astrological, numerological, literary-historical, world historical. But there's one more aspect we should not forget: the materiality of the date itself. Joyce provided the original template on a handwritten copy, sending it directly to Darantière who then put it into placards. And that's where things get a little complicated. I'll discuss this revision stage later on, but for now I want to focus on one curious detail: that line between the two years. Looking at the 1922 edition, that is definitely not an em dash (the kind used to indicate dialogue), but it's not an en dash either (which measures the width of an "n"). Which can only mean one thing: it's a hyphen, that piece of punctuation Joyce despised more than any other even if its absence would inspire so many memorable compound words (*scrotumtightening, snotgreen, loudlatinlaughing* and *buttocksmothered* among them).

That's definitely not the design Joyce made for his dates (figure 5.4). Not only was he more liberal with the spacing between the years, but he also made the line in between a lot longer. In the subsequent revisions that took place during the proof stages, the question was never raised, and the hyphen as set by Darantière made it all the way through to the end. If we consider this first draft as an expression of what Joyce wanted, then we might try and imagine what that longer line means. More time, for one thing, but it also provides more space for an implied sequence of years: 1915, 1916, 1917, 1918, 1919, 1920.

Why stop here? That line could be made even longer, stretched in both directions so that it actually fills the same distance as the "Trieste-Zurich-Paris" looming above (figure 5.5). Time and place, then, would be in sync, the duration of the line corresponding with the wandering in and between the three cities. All of this might sound a little too playful perhaps, more of a fantasy scenario about what this detail in the novel could be instead of an assessment of what it is. But that's precisely what I want to avoid: if all the other pieces of punctuation matter, many of them leading over the years to contentious debates about what *Ulysses* should look like, this line is one of the more provocative examples that has fallen entirely off the radar. So quick are we to calculate the number, that this small segment of line has been ignored.

Once you begin to imagine the line less as the final word (one marking the moment when time passed) and more as the material expression of time passing, then we're getting closer conceptually to Henri Bergson's *durée*. For Wyndham Lewis, "there would be no *Ulysses*" without Bergson.[23] He's referring here to interior monologue, but this same sentiment can extend to the timeline. More specifically, I am referring to what Bergson says about time's qualitative dimension. "Pure duration," Bergson argues, "might well be nothing but a succession of qualitative changes, which melt into and permeate one another, without precise outlines, without any tendency to externalize themselves in relation to one another, without any affiliation with number: it would be pure heterogeneity."[24] Joyce's timeline has the effect of reducing a qualitative, creative experience to a quantitative one. The numbers speak but the emphasis falls on the final sum and not the relations, affiliations, and juxtapositions that are, in the end, so much a part of any creative process no matter how unidirectional or sequential we try to make it seem.

flowers all a woman's body yes that was one true thing he said in his life and the sun shines for you today yes that was why I liked him because I saw he understood or felt what a woman is and I knew I could always get round him and I gave him all the pleasure I could leading him on till he asked me to say yes and I wouldn't answer first only looked out over the sea and the sky I was thinking of so many things he didn't know of Mulvey and Mr Stanhope and Hester and father and old captain Groves and the flameda gardens and Gibraltar as a girl where I was a flower of the mountain and how he kissed me under the Moorish wall and I thought well as well him as another and then I asked him with my eyes to ask again and then he asked me would I to say yes my mountain flower and first I put my arms around him and drew him down to me so he could feel my breasts all perfume and I said I will yes.

Trieste - Zurich - Paris
1914 — 1921

P731-732   L932-933   N782-783

5.4   The first dateline for *Ulysses*.

girls laughing in their shawls and their tall combs and the auctions in the
morning the Greeks and the jews and the Arabs and the devil knows who
else from all the ends of Europe and Duke street and the fowl market all
clucking outside Larby Sharons and the poor donkeys slipping half asleep
and the vague fellows in the cloaks asleep in the shade on the steps and the
big wheels of the carts of the bulls and the old castle thousands of years old
yes and those handsome Moors all in white and turbans like kings asking you
to sit down in their little bit of a shop and Ronda with the old windows
of the posadas glancing eyes a lattice hid for her lover to kiss the iron and
the wineshops half open at night and the castanets and the night we missed
the boat at Algeciras the watchman going about serene with his lamp and O
that awful deepdown torrent O and the sea the sea crimson sometimes like
fire and the glorious sunsets and the figtrees in the Alameda gardens yes
and all the queer little streets and pink and blue and yellow houses and
the rosegardens and the jessamine and geraniums and cactuses and Gibraltar
as a girl where I was a Flower of the mountain yes when I put the rose in
my hair like the Andalusian girls used or shall I wear a red yes and how he
kissed me under the Moorish wall and I thought well as well him as another
and then I asked him with my eyes to ask again yes and then he asked me
would I yes to say yes my mountain flower and first I put my arms around
him yes and drew him down to me so he could feel my breasts all perfume
yes and his heart was going like mad and yes I said yes I will Yes.

Trieste-Zurich-Paris,
1914————1921

5.5   A reimagined extended dateline for *Ulysses*.

I bring this up if only to emphasize how we can imagine these dates as an intrusion, an attempt to control the time in which the work itself, as a creative composition, is being fashioned for the future. Joyce wants the compositional time of *Ulysses* to resemble a line when, as I'll explain in what follows, it is not: dating *Ulysses* was a much more fluid, unfixed process with multiple possibilities. Not only does that line extend forward and backward, it tries to reduce the event to a succession all the while masking the question about what it means for this work, or any work or art for that matter, to begin and end. The timeline, you could say, provides a duration but masks a *durée*. Creation is never so clean and attempts to quantify it are one way to make the process less messy, as if the world within appeared by fiat and not, as we know, through the labor of thinking, writing, and revising.

The timeline in figure 5.6 is one attempt to represent the complexity of compositional time. We may have Joyce's clean and compact version in the novel, but we also know from all the archival evidence that there are other possibilities, and they involve identifying earlier material that was reused, the erratic dating of Joyce himself, and the attempts of critics to identify a prehistory of the novel. This timeline is not complete by any means, but it gives us an opportunity to think seriously about what it might mean not only to imagine different durations for the composition but also different points of beginning and ending. This timeline may not provide a definitive answer to the question of when *Ulysses* began, but it forces us to consider the assumptions we make about the creative process when we go about looking for an answer and then trying to represent it.

II 1914 OR 1912 OR 1909 OR 1906 OR 1903?

So, the beginning: 1914 turned out to be a tragic year in world history, but when Joyce first started writing *Ulysses*, or eventually claimed to, nothing of the sort could have been known.[25] In his early study of the pre-1917 *Ulysses*, Rodney Owen was the first to argue that this date (a year) was a gradually discovered fiction and not even firmly in place until 1920.[26] That, however, is not the story that Herbert Gorman, Joyce's first biographer, recounts: "In the spring of 1914 he began *Ulysses*, setting down,

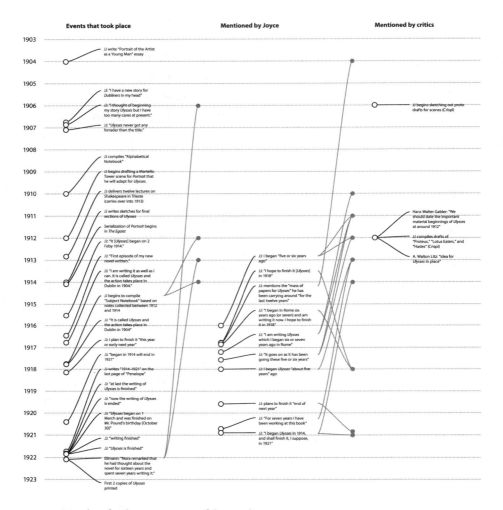

5.6   Timeline for the composition of the novel, 1903–1922.

first of all, the preliminary sketches for the final sections."[27] This particular account may sound objective enough, but only if we are willing to disregard what he told Harriet Shaw Weaver in November 1921: "*Ulysses* began on 1 March (birthday of a friend of mine a Cornish painter) and was finished on Mr Pound's birthday [October 30]."[28] Gorman had the year, but Joyce had an exact day and considering his superstition about numbers and birth dates, he probably an hour and minute. Evidence such as this certainly suggests that Joyce did end up having an exact moment in mind for the beginning and end of his novel, but it was not always fixed. In fact, even this one, as precise as it may be, gets contradicted in other letters addressed to Pound and McAlmon in which the beginning is moved a month earlier and the end a day earlier.

In Gorman's version, one that was likely vetted by the author himself, Joyce begins "first of all" with "sketches" for the final episodes. The term *sketch* could refer to a rough draft, an outline, a series of notes or words, or a few lines or paragraphs, but in an effort to provide some clarification, Gorman goes on to explain that "It would be more precise to say that he began to put *Ulysses* on paper, for the theme as a whole, had been swelling in his mind for some years, growing secretly at first from the seed fecundated in Rome, then blossoming into his consciousness, and finally completely absorbing it."[29] In this tortured organic metaphor, Gorman seems to suggest that beginning can certainly involve putting words down on paper, but it might also coincide with the moment when the seed for the story was first planted (not necessarily involving paper), which in this case would be the period when Joyce was living in Rome and first considered adding it as a short story to *Dubliners*.[30]

So why did Joyce insist on using 1914 and not 1906 or 1907 (figure 5.7)?[31] It wouldn't be the first time he identified the date of writing a novel with the mere seed of an idea. After all, 1904 was not when he actually started writing the novel called *A Portrait of the Artist as a Young Man*: it was the year when he composed the essay "Portrait of the Artist."[32] Whatever the reason, Ezra Pound was not one to get misled, and in a review of *Ulysses* published in the *Mercure de France*, he told his French readers that "les romanciers n'aiment dépenser que trois mois, six mois pour un roman. *Joyce y a mis quinze ans.* Et *Ulysses* est plus condensé (732 grandes feuilles) que n'importe quelle oeuvre entière de Flaubert; on y découvre plus d'architecture."[33] By 1922, Pound's fifteen years puts the beginning of *Ulysses* back in Rome 1906. In an undocumented conversation that was supposed to have taken place on the day *Ulysses* was published that's more in line with Nora Joyce's claim, "he had thought about the book for sixteen years and spent seven years writing it."[34]

It was Joyce, not Pound, who got the last number, and he used Gorman's biography in the 1930s to suggest, in retrospect, that the choice of a date actually had a lot to do with the good fortune he experienced that year with *Portrait* getting serialized, *Dubliners* finally published, and

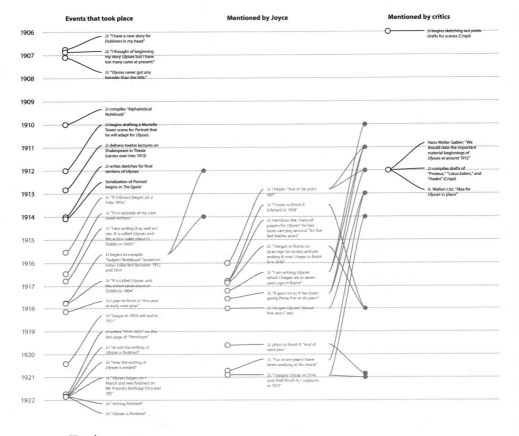

	Events that took place	Mentioned by Joyce	Mentioned by critics

1906 — JJ: "I have a new story for *Dubliners* in my head" — JJ begins sketching out proto-drafts for scenes (Crispi)

JJ: "I thought of beginning my story *Ulysses* but I have too many cares at present."

1907

JJ: "*Ulysses* never got any forrader than the title."

1908

1909

JJ compiles "Alphabetical Notebook"

1910 — JJ begins drafting a Martello Tower scene for *Portrait* that he will adapt for *Ulysses*.

1911 — JJ delivers twelve lectures on Shakespeare in Trieste (carries over into 1913) — Hans Walter Gabler: "We should date the important material beginnings of *Ulysses* at around 1912"

1912 — JJ writes sketches for final sections of *Ulysses* — JJ compiles drafts of "Proteus," "Lotus Eaters," and "Hades" (Crispi)

Serialization of *Portrait* begins in *The Egoist*

1913 — JJ: "It [*Ulysses*] began on 2 Feby 1914." — JJ: "I began 'five or six years' ago" — A. Walton Litz: "Idea for *Ulysses* in place"

1914 — JJ: "First episode of my new novel written." — JJ: "I hope to finish it [*Ulysses*] in 1918"

JJ: "I am writing it as well as I can. It is called *Ulysses* and the action takes place in Dublin in 1904." — JJ: mentions the "mass of papers for *Ulysses*" he has been carrying around "for the last twelve years"

1915

1916 — JJ begins to compile "Subject Notebook" based on notes collected between 1912 and 1914 — JJ: "I began in Rome six years ago (or seven) and am writing it now. I hope to finish it in 1918"

1917 — JJ: "It is called *Ulysses* and the action takes place in Dublin in 1904." — JJ: "I am writing *Ulysses* which I began six or seven years ago in Rome"

JJ: "It goes on as it has been going these five or six years"

1918 — JJ: I plan to finish it "this year or early next year." — JJ: I began *Ulysses* "about five years" ago

JJ: "began in 1914 will end in 1921"

1919 — JJ writes "1914-1921" on the last page of "Penelope"

1920 — JJ: "at last the writing of *Ulysses* is finished." — JJ: plans to finish it "end of next year."

JJ: "now the writing of *Ulysses* is ended" — JJ: "For seven years I have been working at this book"

1921 — JJ: "*Ulysses* began on 1 March and was finished on Mr. Pound's birthday [October 30]" — JJ: "I began *Ulysses* in 1914, and shall finish it, I suppose, in 1921"

1922 — JJ: "writing finished"

JJ: "*Ulysses* is finished"

5.7   Timeline, 1906–1922.

Exiles partially written. In 1914, Joyce was on a roll, and it marked an annus mirabilis in a literary career that had been more *horribilis* up until that point. The beginning of *Ulysses*, then, was bound up with a series of endings involving authorial victories that had so far eluded him, and if in this early biographical account Gorman is clear about where Joyce was in the novel before leaving Trieste for Zurich in June 1915, even going so far as to identify the very line where he stopped in episode 3, he says nothing about the first word, phrase, line, or set of lines, and no evidence has survived to clarify matters.[35]

Ellmann's revisionary account doesn't help much either. Like Gorman, he mentions that Joyce had been "preparing himself to write *Ulysses* since

1907" [imagining a "Dublin *Peer Gynt*"], and he even recycles the point that Joyce had reached "the first pages of the third episode by June [1915]" before leaving for Zurich. Unlike Gorman, however, Ellmann actually had access to letters, which reveal that even if Joyce had started writing sketches of the final episodes in the spring of 1914, he was not talking about beginning *Ulysses* until he finished the first two episodes in June 1915.[36] In a letter to his brother Stanislaus, dated June 16 no less, he writes, "Die erste Episode meines neues Roman 'Ulysses' ist geschrieben" ["The first episode of my new novel *Ulysses* is written"] and to Pound a few weeks later, he reports, "I have written the first two episodes."[37] This lag suggests that even if the writing had begun a year earlier, the novel itself was not ready for any official announcement until the actual beginning was in place.

Once there is a beginning to the plot of *Ulysses*, Joyce sets out to establish one that would coincide with the origins of the novel *Ulysses*. Having told Pound about his progress, he follows up a few weeks later asking if he should send "the first chapters of [his] novel" to Mr. Gosse, adding, "it began on 2 Feby 1914."[38] It would seem logical to assume that in using the phrase "first chapters of my novel" Joyce is referring to *Portrait*, which started serialization in the *Egoist* on that date.[39] However, considering the fact that Pound was the one who had arranged for the serialization and saw each of the installments through, then it would seem strange for Joyce to remind him of the date, and, more to the point, it is worth emphasizing that Joyce informs Pound that he "began on 2 Feby 1914," not *began serialization on*. Equally problematic is the fact that just two weeks earlier, he had already informed Pound that "the first two episodes" of his new novel were written, thereby making it likely that he was picking up the conversation where it had left off.

Whatever the case may be, though, this particular birthdate for the novel did not stick. By September 1916, Joyce was already recalibrating, telling Pound: "All the rest of my stuff is the bewildering mass of papers for *Ulysses* which I carry in a very large envelope that I possess [*sic*] for the last twelve years."[40] That same year, the timeline shifts again, making *Ulysses* begin somewhere around 1909, when he made his penultimate visit to Ireland and discovered both the address of 7 Eccles Street and the possibility of Nora's betrayal (later proven false). That same year, Joyce tells Weaver and his friend C. P. Curran that he began "six or seven years ago" and Pound got a slightly different version shortly thereafter: "As regards

Ulysses I write and think and write and think all day and part of the night. [It goes on as it] has been going on these five or six years. But the ingredients will not fuse until they have reached a certain temperature."[41]

As usual, these dates are approximate, as if Joyce doesn't really want to pin down the beginning. It's always six or seven, five or six, but if you do the math that second number actually brings the beginning of *Ulysses* closer to 1912, the year, Owen suspects, when Joyce began to gather material for Stephen's episodes (2, 3, 9, and possibly 7). Litz agreed: "The idea of Stephen's participation in a later work to be called *Ulysses* must have been well advanced by 1911–12, and the outline of the whole novel was probably visualized as well since Gorman says that Joyce began to make preliminary sketches for the final sections of *Ulysses* early in 1914 immediately after finishing the *Portrait*."[42] Gabler takes this possibility one step further, speculating that 1912 marks the "material beginning" of *Ulysses* when Joyce began to separate scenes, characters, and even sentences for the two novels.[43] Indeed, 1912 might not have been an annus mirabilis like 1914, but it was the year Joyce left Ireland for the last time, the same year he delivered his lectures on Shakespeare.

So, why not 1912 (figure 5.8)? If we believe Frank Budgen, that was the year Joyce alluded to when they met in 1918: "In leaving the café," he recalls, "I asked Joyce how long he had been working on *Ulysses*. 'About five years,' he said, 'but in a sense all my life.' "[44] As usual, the number is left ambiguous: it's *about* five years and there is never an official day or month. One likely reason: Joyce was still unpublished in 1912 and *Portrait* was unfinished, so beginning a new novel when the others were still in progress would end up disrupting the seamlessness of his creative chronology, one that he would eventually maximize to full effect with 1904–1914 (*Portrait*), 1914–1921, 1922–1939 (*Finnegans Wake*). Another reason: the act of gathering material for two different novels at the same time did not mean that a new project was officially underway. Cogitating, gathering, collecting, and rearranging, was not to be confused with writing. And, then, of course, there's always Joyce's numerical superstition. The year 1912 might seem harmless enough until you add the numbers up: $1 + 9 + 1 + 2 = 13$.[45] If this kind of calendrical equation sounds paranoid, consider Joyce's comment to Weaver in 1921 when *Ulysses* was set to appear: "It seems to me as if this year $(1 + 9 + 2 + 1 = 13)$ is to be one of incessant trouble to me."[46] It turned out that the numbers didn't end up counting against him, and by 1921, when

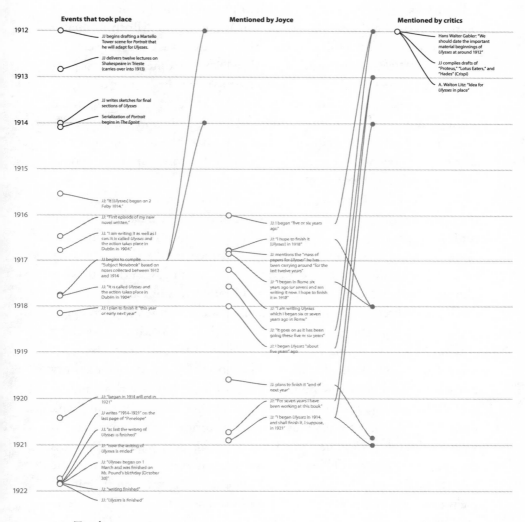

Events that took place | **Mentioned by Joyce** | **Mentioned by critics**

1912 — JJ begins drafting a Martello Tower scene for *Portrait* that he will adapt for *Ulysses*.

Hans Walter Gabler: "We should date the important material beginnings of *Ulysses* at around 1912"

JJ delivers twelve lectures on Shakespeare in Trieste (carries over into 1913)

1913 — JJ compiles drafts of "Proteus," "Lotus Eaters," and "Hades" (Crispi)

A. Walton Litz: "Idea for *Ulysses* in place"

JJ writes sketches for final sections of *Ulysses*

1914 — Serialization of *Portrait* begins in *The Egoist*

1915

1916 — JJ: "It [*Ulysses*] began on 2 Feb 1914."

JJ: "First episode of my new novel written."

JJ: I began "five or six years ago"

JJ: "I am writing it as well as I can. It is called *Ulysses* and the action takes place in Dublin in 1904"

JJ: "I hope to finish it [*Ulysses*] in 1918"

1917 — JJ begins to compile "Subject Notebook" based on notes collected between 1912 and 1914

JJ mentions the "mass of papers for *Ulysses*" he has been carrying around "for the last twelve years"

JJ: "It is called *Ulysses* and the action takes place in Dublin in 1904"

JJ: "I began in Rome six years ago (or seven) and am writing it now. I hope to finish it in 1918"

1918 — JJ: I plan to finish it "this year or early next year"

JJ: "I am writing *Ulysses* which I began six or seven years ago in Rome"

JJ: "It goes on as it has been going these five or six years"

1919 — JJ: I began *Ulysses* "about five years" ago

JJ: plans to finish it "end of next year"

1920 — JJ: "began in 1914 will end in 1921"

JJ: "For seven years I have been working at this book"

JJ writes "1914–1921" on the last page of "Penelope"

JJ: "I began *Ulysses* in 1914, and shall finish it, I suppose, in 1921"

JJ: "at last the writing of *Ulysses* is finished"

1921 — JJ: "now the writing of *Ulysses* is ended"

JJ: "*Ulysses* began on 1 March and was finished on Mr. Pound's birthday (October 30)"

1922 — JJ: "writing finished"

JJ: "*Ulysses* is finished"

5.8 Timeline, 1912–1922.

they had arrived again in a different order, the novel was almost finished and there was a definite end in sight.

Joyce, as I said, needed to have an end date in mind to establish once and for all when he actually got started. By February 1919, ten episodes of *Ulysses* had been serialized in the *Little Review* with an anticipated eight more to go, but that was enough for him to begin guessing when it would all be over. "This year or early next year," he wrote Weaver on

February 25, 1919; "will not be finished probably until the end of next year—if even then," he told Quinn on August 3, 1919. Both estimates were way off. Almost a full year later, the situation was decidedly clearer. Ezra Pound, Carlo Linati, and Henry Davray were some of the first people to get the news and by late November 1920 the beginning of *Ulysses* was an established fact. "I began *Ulysses* in 1914 . . .," he tells Quinn in the bluntest way possible, adding "and shall finish it, I suppose, in 1921."[47] There it is, 1914–1921, a timeline meant to chart the development of a single novel's becoming, one that so many of his contemporaries would identify with the end of an era.

After six years of writing, the dates of *Ulysses* were finally set, though the novel was still another year and two months in the making, with two copies appearing on an express train from Dijon on his fortieth birthday. Joyce was fond of staging publication coincidences like these, and they ended up regulating the entire life cycle of his writing. Contrary to what Thomas Hardy believed, the date of publication was not an "accident in the life of a literary creation."[48] Rather, it was a deliberate astrological event with the power to connect the life of the author with the work he created. In an interesting twist, it was always years and never days that Joyce made public on the last pages of his novels. By the time he was busy calculating the number of hours spent on *Ulysses* (twenty thousand by his tally), 1914 would have meant more to the general public than Frank Budgen's birthday.[49] It was a year of world historical significance, that, on a personal level, determined the direction of his own wanderings across Europe where he was deliberately avoiding any direct contact with the battlefield. This continued act of writing during the war and in spite of the war is what mattered most. "What did you do in the Great War?," one of Tom Stoppard's characters asks Joyce in *Travesties*. "I wrote *Ulysses*," he responds, "What did you do?"[50]

III 1921 OR 1922?

If, as I've been arguing, the beginning of *Ulysses* was a gradually discovered fiction, then so too was its end. The major difference is that we know significantly more about the middle and late stages of the composition process (1918 forward) than we do about the early ones (1912, or earlier, to 1917), in large part, because so much material was preserved, including the detailed correspondence through which Joyce kept friends and admirers abreast of his progress. "A few lines," Joyce wrote to Robert McAlmon on October 29, 1921, "to say that I have just finished the *Ithaca* episode so that at last the writing of *Ulysses* is finished."[51] In this letter and others, Joyce selects an end date in which he distinguishes between writing and revising, and having finished his last rough draft of this episode, he believes that the work he has left to do is fundamentally different: revision and proofreading were not to be confused with composition. Looking through the available typescripts and proofs, however, Gabler and his team concluded to the contrary that Joyce's work was far from over, and that episode 17, in particular, "was by no means ready to go to the printer."[52] In fact, in the following months, he would augment episode 17 by 34 percent, with 16 percent more text added to the notes and typescript and 18 percent to the proofs.[53] Richard Madtes, who first compiled these percentages, concluded that "composition may have been 'at an end' for most of the book, but certainly not for Ithaca [episode 17]."[54]

This flurry of activity in the final months leaves us with an unresolved question: When did *Ulysses* end? The end of writing, as I mentioned, is not something that Joyce identified automatically with the act of revising.[55] They were different activities, the one involving creation from nothing, the other creation from something.[56] In addition, the dates that marked an end to writing were not to be confused with the publication. The original contract was negotiated in April 1921, but by the end of August, Darantière was already warning Joyce, "it will not be possible to finish *Ulysses* before the end of this year 1921" ["il ne sera pas possible d'achever 'Ulysses' avant la fin de cette année mil neuf cent vingt et un"].[57]

The evidence from one of the fliers for *Ulysses* reveals that Joyce didn't care.[58] Along with the woodcut image of a meditative bard in the middle of the page is an announcement that "Ulysses by James Joyce will be published in the Autumn of 1921" with a correction to the date, "January 1922." This move from season and year to month and year was obviously intended as a necessary point of clarification, but what's so striking here is Joyce's explicit acknowledgement that *Ulysses* was not going to be ready for publication before the year's end. In fact, since this correction to the flier was made while the book was still being revised/written, it also suggests that the end of *Ulysses* was in sight though it was not yet an event that would coincide with his birthday.[59]

None of this, however, was enough to make Joyce consider revising the one detail in his novel that could have used it: 1921.[60] Here the genetic evidence is hard to ignore. Joyce wrote a version of the final sentence of episode 18 between the end of August and late September when the final *yes* was still uncapitalized. But even then, with several months of revisions before him and episode 17 still unfinished, 1921 was going to be the year when *Ulysses* came to an end.

In these final months, Joyce was not just adding more material to his already massive novel: he was counting the time it took. And in doing so, he refused to keep the clock running as the revisions took him and his printers into another year. Indeed, Joyce may have designated October 30, 1921 as the official end, but the proofs are evidence enough that the work actually took three months more and up to January 31, 1922, two days before the first two copies were printed and delivered. All of this might seem trivial enough. Joyce's distinction between writing and revising, one could argue, provides enough justification for this choice. Yet that's only convincing if we are willing to ignore the fictionality of the beginning as well, a fictionality that actually determined when the novel itself could end in the first place. By November 1920, and with thirteen episodes already printed in the *Little Review*, there really was no choice for another end date. Joyce had to finish in 1921 in order for the numbers to add up. Instead of a Homeric ten years, *Ulysses* would take seven.[61]

IV 7 OR 8 YEARS?

Why seven?[62] Kenner, as I mentioned in the introduction, was the first critic to pick up on the fact that *Ulysses* is a title made up of seven letters and is the "sole *remark* the author . . . permits himself amid a quarter-million words."[63] In the novel itself, seven is the number of monsters Bloom must bypass (episodes 4, 8, 12, 11, 5, 9, 13). John Eglinton reminds Stephen, seven is "dear to the mystic mind" and Bloom, while farting, conflates Robert Emmet's last words with the "seven last words" of Jesus Christ (*U*, 151, 238). This number appears again in a poem by Yeats, in reference to the number of known planets in 1895, and to identify the years D. B. Murphy has been at sea and the miles Bloom can stick his tongue up Molly's "hole." In Hebrew, Greek, Egyptian, and Eastern traditions, Seidman and Gifford tell us, it was a number representing, "the embodiment of perfection and unity, mystically appropriate to sacred things," and for early Christian writers, it was "the number of completion and perfection," corresponding as it did with the days of creation.[64] Of course, seven is also the number of signatories on the proclamation of the Irish Republic, the colors of the rainbow, the continents and seas, the notes on a numerical scale, the stars of the Big Dipper, the feelings of mankind (joy, anger, sadness, fear, love, liking, disliking), the wonders of the world, the cardinal and theological virtues (prudence, temperance, fortitude, justice, faith, hope, charity), the classical planets to the ancients, the liberal arts in the Middle Ages, and the days of the week.

On the last page of *Ulysses*, seven, as I mentioned, is not a number that gets mentioned explicitly. Rather, it is the sum derived from an equation that can involve either subtraction ($1921 - 1914 = 7$) or addition ($1914 + 7 = 1921$). Once discovered it can suggest unity and perfection while also corresponding with the life cycle of the novel, a novel, Joyce once claimed, that was an epic of the human body, which, if you take the analogy far enough, involves the inevitable aging process for author and book alike. Consider, for instance, his original, unrealized plan for *Stephen Hero* in 1903: an autobiographical novel that was to be comprised of nine sections each one made up of seven chapters. Gabler has argued that the sixty-three "seems to have been numerologically related to the periods of life of a man" that would include infancy, boyhood, adolescence, young adulthood, middle age, early old age, and later old age. As much as *Ulysses* was arranged by organ and divided by hour, it was also intended as a document of an entire human life, and each year of its becoming corresponding with one of these seven stages compressed into the hours of a single day. Considering the number of allusions to *As You Like it*, in fact, it's impossible to believe that Shakespeare was not somehow behind the idea. "All the world's a stage," Jaques says to

Duke Senior, "And all the men and women merely players;/They have their exits and their entrances,/And one man in his time plays many parts,/ His acts being seven ages."[65]

Seven ages, seven acts, seven stages. If Shakespeare's stage (set in a Globe no less) could contain worlds and reveal the lives of so many players moving across it, then why not a novel in Dublin that begins and ends on 7 Eccles Street? The dates at the end are, in a sense, an attempt to reaffirm just that with the emphasis always on the time and place of creation. *Ulysses*, like every novel before and after it, must come to an end, but the seven years are there as evidence that something transcendent has happened in the process. No matter how many times this novel ends, no matter how many readers flip to that final page, something mystical takes place, an experience in fictional time and in a fictional world that leads outside of time, and much like Stephen and Bloom entering the cosmos with the final "Where?" of episode 17 (the first ending) or Molly Bloom passing into eternity after her emphatic "Yes" in episode 18 (the second ending), readers of *Ulysses* have no choice but to come face to face with a set of numbers waiting to be counted. Joyce, Ellmann tells us, looked forward to the "expiration of [his] seven years' sentence," picking up, no doubt from Gorman, who, in the first authorized biography, claimed "It was a long period—seven years, and it seemed even longer because of the hectic era that had been packed into those years."[66]

An age, a stage, but all together seven years that define an era. That helps to explain why none of these numbers matter much on their own. This paradoxical condensation and dilation of time requires the simple act of solving an equation, and the dates, the novel's last word, are a way of summing up the larger point that the time of composition is strangely equivalent to the chronology of the plot. The labor of *Ulysses* might have continued up until the last day in January 1922 (with the first copy arriving at 7 A.M. on February 2), but in order for it all to add up, the novel itself had to end before the writing was done, and in doing so, Joyce put Pound's statement about dates to the test. It's *the time spent on the novel that counts*. If you take Pound at his word, it all adds up: 1 novel=7 years. Seven, it's the number of perfection, unity, days of the week, the stages of life, the years Odysseus spends on Calypso's island, and, from that moment forward, it is the amount of time Joyce took to write a novel that would mark the end of one era and the beginning of another.

V P.S.U.

The high watermark for modernism might be 1922, but Joyce's contemporaries weren't entirely sure if the arrival of *Ulysses* marked a beginning or an end to writing, to the novel as a genre, to modern literature, or even to civilization. "If it does not make an epoch—and it well may!" Ford Madox Ford wondered, "it will at least mark the ending of a period."[67] T. S. Eliot agreed, and his positive assessment recalled decades later by a more skeptical Virginia Woolf: "How could anyone write again after achieving the immense prodigy of the last chapter."[68] For Pound, *Ulysses* represented a "dead-end" in the history of the novel, and he identified it more broadly with "the end of an era or a cycle of composition."[69] "*An END not a start*," he told Wyndham Lewis. This end may signify an irrevocable break with the past, but Pound also saw it as a unique opportunity to begin again, telling H. L. Mencken: "The Christian Era ended at midnight on Oct. 29–30 of last year. You are now in the year 1 p.s.U., if that is any comfort to you."[70] p.s.U., as I mentioned in the introduction, was Pound's acronym for "post scriptum *Ulixes*," inspiring the calendar which he published in the spring 1922 issue of the *Little Review*.

In this *incipit* of a p.s.U. generation there lies another calendrical contradiction. Here, Pound identifies not just a month and a day but an exact hour for the transition from one era to another, but when, to return to the question I raised earlier, was *Ulysses* finished? In Joyce's letter to McAlmon, October 29 was the day when he "just finished" episode 17, but in his subsequent letter to Weaver it was pushed back a day later ("Mr Pound's birthday"). Given Joyce's intense fascination with birthdays, it's likely that the timing for the coincidence could be tweaked easily enough, but what's looming behind it all is a fantasy that *Ulysses* was finished on the same day when Pound, the midwife for the novel if there ever was one, was born.[71] Joyce may have stressed an actual birth day, but it was Pound who emphasized the diurnal transition so that the move from one day to another represented the dramatic shift from one era to another and the full meaning was less biographical (or biological) than it was literary and world historical.

Under this new calendar *Ulysses* was a morphological nightmare from which literary history would need to awaken, one that forced readers and

writers back to the past to try and figure out where it came from, and
for world history, it was a publishing event with the power to provide a
glimpse into an uncertain future. In both cases, supporters and detractors
alike were left trying to assess what the birth of *Ulysses* did to literature
in general. Though opinions certainly varied, there was consensus from
Joyce's contemporaries that from February 2 forward the world of letters
was never quite the same. It was *Ulysses* that made 1922 memorable and
not the other way around.

The afterlife of *Ulysses* was not something Joyce could control, but that
in itself can help us understand how we might continue to decode those
numbers on the last page. They are, as I've already mentioned, one way to
affirm the act of authorial creation by situating the novel's production *in
time*. But what's left on the rest of the page matters as well. In the handwritten fair copy draft, there is no punctuation in his timeline. Instead,
the bottom half of the page is mostly blank, which could signal creation
ex nihilo and/or the destruction ex post facto. When Darantière's printers decided to insert a period after 1921 in the typescript, however, they
inadvertently changed what both dates meant, cordoning them off as if
to stop the clock from ticking, and by the time the proofs arrived for the
final episodes, that was it (figure 5.9). *Ulysses* was already a book with a
clearly defined lifespan, those dates on the page reminiscent of the ones
found on tombstones. A strange idea, maybe, but it's one inspired by an
observation Pound himself made in a 1941 radio broadcast comparing
Ulysses to a "tomb and muniment of a rotten era portrayed by [the] pen
of a master."[72]

In the final months, the periods in *Ulysses*, inserted to mark definitive
ends, would cause a great deal of confusion with printer and author
alike. Not only did Joyce have to remind Darantière and his fellow compositors that the enlarged em dash in episode 17 was the answer to the
final question, but he also had to decide whether or not episode 18 should
even have a period.[73] Joyce may have claimed that episode did not have a
beginning, middle, or end, but he had still not arrived at the kind of inventive syntactical solution he found for *Finnegans Wake*, a novel that begins
and ends in the middle of a sentence.[74]

Putting a period at the end of episode 18 may have been necessary for
Joyce to stop the flow of the eight paragraphs, but it also represents one
of the novel's least experimental moments, since the final period closes the

all who ah that they don't know neither do I so there you are they might as
well try to stop the sun from rising the sun shines for you he said the day we
were lying among the rhododendrons on Howth head in the grey tweed suit
and his straw hat the day I got him to propose to me yes and it was leapyear
like now yes sixteen years ago my God after that long kiss I near lost my breath
yes he said I was a flower of the mountain yes so we are flowers all a woman's
body yes that was one true thing he said in his life and the sun shines for you
today yes that was why I liked him because I saw he understood or felt what
a woman is and I knew I could always get round him and I gave him the
pleasure I could leading him on till he asked me to say yes and I wouldn't
answer first only looked out over the sea and the sky I was thinking of so
many things he didn't know of Mulvey and Mr Stanhope and Hester and father
and old captain Groves and the figtrees in the Alameda gardens and cactuses
and Gibraltar as a girl where I was a flower of the mountain when I put the
red rose in my hair like Andalusian girls used shall I wear a white rose and
how he kissed me under the Moorish wall and I thought well as well him as
another and then I asked him with my eyes to ask again and then he asked me
would I to say yes my mountain flower and first I put my arms around him
and drew him down to me so he could feel my breasts all perfume yes and his
heart was going like mad and I said I will yes.

Trieste-Zurich-Paris,
1914-1921.

and the sailors playing all birds fly
and I say stoop on the pier and
the Spanish girls laughing in their
shawls and the auctions in the morning
the Greeks and the jews and those
handsome Turks all in white like
kings

Moors

5.9 Revised dateline in the proofs for *Ulysses*.

novel but creates an artificial break in the narration. After her crescendo, Molly is wide awake and still walking down memory lane, but as readers we are cut off.[75] Therefore, instead of beaming off into infinity, the novel closes with an abrupt stop, which should be a reminder that the end of *Ulysses*, like the beginning, was a fiction from the start, a set of points that had to be chosen so that a single day in Dublin could finally be contained.

Are these particular novelistic fictions so strange? After all, we don't know when Stephen, Buck, or Bloom wake up in the morning, much like we don't know when they fall asleep. And even if Molly is in the same place when the novel opens and closes, not even that final period in her monologue is enough to keep her thoughts from continuing, a point, which may help explain just why Joyce added dates after the fictional plot was presumably over. They are an afterword to the novel's becoming instead of an afterward to the plot's inevitable end.

1914–1921 may represent a grandiose intrusion by the author but considering what I just said about that last sentence (which really could culminate in an exclamation point or an ellipses), it reminds us that the composition of *Ulysses*, could have kept on going at least until Molly had fallen asleep. The actual publication of the novel functioned as an interruption in the same way as well. If you consider all of the possible beginnings for *Ulysses*, the book was eighteen, fourteen, twelve, nine, eight, or seven years in the making, and without the serialization, the legal battles, censorship, eye surgeries, search for a publisher, and an attenuated printing process, the composition could certainly have continued far beyond 1922.[76] Joyce may have finally stopped writing and revising, but I agree with Groden that he "never really 'finished' *Ulysses*."[77] As much as the novel resembles a tomb, muniment (Pound's phrase), body, machine, city, or cosmos, it is also a lot like *non-finito* sculpture, not because the artist didn't have a vision for what he wanted to create but because the experiments could have continued if he didn't finally put his pen down.[78]

The dates of *Ulysses* have been convenient facts that we as readers latch on to try and make sense of what this novel is, where it came from, and what it did, and it involves attributing value to an arbitrary connection between real events and concrete numbers. We can continue to do so, of course, if we are willing to acknowledge that Joyce at least refused to let the arbitrariness of compositional time disrupt any correspondence with world history. In one of the more popular interpretations, which follows

Siegfried Kracaeur's reminder that "the date of the event is a value laden fact," the beginning and ending of *Ulysses* coincide with the outbreak of World War I and Irish independence.[79] This epic perspective on the timing of his novel is one that Joyce encouraged early on when he reminded Budgen that "the history of *Ulysses* did not come to an end when the Trojan War was over. It began just when the other Greek heroes went back to live the rest of their lives in peace."[80] What the Trojan War and the journey back to Ithaca were for Odysseus and Homer, then, the Great War, which anticipated the Anglo-Irish war, were to Leopold Bloom and Joyce. But as much as readers are free to decide what does and does not happen in the novel, they can never choose the when. That was Joyce's job, and as Gorman colorfully recounts it in his biography, the definitive moment when the pages of *Ulysses* were all set by Darantière and his compositors and unable to be revised further, the overworked author could finally "sit back and stretch his legs a bit and regard the world at his leisure."[81]

His friends and family, it turns out, were not afforded the same luxury. Once the novel was in print, Joyce was anxious for it to get read, and the question "Have you finished *Ulysses*?" was a common refrain in the subsequent months, even though he was soon left wondering if the delays with reviews had something to do with the fact that his book was "so long."[82] By March 1923, though, he was at it again telling Weaver that he had written the first "two pages" of another novel.[83] When he revised the proofs for *Finnegans Wake* fifteen years later, there was no question about when it all began: 1922. At this point, it had to be if he wanted to imagine his life and work fused together. The clock of his career was already ticking, the sequence of his novels tocking, and it would all come to an end in 1939 just as he could have never counted on, with another world war erupting.

VI *IL N'Y A PAS D'HISTOIRE SANS DATES*

1914–1921 does not only belong to the production of a single novel: it is part of an ever-evolving literary-historical timeline. And what Claude Lévi-Strauss said about *histoire* ("Il n'y a pas d'histoire sans dates") is true of *histoire littéraire* as well: there is no literary history without dates.[84]

Just try describing Dante's *Commedia*, the age of the Victorians, the rise of the bildungsroman, or the end of the epic without identifying at least one or two numerical points of reference along the way.[85] It's common enough to start with vague approximations about time when literary histories are involved, but eventually, there's a moment when a before and after needs to be established, and that's when the date emerges with all of its peculiar force.[86]

Every major period in literary history is marked by one or another significant date, too many, in fact, to list here. It can be a day, but more frequently it's a year or a well-rounded decade, and they all get used to define shifts in sensibility, innovations in technique, or generic inventions.[87] But as convenient as dates can be for anchoring chronologies, Hayden White, following Lévi-Strauss, has suggested that they are really problems that need to be solved.[88] What looks like coherence with dates is abstraction, and what seems like historical truth is something conceptually closer to myth.

Laurence Sterne responded to his own timeline-obsessed age by including a page filled with different squiggly lines in *Tristram Shandy* mapping out the plot of his novel. The *linearity of the line* in an otherwise fictional story made of digressions was the target of Sterne's joke, but he was responding to the incredibly innovative work of contemporaries such as Joseph Priestley who were developing diagrams to visualize history, one of his most famous, a biographical chart (1765) laying out the lives and deaths of the men involved with the science of optics from 1000 C.E. to the late eighteenth century. It was intellectual history at a glance, each scientist building on the discoveries of his predecessor, the ideology of progress clearly on display for all to pick up on, Sterne included.[89] Priestley and others were playing with the illusion that time is quantifiable, something that can not only be measured but also made visible to document the forward movement of human progress.

With literary history, these ideologies of progress are certainly suspect. Time moves forward, but literature is not better or worse as a result. Still, there remains a fascination with the origins of literary works *in their time*, and it is one, at its very core, intended to help explain how a work of art happened. The when is a qualitative designation to help us understand the what. Alan Liu faced this challenge more than thirty years ago when he set out to create a "visual flowchart" plotting "the whole course of

Wordsworth's compositional history (using the best available dates)" and soon discovered that critical information was missing, eventually forcing him to abandon the original plan. In the process, he realized that there was still a "need for a visual representation to complement our current, elaborately detailed chronologies with all their repetitions, syncopations, overlaps, local mysteries, and strange loops."[90] When, Liu wanted to know, did *The Prelude* really begin? Was it the seed of the idea for the poem before a single word was even down on paper? Was it the moment when the first draft had been made or earlier when words, notes, and lines were collected.[91] Instead of providing any real clarity, the collection of dates in his Wordsworth chronology reminded Liu more and more of the fruitless search for the "dream's navel," one involving an interpretive process in which dream thoughts cannot be traced to a single origin.[92]

The same is true of Joyce's dates on the last page of *Ulysses*. They are the riddle to the mystery of compositional time and not the answer. But what, finally, are they asking us? So far, we know that they are a highly personalized timeline with historical, biographical, and other symbolic correspondences, but we must also consider the fact that this is Joyce's version, one with a whole range of distortions, omissions, and obfuscations that I've discussed throughout this chapter. As was true with the rest of the paratext, he wanted to manage the expectations of his audience as best he could, and this would include situating *Ulysses* not just *in time* but across time. This sequence of years is part of a much longer continuum absent from the page. That is how these dates work. They are an interruption in the timeline of literary history, but only temporarily, before the calibration process restarts and the weighing and measuring of reputation, influence, and achievement can take place. And you should feel free to tweak that line yourself: every direction you extend or shorten will modify what the numbers mean together and separately (figure 5.10). It is a simple act making you an active participant in the process and foregrounds how that qualitative dimension of those numbers can change.

Putting that date on the last page does not pull *Ulysses* out of history. Rather, it anchors *Ulysses* in history, one with a previously established chronology, as the definition of the term *dating* itself implies.[93] But, in this case, it's a chronology whose own beginnings will remain forever uncertain. Homer, whether an individual or the name for a collective tradition, may have been responsible for setting Western literary history in motion, girls laughing in their shawls and their tall combs and the auctions in the morning the Greeks and the jews and the Arabs and the devil knows who else from all the ends of Europe and Duke street and the fowl market all clucking outside Larby Sharons and the poor donkeys slipping half asleep and the vague fellows in the cloaks asleep in the shade on the steps and the big wheels of the carts of the bulls and the old castle thousands of years old yes and those handsome Moors all in white and turbans like kings asking you to sit down in their little bit of a shop and Ronda with the old windows of the posadas glancing eyes a lattice hid for her lover to kiss the iron and the wineshops half open at night and the castanets and the night we missed the boat at Algeciras the watchman going about serene with his lamp and O that awful deepdown torrent O and the sea the sea crimson sometimes like fire and the glorious sunsets and the figtrees in the Alameda gardens yes and all the queer little streets and pink and blue and yellow houses and the rosegardens and the jessamine and geraniums and cactuses and Gibraltar as a girl where I was a Flower of the mountain yes when I put the rose in my hair like the Andalusian girls used or shall I wear a red yes and how he kissed me under the Moorish wall and I thought well as well him as another and then I asked him with my eyes to ask again yes and then he asked me would I yes to say yes my mountain flower and first I put my arms around him yes and drew him down to me so he could feel my breasts all perfume yes and his heart was going like mad and yes I said yes I will Yes.

Trieste-Zurich-Paris,
——*1914—1921*——

5.10   Dateline for *Ulysses* reimagined as a continuation of literary history.

but there was no book that he, or it, could ever put a date on. Turns out that wasn't necessary. Joyce would do it instead. "The most beautiful book that has come out of our country in my time," Buck Mulligan, (distorting a line by William Butler Yeats) jokes, before adding, "One thinks of Homer" (*U*, 178). The wink here is as much for Stephen as for us: the book is *Ulysses*, the time is 1922, and the whole process started thousands of years earlier long before the Republic of Ireland, books, Mulligan, or Leopold Bloom even existed.

3pilogue

Miscounts, Missed Counts

Todo puede ser, respondió Sancho, mas yo sé que en lo de mi cuento no hay mas que decir: que allí se acaba do comienza el yerro de la cuenta del pasaje de las cabras.

—Sancho Panza to Don Quixote

After reducing *Ulysses* to so many sums, ratios, totals, and percentages, it's only fair to end with some reflection on the other inescapable truth that literary numbers bring: *the miscounts*. Poor Sancho, cited in the epigraph above, is not alone in his plight and "mistakes in counting" (*el yerro de la cuenta*) are not restricted only to stories that you tell about "goats" (*las cabras*). The term *miscount*, as I'll be using it, suggests that something went wrong along the way, either during the collection stage, when the data was first identified and assembled, or the calculation stage, when the numbers were run. But here, I'm also playing around with the concept of *missed counts*, the ones connected to a critical tradition that has chosen to ignore the presence of both precise and approximate numbers. Since the publication of *Ulysses* a century ago, a few of the numerical puzzles have been picked up, but they are never treated as anything more than the expression of light-hearted authorial pranking: seven letters in the title, fifteen lines for a letter by the fifteen-year-old Milly Bloom, twenty-two words in the opening line, 366 pages marking the middle of the book and end of daylight, and so on.

To this day, Joyce remains in control of the abacus for readers who may or may not have the capacity (or desire) to keep count as they read. But *"Ulysses" by Numbers* is one attempt to refocus our attention on *all the numbers*, including the ones to which we barely give a thought. They are there, but it takes some work to figure out not only how to *operationalize* them but also how to use them for more substantive interpretation of the novel. Think again of the quasi-paradox identified by William James: "something comes by the counting that was not there before. And yet that something was ALWAYS TRUE."[1] James is referring here to the discovery of planets that preexist computation, but the same is true for the words, paragraphs, and characters in Joyce's novel. They will always be there, but the act of counting these words, paragraphs, and characters makes it possible to discover something about the structure, design, and pacing of *Ulysses* we didn't already know even if it was ALWAYS TRUE.

Miscounts are built into the computational process, and anyone working with numbers knows that they can appear without warning and derail any quantitatively-inclined investigation. Working at a much larger scale, Ted Underwood, for instance, admits that there are "thousands of errors" in the data he used to examine genre, literary prestige, and gender, with the added caveat that the error can be measured but not eliminated.[2] Not only would some of the data used in his investigations be inaccurate, but Underwood also expects that his "book will be wrong on some topics."[3] Still, for Underwood or anyone else working with numbers, miscounts are not always as disruptive or undesirable as they might seem. There are the more blatant errors, which Stephen Dedalus, in a moment of defensive optimism, calls "portals of discovery," but others are harmless enough to warrant a mere shrug of the shoulders (*U*, 156). Does it really matter, for instance, that Joyce counted 138 characters in his list when there were 140 or that the episodes he first delivered to the *Little Review* weighed in at *about 6,000 words*, give or take a few hundred, with no agreement from his critics about the final tally? It certainly wouldn't seem so, and it's hard to imagine why anyone would need such *exact calculations* down to last character or word. But this tension between accuracy and approximation is on display in all of the examples I focus on. At some point in the analysis, the questions about accuracy arise: Just how many characters make an appearance in *Ulysses*? When, exactly, was *Ulysses* written? Each answer has a number with a qualification. There are 592 characters in *Ulysses*, but only if you count those present (i.e., in the plot on June 16, 1904). It took Joyce seven years to write *Ulysses*, but only if you ignore the fact that he was generating new content before 1914 and after 1921.

Miscounts, then, can be another way of describing the nature of literary quantities: they can be in the ballpark but still imprecise. And this tension between approximation and precision, accuracy and inaccuracy, ballpark and left field, can complicate how we imagine what it is we're looking for in the first place. Approximation is often all we have. It's not inaccurate, but it's not precise either. The in-betweenness is what makes the approximation more like a miscount. It's not wrong, as the general definition of the term implies, but it could be refined further, made more precise. Whenever the measuring begins, questions about scale will emerge, and they will involve defining the limits of knowledge that enough is enough based on the available evidence at a given time.

So let me return to the line with which I began this book and provide a qualification: numbers are *everywhere in Ulysses*, but they are not always precise, and the motivation for discovering them is by no means self-evident. Take the addresses of those subscribers linked to the one thousand printed copies as an example. Though a widely known fact in the novel's publication history, the numbered copies are not what they seem. Not only were there more copies printed than advertised, but the task of pinning them down to a person or location (then and now) also proves incredibly complicated. Different numbered copies and addresses could be found with some archival digging, but the more important takeaway involves the pointed questions that these breakdowns raise about the reception history of the novel. We can identify, more or less, which cities, continents, and countries a majority of the copies ended up, but then what does the incomplete distribution across the various locations around the world tell us? For starters, the maps generated from ArcGIS, a platform that visualizes spatial data, make us see what the audience looked like at a specific moment in time and within the representational parameters of a geographic information system. They are two-dimensional diagrams documenting the gradual dispersal of a reproduced object that would, over time, generate a truly global audience but never as quickly or seamlessly as we've been led to believe.

The data points connected to the circulation of the individual copies, however, are there to reaffirm the disjuncture that exists between the reality of this moment in literary history and its rapid transformation into myth. *Ulysses*, so the stories go, was either seriously limited in its distribution around 1922 (when still banned in the United States and the United Kingdom) or it was everywhere all at once. And if there's a miscount here, it is not because the number is wrong. Rather, the dataset is incomplete so conclusions based on it will be provisional. We have collected as many addresses as we can, but that still does not include all of the recipients, particularly those who got their copies by proxy or through bookstores or the many that still remain off the radar.

For some critics, approximation might be enough to make them want to steer clear of computational reading. That's unfortunate because it misunderstands what function these approximate numbers can serve. They are not the *answer* to the question, as I've said many times already. Instead, they can be put at the service of a close reading that privileges context. Approximation in an interpretive exercise of this sort is an opportunity to consider why it's one particular number at a specific moment in time and in a specific place and not another, a way of understanding why certain quantities or figures or percentages or ratios appear when they do.

Context needs approximation. That's one of the lessons I've learned. Every one of these chapters involves sets of data that can be calculated. In some cases, my efforts were hampered by the lack of access to information, but even when I had everything I needed, it was often the novel that disrupted the calculation, in large part by refusing to make a clear designation of what counts or by what measure: What is a character or a word or a paragraph or a reader/subscriber? These categorical distinctions are not just confined to basic linguistic units or typographical, syntactical choices, they involve more expansive questions about style and authorship, audience and writing time. Thinking with the fuzziness of numbers, is, in its own way, to engage with the work as a critic who is in a position to weigh, evaluate, and determine what can and cannot be measured and to what end.

This fuzziness, then, is a condition knowledge, one that tells us how we as readers and critics engage with certain kinds of literary facts. I use these numbers to read *Ulysses* closely from a variety of angles, but there may be others in the future keen to put them at the service of a distant approach in the hope of perhaps discovering laws about the novel, modernism, or the twentieth century. I'm not convinced that would be the best use of the numbers, and that's because an expanded sample loses the grain of the critical and creative context. Five hundred and ninety-two characters or six-thousand-word episodes are meaningful to the way we read not because they are like or unlike so many other novels. These numbers indicate their singularity: together, they are evidence of an organic process by which the novel came into the world. Reading with and against them gives us the chance to encounter that burst of imagination coming to terms with the urgency of the fictional plot as it was being written, discoveries of experimental techniques for representation of character, time, and space, and even the inevitable aging of the writer, an experience with time that shapes how any work of art comes into being before it is let go.

Coming up against miscounts has taught me something else. Far from being an unwelcome element in the process, the miscounts are the expression of an imprecision, vagueness, and inaccuracy that belongs both to the literary object and to literary history. In saying that, you probably don't need to be reminded that literary criticism is not a hard science with the empirical as its goal, and critics do not need to measure the value of their arguments against the catalogue of facts that they can, or cannot, collect. The theories generated from approximations and small samples have been used to generalize about all kinds of ideas, processes, and things, including genre, form, reader reception, historical, social, and political contexts, etc. If all of these theories had to be based on the largest-known samples or corroborated by empirical facts, then many of them would simply not exist. The size of the sample and the desire to work approximately have made literary criticism possible as a field. That is what initially jump-started the computational turn with critics beginning to wonder if the availability of digital archives, which provided access to more and more of the "great unread" (Margaret Cohen's phrase), would corroborate or disprove so much of what we think we know about literature.[4]

I'm not making any new claim here, but at a time when computational approaches to literature generate so much enthusiasm and skepticism, we need to be honest about the nature of the measurements we're taking in the first place and what we expect to do with them. Any honest evaluation will include thinking about the tools and methods implemented along with the visualizations that have become so central to the interpretation of *literary data*. In the process, we need to address an equally basic question regarding literary measurements: What makes them valuable for critical analysis? If I read *Ulysses* by numbers all the while embracing this ambiguity, imprecision, and approximation, then what is the payoff? Wouldn't it be easier to return to the good old precomputational days when all the numbers were more or less kept at bay?

In the course of writing this book I've thought deeply about both questions and have come to the conclusion that we can *miss the counts* but only at our peril. They may not upend a century's worth of interpretations about *Ulysses* (and, really, how could they?), but they contribute significantly to the ongoing critical investigations about what this novel is made of and, on a related note, how it happened. As things stand now, we still rely heavily on the biographical, historical, and genetic contexts to provide answers—some more convincing than others—and all of them focused on the life and work, with an intense appreciation for those moments when the two intersect. To know *Ulysses*, for better and for worse, means to try to know what Joyce was doing, thinking, reading at specific moments in time, and to this day, there is still a great deal of critical admiration for uncovering the original sources behind the novel.

The so-called genetic approach has been firmly in place since the 1970s when a massive amount of archival material was made available in bound, photocopied volumes, but it has gained momentum in recent years not only because of the discovery of new materials but also due to the widespread proliferation of digital documents. A relatively small group of critics continue to sift through every scribbled sheet searching for answers to questions about the novel's development, and though the focus can vary, they all have one goal in mind: to demystify the process by which words, sentences, paragraphs, pages, episodes, and characters were constructed over a relatively short period of time. What the genetic critics want most of all is concrete evidence to weigh decisions and check conclusions.

Given the wider availability of these resources, along with other digital platforms for the novel, readers are increasingly in a position to read genetically. And this is really an opportunity to read computationally. That's what Gabler and his team did as they learned to navigate the different numerical systems holding the novel together. The major difference now involves addressing not only where those numbers are but also how we might find and process them. Working with numbers today may still involve asking the old intentionality question (Did Joyce or didn't Joyce put them there?), but that's a dead end. He mobilized some to organize his ideas, but there are just too many to keep track of. What's more generative is an approach that lets us consider all the ones he was completely oblivious to. I used the term *numerical unconscious* before to describe a compositional process that was out of Joyce's control. That's not to say there was no intention guiding them. In this case, I use the term to identify forces, processes, and impulses that get channeled into the structure of a work without any conscious deliberation. And that gets us to think about the creative process not in terms of what he meant to do or not do with numbers. Rather, it is another way of thinking about what he did without having any idea it was even possible.

Gertrude Stein points out after Seneca that counting may be the "only difference between man and animals," but it is not a meaningful activity in and of itself.[5] In fact, it's too often the case that instead of revealing meaning, the measurements mask its absence, bringing to mind T. S. Eliot's stern warning that the critic's tools should be "handled with care, and not employed in an inquiry into the number of times giraffes are mentioned in the English novel."[6] Just because you can count the giraffes does not make them worth counting, and that was the problem Kenner had with the "empirical variousness" of Richard Kain's early book on *Ulysses*: "Doubtless he couldn't have told you why it mattered that a huge novel had been grounded in Thom's *Directory*, or why a mimeographed *Word-Index* was a useful portal of access (That's not how we gain access to *David Copperfield*)."[7] Take the measurements of *Ulysses* all you want was Kenner's advice, but at least try and explain why it's worth the effort.

Which brings me back to the miscounts. Try as readers might with the punch cards, calculators, or computers, the numbers will not always add up. This was as true with the 150 characters Kain first counted (a perfectly round number that he refused to document for later recounts) as it was with the unsubstantiated claim embraced by Joyce and his critics that *Ulysses* "grew by one third in proofs," or the number of copies logged by Darantière when sending the book crates to Beach, or the number of responses from the U.S. librarians collected by Morris Ernst's legal team.[8] In the process of identifying so many miscounts, I was just as guilty.

Counting can be an incredibly time-consuming process that carries on for several years as the data gets cleaned and reorganized. And even when all the data points seemed to be accounted for, the tallying did not always go as planned—and this was as true with the 106 characters of episode 10 (or was it 100 characters?) as it was with the 63 (or was it 62?) paragraphs of episode 14.

Like it or not, counts can be accurate even when they are *close enough*, *almost there*, *just about*, and have the ring of rightness about them that Kenner relished. Alexandre Koyré, a historian of science, called them the à-peu-près, or "more or less," of scientific measurement before the precision of modern science arrived.[9] Not only were individuals such as Galileo and Newton helping to transform the laws of the universe into a catalog of mathematically supported facts, but this persistent desire for precise measurements in the centuries that followed also effectively downplayed the relevance of things that were either left unmeasured or remained stubbornly approximate.

When tracing the passion for precise numbers, Koyré focuses on the moment when Galileo experimented with the laws of motion using an inclined wooden plank, a bronze ball, and a pendulum. Galileo, he points out, was on the right track with his theory about motion, but the numbers he compiled to document the acceleration ($s = \frac{1}{2} at^2$) were all wrong because there was no accurate way to measure time.[10] Still, for Koyré, the experience of the scientist with imprecise instruments and inaccurate numbers serves an important lesson: if its only numbers you want, then you can miss out on the rest of what's happening in the experiment. The world may get measured by people searching for laws, but it is rare that the measurements alone, even the most accurate ones, can lead to a theory of anything.

The history of science, he reminds us, is filled with hunches, flashes of intuition, and general theories before there were any accurate numbers to support them, raising the question: What comes first, the theory or the measurement? Thomas Kuhn believes that Galileo was the kind of genius who could "leap ahead of the facts," but when considering the broader history of measurement, he argues that the numbers get generated either to discover something that the scientist intuits or to confirm something the scientist already knows.[11] Without a theory or law or even "some knowledge" leading the way, the numbers, he argues, remain "just numbers."

Considering the nature of the arguments I work through in this book, Kuhn's conclusion, when I first read it, gave me pause. How much knowledge is enough? And when are literary numbers *just numbers*? I never set out to discover any general laws about *Ulysses* or the novel as a genre, and I was never guided by the desire to try and confirm (or deny) the validity of a single theory or critical approach. All of the measurements in the preceding pages rely on the data of a single novel, which means, of course, that the conclusions, when there are any, are not generally applicable, thereby making the title— *"Ulysses" by Numbers*—all the more ironic. If *Ulysses* was, at some level, written *by numbers*, reading by them with historical sensitivity and methodological self-awareness and with the hope of understanding what that act of writing meant *in its own time and in ours* actually requires a lot of context. The numbers on their own are never enough when faced with this kind of challenge. What's more, nothing particularly meaningful will come of readers armed only with punch cards, a calculator, or a computer, counting paragraphs, for instance, without ever having understood what's inside them.

In computational literary criticism the big data is part of the allure: Who needs one novel when you can run the numbers on a corpus of 100,000 or more? Computational literary analysis has been making promises on the big data, with studies involving "millions of digitized books," "2,958" nineteenth-century British novels, and essays by thirteen thousand scholars. None of the people running the numbers actually read all the words, and that seemed to be the beauty of it: there was no need to. The data, once processed and visualized, would provide an opportunity for macro-interpretation. The critical move from the particular to the general using empirical data signaled a break from the close reading that traditionally involved smaller samples, and none of them were organized by number: no seventeen novels for the seventeenth century or 290 French poems for the future of poesy. But to stay on topic here, there's no way that the exact numbers of these much larger samples really matter. If there are 1.5 million books or 2,500 nineteenth-century novels, nothing will change in the analysis or the conclusions. The point here is that these sums render the specificity obsolete: what matters is that the number is very large, which means, by extension, that the conclusions derived from that very large number will be widely applicable.

Or maybe not. There are many still hoping that the laws of the literary universe are there waiting to be discovered in big data sets. Until then, the small data is there like William Blake's grain of sand waiting for a universe to be projected. But in identifying what the benefits of small literary data might be, it's worth returning once more to that distinction between literary numerology and humanities computing. The 1960s saw the brief coexistence of the two, the numerologists excavating texts for hidden patterns while the computer humanists (many of them from fields other than literature) were busy compiling concordances, indexes, and experimenting with translation. In these early days, the numerologists were the ones reading by numbers, the computer humanists focused more on the tools that would keep readers with their noses in the codex. Together they reveal different attitudes about where the numbers might be found and related questions involving where they originated.

The origin of literary numbers distinguish the numerologist and computer humanist in some provocative ways. If the former wants to see the numbers as part of a preexisting interpretive system, the latter wants to show that the system itself is not made by God or man. Even in the early days when the concordances were a primary consideration, there was already the idea in place that these machines can reveal a structure no one knew existed, and it was connected, of course, to the idea that meaning in the literary work is not guided by authorial intention alone. The numerologists lost the battle over literary numbers in the end, but the efficiency of the computer is not the only reason. As different kinds of programs and platforms were created, the computer was increasingly able to perform complicated tasks on literary works. Instead of only saving time with their magnificent indexing capacities, they could be adapted to generate editions involving multiple levels of revision, and with digitization would soon be running programs on works that had been transformed into strings of numerical code.

If numerology was once tasked with locating numbers supposedly hidden within and behind the pseudosacred words, paragraphs, and pages of literary works (always the most canonical, of course), the computer humanists were literally transforming these same literary works and words into numbers. Consider, for instance, an early description of this process from a paper in 1967 with the blandest of titles, "The Computer and the Humanist." "The computer holds data in a form which can be thought of as numbers, and sentences of text or lists of musical data can, if desired, be added up arithmetically at any moment." But there's more: "Since we can move data around in a computer and compare, say, each letter with 'blank' to see whether we are at the end of a word, we need never think of our data as numbers, even though the machine treats the data as such."[12]

We need never think of our data as numbers . . . That was bad advice back in the 1960s and remains so today. At this early coupling of man and machine was a desire to pretend as if the humanists were operating in a realm beyond the numbers with all the computational grunt work left for the computer alone. Much has changed—in part, because so many of the programs that we have at our disposal make the numbers a primary and not a secondary consideration. Network analysis, geographic information systems (GIS), the word and paragraph counts, and timelines are all part of a computational approach that needs to see the literary data as data—to see the words, characters, subscribers, paragraphs, and years of composition as numerical sequences—precisely so that we can then work our way into various qualitative considerations involving the who, what, where, when, and why of *Ulysses*.

In one of the most sophisticated, and scathing, critiques of data-minded humanists, Nan Z. Da concludes that "CLS [Computational Literary Studies] has no ability to capture literature's complexity."[13] Though I'm certainly sympathetic to much of what she says about the overblown claims, misleading evidence and misuse of statistical tools at the big-data level, I'm less inclined to agree with the wholesale dismissal of an entire critical approach, one that I have insisted on associating with a longer history of a computational literary criticism with philological roots. No, I don't think a revamped numerological criticism is a viable alternative, but there is a need to continue weighing the benefits and limits of quantitative literary measurement more generally and at a much smaller scale. Computational analysis is not opposed to literary complexity. It is a way into that complexity, in part, because the object itself resists facticity and statistical modeling, but what's more it has the potential to benefit from a long humanist tradition that imagines not just the object but the practice as something with genuine interpretive power. The numbers are not incidental, and they do not serve as a deviation from qualitative analysis. Instead, they are part of what makes literature stubbornly abstract and occasionally rebarbative.

And in saying this, I'm acutely aware that the idea of counting at this or any other moment means nothing if not guided by an awareness of what concepts such as *computation* and *literature* mean in specific times and places. Like it or not, the literary object has changed irrevocably. The book will continue to stick around, but digital procedures and practices have transformed how we as readers can continue to interact with it. In the meantime, a literary mode of computation has moved far beyond the concordance and the punch card, but realizing its potential requires a lot of fine-tuning and experimentation. In my extended computational close reading of one of literary history's most canonical works, I demonstrate that there is much to be gained from new and old numbers alike, many of them belonging to quantities we miscounted and *missed counting*. But as you probably noticed, those numbers, once found and corrected, are only the beginning. They require reading against the grain of *Ulysses*, largely because a particular kind of critical distance is required, and it is one that could never have been achieved through the navigation of words alone.

But that distance has always been there. Try as readers might to bridge the gap, *Ulysses* will remain a work in progress, a novel left behind for other generations to finish. Reading by numbers is one way to recover some of the mystery behind the creative process. *Every Man a Joyce, indeed!* Far from being a coherent method that gets applied mechanically from without, it is part of a reading experience that happens from within, allowing us to pause and consider those moments when the outline of the structure itself becomes visible before disappearing again. In the end, that is no small feat, since reading is a practice encouraging all of us to try and imagine what it might have been like to build something so monstrous, beautiful, and complex using only a pen and paper. Writing in the 1930s, it was Pound who observed that the "careful historian of the 1910s is not yet busy in numbers."[14] Reading *Ulysses* by numbers a century later, it makes you wonder what took so long.

Notes

OVERTURE

1. Hugh Kenner, "Shem the Textman," in *Languages of Joyce: Selected Papers from the 11th International James Joyce Symposium, Venice 1988*, ed. Rosa Maria Bosinelli (Philadelphia: John Benjamins, 1992), 146. Kenner's computational optimism runs contrary to Roland Barthes's more pessimistic poststructuralist claim that "the TEXT is not to be thought of as an object that can be computed." See Roland Barthes, "From Work to Text," in *Image-Music-Text*, trans. Stephen Heath (New York: Hill & Wang, 1977), 155–64.

2. Joyce, *Letters of James Joyce*, vol. 3, ed. Richard Ellmann (New York: Viking, 1957–1966), 58. Hereafter referred to as *L* and identified by volume (I, II, or III). In a personal email (February 8, 2019), Daniel Ferrer mentioned that he never noticed it before, but pointed out that the double numbering was occasionally done at the end of the nineteenth and beginning of the twentieth century. A good example, one mentioned by Daniel Ferrer to Michael Groden in an email exchange, can be found on the cover of *La Nouvelle Revue Française*: 78, Rue d'Assas, 78.

3. Consider as well that the correct numbering of the address occurs on the announcement and subscription forms for the novel: 12 rue de l'Odéon, Paris—VIe. There is no 12 in the second impression done for the Egoist Press in October 1922 (because the address had changed), and the second 12 is dropped in the 1924 edition and after. It's worth noting that the first and second 2s, taken from 12, occupy the same position: 10 + 2. This correspondence with the date would not work, for example, if they were positioned in 20 (2 tens) or 230 (2 hundred plus 3 tens).

4. Guy Davenport, "Joyce's Forest of Symbols," *Iowa Review* 6, no. 1 (Winter 1975): 75–91. Joyce's idea for twenty-two (4, 15, 3) episodes was divulged to his brother

on June 16, 1915. See Richard Ellman, ed., *Selected Letters of James Joyce* (New York: Viking, 1957), 209. Hereafter referred to as *SL*.

5.   When serialized in the *Little Review*, each episode was identified by a roman numeral in the contents page. In the fair copy manuscript Joyce copied himself, each episode has an arabic numeral but each section a roman one.

6.   Richard Ellmann, *"Ulysses" on the Liffey* (London: Faber & Faber, 1974), 2; Vincent F. Hopper, *Medieval Number Symbolism: Its Sources, Meaning, and Influence on Thought and Expression* (New York: Columbia University Press, 1938), 4, 5, 11.

INTRODUCTION: *ULYSSES* BY NUMBERS

1.   Appearing six times each, 133 and 102 are the numbers with the highest frequency.

2.   Weight reported by Sylvia Beach, *Shakespeare and Company: The Story of an American Bookshop in Paris* (New York: Harcourt, Brace, 1959), 86. The dimensions provided by Sisley Huddleston in Robert H. Deming, ed., *James Joyce: The Critical Heritage*, vol. 1 (London: Routledge & Kegan Paul, 1970), 242. Bulk provided by John Ryder, "Editing *Ulysses* Typographically," *Scholarly Publishing* 18, no. 2 (1987): 119.

3.   Katherine Q. Seelye, "Dan Robbins, Who Made Painting as Easy as 1-2-3 (and 4-5-6), Dies at 93," *New York Times*, April 5, 2019, https://www.nytimes.com/2019/04/05/obituaries/dan-robbins-dead.html.

4.   Thomas Kuhn, "The Function of Measurement in Modern Physical Science," in *The Essential Tension: Selected Essays: Selected Studies in Scientific Tradition and Change* (Chicago: University of Chicago Press, 1977), 183.

5.   T. S. Eliot, "The Function of Criticism," in *T. S. Eliot: Selected Essays, 1917–1932* (New York: Harcourt, Brace, 1932), 21.

6.   Aristotle, *Metaphysics* 1, 980a., 21, http://www.perseus.tufts.edu/hopper/text?doc=Perseus%3atext%3a1999.01.0052.

7.   Alan Turing, "On Computable Numbers, with an Application to the Entscheidungsproblem," *Proceedings of the London Mathematical Society* s2, 42, no. 1 (1937): 230–65.

8.   Friedrich Kittler, "Number and Numeral," *Theory, Culture, & Society* 23, no. 7–8 (2006): 55.

9.   Stuart Gilbert, *James Joyce's "Ulysses": A Study* (New York: Vintage, 1955), 3, 8–9.

10. I've chosen to refer to the eighteen episodes of *Ulysses* by number and not Homeric title for the simple reason that these titles did not exist in the original 1922 edition. In fact, the episodes did not contain any numbers at all. But to impose a Homeric title retroactively not only presupposes a specific

interpretation but also has the effect of further erasing the presence of numbers that were meaningful to the specific episodes in question.

11. John Kidd, "Editor's Preface" for an unpublished Dublin edition of *Ulysses*, 1994.

12. Kidd reportedly wondered if Gabler encouraged his pursuit of numerological criticism "in order to dissuade him from this critique of the 1984 *Ulysses*." See David Remnick, "The War Over *Ulysses*," *Washington Post*, April 2, 1985, https://www.washingtonpost.com/archive/lifestyle/1985/04/02/the-war -over-ulysses/5bc5964b-0486-4005-beb7-1e56e36590d2/.

13. For some of the history of numerology see Hopper, *Medieval Number Symbolism*; Tobias Dantzig, *Number: The Language of Science* (New York: Plume, 2007); E. T. Bell, *Numerology* (Baltimore, MD: Williams & Wilkins, 1933).

14. Dante Alighieri, *Vita Nuova*, trans. Mark Musa (Bloomington: Indiana University Press, 1973), 62.

15. As Dante outlines it here, that number only becomes legible because he is able to recognize God's design. Nine is literally embodied in the original event (written in the stars), but it also gives shape to the structure of the work in which the entire experience is then narrated. The twenty-eight poems that appear in between the prose sections are also punctuated by three canzone. The 10 I 4 II 4 III 10 arrangement can also be subdivided into 1–9 I 1–3 II 3–1 III 9–1, each breakdown of four and ten necessitated by the introduction of a new theme or topic. What it all reveals, according to Mark Musa, is not only Dante's obsession with nine, and its square root but also the prominence of the second canzone placed in the middle, which looks forward to and backward on Beatrice's death.

16. See John A. Shawcross, "The Balanced Structure of *Paradise Lost*," *Studies in Philology* 62 (1965): 697–718; Alastair Fowler, *Spenser and the Numbers of Time* (London: Routledge, 1964); Clyde Murley, "The Structure and Proportion of Catullus LXIV," *Transactions of the American Philological Association* 68 (1937): 3305–17.

17. R. G. Peterson, "Critical Calculations: Measure and Symmetry in Literature," *Publication of the Modern Languages Association* 91, no. 3 (May 1976): 373.

18. Alastair Fowler, *Spenser and the Numbers of Time*; Fowler, *Triumphal Forms: Structural Patterns and Elizabethan Poetry* (Cambridge: Cambridge University Press, 1970); A. Kent Hieatt, *Short Time's Endless Monuments: The Symbolism of Numbers in Edmund Spenser's "Epithalamion"* (New York: Columbia University Press, 1960); Maren-Sofie Røstvig, *Fair Forms: Essays in English Literature from Spenser to Jane Austen* (Cambridge: Cambridge University Press, 1975); Gunnar Qvarnström, *Poetry and Numbers: On the Structural Use of Symbolic Numbers* (Lund, Sweden: Lund C. W. K. Gleerup, 1966); Christopher Butler, *Number Symbolism* (London: Routledge & Kegan Paul, 1970).

19. Peterson, "Critical Calculations," 374.

20. Franco Moretti, *Canon/Archive* (New York: N+1 Foundation, 2017), 98.

21. James Joyce, *Ulysses*, prepared by Hans Walter Gabler (New York: Random House, 1986), 224, 621. Hereafter referred to as *U*. Other editions will be identified when necessary; my emphasis.

22. Fowler, *Triumphal Forms*, 202.

23. György Lukács, *Theory of the Novel* (London: Merlin, 1971), 88; Ernst Robert Curtius, *European Literature and the Latin Middle Ages* (Princeton, NJ: Princeton University Press, 504; *Kidd*, "Editor's Preface," 50.

24. Pound, *How to Read*, 27.

25. To prove his point, Pound directs his readers to the alleged "40 books" that belonged to Chaucer and the "half dozen" or so of Shakespeare.

26. As conveyed to me by Moretti in an email. Virginia Woolf, "How It Strikes a Contemporary," *Common Reader* (London: Hogarth Press, 1948), 297.

27. Nan Z. Da includes a variety of computational approaches under this label including cultural analytics, literary data mining, quantitative formalism, literary text mining, computational textual analysis, computational criticism, algorithmic literary studies, social computing for literary studies, and computational literary studies. See "The Computational Case against Computational Literary Studies," *Critical Inquiry* 45, no. 3 (Spring 2019): 601.

28. Richard So and Hoyt Long, "Literary Pattern Recognition: Modernism between Close Reading and Machine Learning," *Critical Inquiry* 42, no. 2 (Winter 2016): 235–67; *On Paragraphs: Scale, Theme and Narrative Forms*, pamphlet 10 (Stanford, CA: Stanford Literary Lab, October 2015); Ted Underwood, David Bamman, and Sabrina Lee, "The Transformation of Gender in English-Language Fiction," *Journal of Cultural Analytics* (February 2018) https://culturalanalytics.org/article/11035-the-transformation-of-gender-in-english-language-fiction; Andrew Piper, "Characterization," in *Enumerations: Data and Literary Study* (Chicago: University of Chicago Press, 2018), 118–46.

29. On this point, then, I am not in agreement with Underwood's claim that "even when an argument relies on a single data set, quantitative researchers implicitly understand its claims as part of a larger conversation, organized by a goal of replicability that entails comparisons between different kinds of samples." Underwood, *Distant Horizons*, 176.

30. And this emphasis was further encouraged by the publication of Matt Jockers, *Macroanalysis: Digital Methods and Literary History* (Champaign: University of Illinois Press, 2013).

31. Ted Underwood, for instance, mentions that his own investigations of the novel do not move beyond 1800 because the data is harder to gather. Taken another way, you could say that his inquiry is restricted by the availability of the resources. This restriction shapes the scope of the investigation.

32. See Ted Underwood, "A Genealogy of Distant Reading," *Digital Humanities Quarterly* 11, no. 2 (2017): http://www.digitalhumanities.org/dhq/vol/11/2 /000317/000317.html.

33. For a representative sample, see Jacob Leed, *The Computer and Literary Style: Introductory Essays and Studies* (Kent, OH: Kent State University Press, 1966).

34. Leo Spitzer, "Linguistics and Literary History," in *Representative Essays*, ed. Alban K. Forcione, Herbert Lindenberger, and Madeleine Sutherland (Stanford, CA: Stanford University Press, 1988), 22.

35. "The object of study in literary science," Roman Jakobson writes, "is not literature but *literariness*, that is, what makes a given work a literary work." Quoted in Boris Eichenbaum, "The Theory of the 'Formal Method,'" in *Russian Formalist Criticism: Four Essays*, trans. Lee T. Lemon and Marion J. Reis (Lincoln: University of Nebraska Press, 1965), 107.

36. Franco Moretti and Oleg Sobchuk, "Hidden in Plain Sight: Data Visualization in the Humanities," *New Left Review* 118 (July–August 2019): 86.

37. P. Shannon et al., "Cytoscape: A Software Environment for Integrated Models of Biomolecular Interaction Networks," *Genome Research* 13, no. 1 (November 2003): 2498–504.

38. R. P. Blackmur, "A Critic's Job of Work," in *The Selected Essays of R. P. Blackmur*, ed. Denis Donoghue (New York: Ecco Press, 1986), 45.

39. More than simply providing the factual information about where and when a particular title appeared, the paratext, he explains, also establishes how it can be read. Title, copyright, and limitation pages, Genette explains, are "the conveyor of a commentary that is authorial or more or less legitimated by the author, constitut[ing] a zone between text and off text, a zone not only of transition but also of *transaction*: a privileged place of a pragmatics and a strategy, of an influence on the public, an influence that . . . is at the service of a better reception for the text and a more pertinent reading of it." See Gérard Genette, *Paratexts: Thresholds of Interpretation*, trans. Jane E. Lewin (Cambridge: Cambridge University Press, 1997), 1–2.

40. Kidd, "Editor's Preface," 52–53.

41. See David Kurnick, "Numberiness," a response to my essay, "'*Ulysses* by Numbers," *Representations* 127 (2014). http://www.representations.org/response -to-ulysses-by-numbers-david-kurnick/

42. These "hidden line counts" belong to Kidd, "Editor's Preface," 51, 52.

43. Kenner, *Ulysses* (Baltimore, MD: Johns Hopkins University Press, 1987), 156.

44. Unsigned Review, *Evening News* (London), April 8, 1922; Arnold Bennett, *Outlook* (London), April 29, 1922; quoted in Deming, *James Joyce*, vol. 1, 194, 220.

45. Edmund Wilson, "*Ulysses*," *New Republic*, July 5, 1922. See also Ezra Pound (who gets the page numbers right) "James Joyce et Pécuchet," *Mercure de France* 106 (June 1, 1922): 307–20.

46. Hugh Kenner, *Flaubert, Joyce, and Beckett: The Stoic Comedians* (London: Dalkey Archive Press, 1962), 34.

47. Maurice Darantière to Sylvia Beach, October 17, 1921. The Darantière letters to Beach are in the James Joyce Collection at the University at Buffalo.

48. It is likely that this calculation was intended for Harriet Shaw Weaver. On October 7, 1921 Joyce wrote: "I expect to have early next week about 240 pages of the book as it will appear ready and will send on [i.e. through the end of 'Cyclops']." *L* I, 172.

49. Maurice Darantière to Sylvia Beach, April 18, 1921.

50. Maurice Darantière to Sylvia Beach, September 30, 1921.

51. An additional 9.806,25 francs were added for corrections (fr. 4,75 per hour). Compare that with the original estimate of 10.349, 64 francs for the paper required for one thousand copies under six hundred pages in 10-point Elzevir. The final paper cost with 732 pages and 11-point Elzevir was 14.060,85 francs.

52. Thanks to Ronan Crowley for providing clarification here (and elsewhere).

53. Ryder, "Editing *Ulysses* Typographically," 111.

54. Wim Van Mierlo, "Reflections on Textual Editing in the Time of the History of the Book," *Journal of the European Society for Textual Scholarship* 11 (2013): 144–45.

55. On March 16, once the copies of the first edition were all printed and shipped, Darantière wrote to Beach: "Il faut s'en tenir au nombre de cette première édition ou bien couler le volume en entier. Un tirage sur clichés vous permettrait d'augmenter l'édition de 100 ou 200 exemplaires à votre convenance."

56. "The book grew by one third in proof": Richard Ellmann, *James Joyce*, rev. ed. (Oxford: Oxford University Press, 1982), 513; "Joyce had told me that he had written a third of *Ulysses* on the proofs": Beach, *Shakespeare and Company*, 58; Stacy Herbert, "Composition and Publishing History," in *Joyce in Context*, ed. John McCourt (Cambridge: Cambridge University Pres, 2009), 10; "In all, *Ulysses* grew approximately one-third longer from additions Joyce made on the proofs": Luca Crispi, "Manuscript Timeline, 1905–1922," *Genetic Joyce Studies* 4 (Spring 2004) https://www.geneticjoycestudies.org; "Joyce enlarged *Ulysses* by approximately one-third through additions to the proofs": Derek Attridge, *James Joyce's* Ulysses: *A Casebook* (Oxford: Oxford University Press, 2004), 9; "For *Ulysses'* 732 pages forty-six gatherings were required: somewhat more than the thirty-seven figured in the printer's castoff—i.e. in the initial typographic estimate to work out the space copy would require. Such an underestimation (155 pages short) goes some way to substantiating the familiar claim that Ulysses 'grew by one third in proof'": Luca Crispi and Ronan Crowley, "Proof^finder: Page Proofs," *Genetic Joyce Studies* 8 (Spring 2008) www.genetic joycestudies.org.

57. Thanks to Hans Walter Gabler for saving me countless hours by running his typed version of the Rosenbach manuscript against the 1984 edition. Here's

his explanation (July 21, 2019): "Roughly, it [Rosenbach Manuscript] runs to 220,000 words. The word count for the 1984 edition, according to the *Handlist*, is approx. 264,500 words. The difference then is approx. 44.500 words by which the text of the Rosenbach was eked out. Which—I admit—approximates 20 percent augmentation, not 33 percent. There goes another almosting."

58. A note handwritten by Beach on the back of a letter typed by Darantière dated August 31, 1921, indicates that he did know what would constitute one-third of his book: "15th June Joyce gave him 1 3rd of book which he has now printed (in 3 months) with a few pages of the second part."

59. Kenner, *Joyce*, 168.

60. From a letter to Weaver, it is clear that Joyce was aware of the relative value of pages, *L* I, 196: "It [*Ulysses*] is an extremely cheap (considering paper and type) edition of the equivalent of 8 English novels of standard size (75,000 to 80,000 words) at the normal selling price today or less, as 8 10/- novels would sell at 270 francs a copy."

61. In *James Joyce's* Ulysses: *A Study*, 31, Gilbert explains that the symmetry is contained within a prelude of three episodes, a central section of twelve, and a finale of three.

62. I am grateful to Aaron Matz for leading me here.

63. Hopper: "The great astrological numbers being 4, 12, 7, the age of the world was known to be divided into 4 periods, into 12 parts, or into 7,000 days, 70 generations or 7 weeks." Hopper, *Medieval Number Symbolism*, 30–31.

64. Kidd: "It remained to be discovered decades later that the book is arranged and proportioned in accordance with a concealed numeric pattern. *Ulysses*, meticulously adjusted during months of revision in proof, is as consummately ordered as Dante's *Divine Comedy* or Spenser's *Faerie Queene*. In the editions since the printings of 1922–1925, the geometric form of Ulysses has been obscured beyond recognition." Kidd, "Editor's Preface," 49–50.

65. Kidd's theory as laid out by D. F. McKenzie, *Bibliography and the Sociology of Texts* (Cambridge: Cambridge University Press, 1999), 58.

66. When would it have been likely for Joyce to know the middle? And how likely is it that this would have been possible given the chaotic nature of the revision in the fall of 1921? Here's Joyce to McAlmon: "I have now written in a great lot of balderdash all over the damn book and the first half is practically as it will appear." September 3, 1921, *L* III, 48.

67. John MacQueen, *Numerology: Theory and Outline History of a Literary Mode* (Edinburgh: Edinburgh University Press, 1985), 4; emphasis added.

68. Robert Spoo, "Copyright Protectionism and Its Discontents: James Joyce's *Ulysses* in America," *The Yale Journal* 108, no. 3: 633-667.

69. James Joyce, *Ulysses: A Digital and Critical Synoptic Edition*, ed. Hans Walter Gabler, Ronan Crowley, and Joshua Schäuble (New York: Garland, 1984), http://ulysses.online/index.html. For more background on the process and its

implications, see Hans Walter Gabler, "Seeing James Joyce's *Ulysses* into the Digital Age," *Joyce Studies Annual* (2018): 16–18.

70. Kidd's Dublin edition was going to retain the original pagination and line counts in order to restore the novel's "geometric form." He writes: "This is the only edition to account for number symbolism more often associated with classical, medieval, and renaissance artists than with modernists." Kidd, "Editor's Preface," 50.

71. The TEI XML versions of each episode can be accessed in the GitHub repository at https://github.com/open-editions/corpus-joyce-ulysses-tei.

72. For an in-depth account of the steps involved in this process, see Hans Walter Gabler "Towards an Electronic Edition of James Joyce's Ulysses," *Literary and Linguistic Computing* 15, no. 1 (2000): 115–20.

73. Hugh Kenner, *Joyce's Voices* (Oakland: University of California Press, 198), 166.

74. Hugh Kenner, "Reflections on the Gabler Era," *James Joyce Quarterly* 26, no. 1 (Fall 1988): 18, 19.

75. Kenner, "Reflections," 19.

76. Hanley never includes the word counts, but by Zipf's estimation, there are 28,899 unique words in 260,430. Compare with Gabler's version of 39,801 and 264,448.

77. Charles Kingsley Zipf, *Human Behavior and the Principle of Least Effort: An Introduction to Human Ecology* (Cambridge, MA: Addison-Wesley, 1949), 546n3.

78. Zipf, *Human Behavior*, 24, 35.

79. See Zipf, *Human Behavior*, 40–47.

80. Zipf, *Human Behavior*, 51.

81. I'm using the term *law* here realizing that it is neither a law, because of the deviations in most languages and its nonuniversality, nor entirely Zipf's, because it was already discovered by Jean-Baptiste Estoup in 1912. See Erez Aiden and Jean-Baptiste Michel, *Uncharted: Big Data as a Lens on Human Culture* (New York: Riverhead, 2014), 249n34.

82. René Wellek, *A History of Modern Criticism*, vol. 5 (New Haven, CT: Yale University Press, 1986), xix.

83. Pound uses "dateline" in an essay by the same name, but I take it here from A. Walton Litz in the opening line to *The Art of James Joyce: Method and Design in "Ulysses" and "Finnegans Wake"* (Oxford: Oxford University Press, 1961), 1.

1. MAKING STYLE COUNT

1. See, for instance, James Shapiro, *Contested Will: Who Wrote Shakespeare?* (New York: Simon & Schuster, 2010).

2. Harry Mathews, "For Prizewinners," *Review of Contemporary Fiction* 7, no. 3 (Fall 1987): https://www.thefreelibrary.com/For+Prizewinners.-a059410485.

3. As reported to me by Kevin Dettmar, who heard it firsthand from an unnamed woman waiting in line at the British Library.

4. Frederick Mosteller and David L. Wallace, "Inference in an Authorship Problem," *Journal of the American Statistical Association* 58, no. 302 (June 1963): 275–309.

5. A. Q. Morton, "Who Wrote St. Paul's Epistles," *Listener* (March 21, 1963): 489ff. See also Morton, "The Authorship of Greek Prose," *Journal of the Royal Statistical Society*, series A, 128, no. 2 (1965): 169–224.

6. A. Q. Morton and J. McLeman, *Christianity in the Computer Age* (New York: Harper & Row, 1964).

7. McCandlish Philips, "Computer Flouts Test by Another: Study on St. Paul's Epistles Questioned at Yale Parley," *New York Times*, January 23, 1965, 17. The talk in which Ellison made these comments appeared in an edited collection from the conference proceedings. See "Computers and the Testaments," in *Computers for the Humanities: A Record of the Conference Sponsored by Yale University on a Grant from IBM, January 22–23, 1965* (New Haven, CT: Yale University Press, 1965), 64–74.

8. See, for instance, G. Udney Yule, "One Sentence-Length as a Statistical Characteristic of Style in Prose: With Application to Two Cases of Disputed Authorship," *Biometrika* 30, nos. 3/4 (January 1939): 363–90; C. B. Williams, "A Note on the Statistical Analysis of Sentence-Length as a Criterion of Literary Style," *Biometrika* 31, nos. 3/4 (March 1940): 356–61; Franco Moretti, Sarah Allison, Marissa Gemma, et al., *Style at the Scale of the Sentence*, pamphlet 5 (Stanford, CA: Stanford Literary Lab, June 2013), https://litlab .stanford.edu/LiteraryLabPamphlet5.pdf.

9. Here's how they describe it in their results: "Multifractals are not simply the sum of fractals and cannot be divided to return back to their original components, because the way they weave is fractal in nature. The result is that in order to see a structure similar to the original, different portions of a multifractal need to expand at different rates. A multifractal is therefore non-linear in nature."

10. Stanislaw Drożdż, "The World's Greatest Literature Reveals Multifractals and Cascades of Consciousness," Institute of Nuclear Physics (website), January 21, 2016, https://press.ifj.edu.pl/en/news/2016/01/.

11. T. S. Eliot, "Lettre d'Angleterre: Le Style dans la prose anglaise contemporaine," *La Nouvelle Revue Française* 19 (July–December, 1922): 751–56. The landmark book on the subject is Karen Lawrence, *The Odyssey of Style in "Ulysses"* (Princeton, NJ: Princeton University Press, 1981), with the focus on the narrative discontinuities that modify readerly expectations over the eighteen episodes.

12. T. C. Mendenhall, "A Mechanical Solution of a Literary Problem," *Popular Science Monthly* 60 (1901): 97–105.

13. Throughout this chapter, I am using the paragraph counts from the xml files that were prepared for the *Ulysses: A Digital and Critical Synoptic Edition*. These files are based on the reading text of the novel that was generated by the TUSTEP program for Gabler's original 1984/1986 edition. The online edition, *DCSE*, is being overseen by Ronan Crowley and Joshua Schäuble. There are some discrepancies in the paragraph breaks between the *Little Review* episodes and the 1922 edition that Gabler corrected, consulting typescript and other drafts when possible. Those interested in these differences are encouraged to consult Philip Gaskell and Clive Hart, *"Ulysses": Review of Three Texts* (Gerrards Cross, UK: Colin Smythe, 1989).

14. Gertrude Stein, "Lectures in America," in *Gertrude Stein: Writings, 1932–1946*, ed. Catharine R. Stimpson and Harriet Chessman (New York: Library of America, 1998), 218.

15. Franco Moretti, Ryan Heuser, Mark Algee-Hewitt, "On Paragraphs: Scale, Themes, and Narrative Form," pamphlet 10 (Stanford, CA: Stanford Literary Lab, October 2015), 69.

16. Fredric Jameson, "Joyce or Proust?" in *The Modernist Papers* (New York: Verso, 2007), 181.

17. Jean-Michel Rabaté and Daniel Ferrer, "Paragraphs in Expansion (James Joyce)," in *Genetic Criticism: Texts and Avant-Textes*, ed. Jed Deppman, Daniel Ferrer, and Michael Groden (Philadelphia: University of Pennsylvania Press, 2004), 132–52.

18. Hugh Kenner, "The Most Beautiful Book," *English Literary History* 48, no. 3 (1981): 604.

19. Michael Groden, Ulysses *in Progress* (Princeton, NJ: Princeton University Press, 1977), 160.

20. Groden, Ulysses *in Progress* 160.

21. *Oxford English Dictionary* online, s.v. "paragraph," accessed May 7, 2020, https://www-oed-com.ccl.idm.oclc.org/view/Entry/137422?rskey=Tp6W8b &result=1&isAdvanced=false#eid

22. "Coleman's Writing Class," Faulkner at Virginia (University of Virginia), accessed March 18, 2020, http://faulkner.lib.virginia.edu/display/wfaudio001 _2#wfaudio001_2.

23. For one of the few books of criticism devoted entirely to the subject, see Jean Châtillon, ed., *La Notion de paragraphe* (Paris: Éditions du Centre national de la recherche scientifique, 1985).

24. Jason Pamental, "Life of ¶" *Print* 69, no. 4 (2015): 24–26.

25. Robert Bringhurst, *The Elements of Typographic Style* (Vancouver: Hartley & Marks, 1992), 80.

26. Henri Mitterand, "Le paragraphe est-il une unité linguistique?" in Châtillon, *La Notion de paragraphe*, 85.

27. Thanks to Jonathan Reeve for giving me a record of the conversation that took place between the various members working with Gabler on the digital edition.

28. Kidd, "Dublin Edition," 50.

29. Kenner, "Reflections on the Gabler Era," 17.

30. Joyce, *Finnegans Wake*, 123. I say "came to think" here because we know from a letter to Budgen that Joyce had in mind sentences as he was writing episode 18: "There are 8 sentences in the episode."

31. Moretti et al., "On Paragraphs," 5.

32. See, for instance, E. H. Lewis, *The History of the English Paragraph* (Chicago, IL: University of Chicago Press, 1894), 173.

33. Lewis, *History of the English Paragraph*, 156–57.

34. Lewis, 157.

35. *On Paragraphs*, 93. That wasn't exactly the plan when they started. The Literary Lab was originally hoping that the unit of the paragraph could provide a way into thinking about style as they discovered earlier in the discrete elements of the sentence. It did not. But that, they came to realize, was because paragraphs *are not* sentences, and we should not assume just because they are made up of sentences that they would function according to the same rules. See Moretti et al., *"Style at the Scale of the Sentence,"* pamphlet 5 (Stanford, CA: Stanford Literary Lab, 2013), 58–59.

36. Adrienne Monnier, *The Very Rich Hours of Adrienne Monnier*, trans. Richard McDougall (Lincoln: University of Nebraska Press, 1996), 115.

37. S. L. Goldberg, *Joyce: The Man, The Work, The Reputation* (Edinburgh: Oliver & Boyd, 1962), 90.

38. Lewis, 102.

39. Theodor Adorno, "Punctuation Marks," in *Notes to Literature*, vol. 1, trans. Sherry Weber Nicholsen (New York: Columbia University Press, 1991), 91.

40. Wolfgang Iser, *The Act of Reading: A Theory of Aesthetic Response* (Baltimore, MD: Johns University Press, 1978), 113.

41. For a fascinating account of the subject, see Rudolf Arnheim, "The Images of Thought," in *Visual Thinking* (Berkeley: University of California Press, 1969), 97–115.

42. Stéphane Mallarmé, *Divagations*, trans. Barbara Johnson (Cambridge, MA : Harvard University Press), 298. French reads: "Mobiliser, autour d'une idée, les lueurs diverses de l'esprit, à distance voulue, par phrases: ou comme, vraiment, ces moules de la syntaxe même élargie, un très petit nombre les résume, chaque phrase, à se détacher en paragraphe gagne d'isoler un type rare avec plus de liberté qu'en le charroi par un courant de volubilité. Mille exigences, très singulières, apparaissent à l'usage, dans ce traitement de l'écrit, que je perçois peu à peu: sans

doute y a-t-il moyen, là, pour un poète qui par habitude ne pratique pas le vers libre, de montrer, en l'aspect de morceaux compréhensifs et brefs, par la suite, avec expériences, tels rythmes immédiats de pensée ordonnant une prosodie."

43. Mallarmé may have singled out the press for this discovery of prose distillation and layout, but it's also worth noting that Joyce actually used the abbreviated term *par* as journalist slang for paragraph. And when the word appears in *Ulysses*, Bloom uses the unabbreviated version but in reference to an advertisement he hopes to place in the newspaper (see epigraph). "Get a par," he once ordered his brother when trying to publicize a business venture in Dublin back to his adopted home in Trieste. *L* II, 277.

44. The recent discovery of the earliest known draft for this episode would seem to support this decision: it includes fifteen different sections (beginning on page 5 of the notebook) separated by a line of asterisks, with dialogue dashes extending outside of the paragraphs, thereby keeping narration and dialogue on the same level. A digital copy is publicly available from the National Library of Ireland. See http://catalogue.nli.ie/Record/vtls000357767. Critics are already in the habit of referring to these different sections as fragments, but that obfuscates what is otherwise an important point: Stephen is already thinking in complete paragraphs. See, for instance, Sam Slote, "Epiphanic 'Proteus,' " *Genetic Joyce Studies* 5 (Spring 2005); Luca Crispi, "A First Foray into the National Library of Ireland's Joyce Manuscripts: Bloomsday 2011" *Genetic Joyce Studies* 11 (Spring 2011). Daniel Ferrer wonders if Joyce considered using a "fragmentary form" for this episode, something more in line with episode 10. Whatever happened along the way, it wasn't fragments that Joyce collected for episode 3, it was paragraphs, then arranged in a sequence, which would allow him to weave together the movement of thoughts in Stephen's head with the movement of his body along the beach. Daniel Ferrer, "What Song the Sirens Sang . . . Is No Longer beyond All Conjecture: A Preliminary Description of the New 'Proteus' and 'Sirens' Manuscripts," *James Joyce Quarterly* 39, no. 1 (Fall 2001): 53–67.

45. Gerhard Dohrn-van Rossum, *History of the Hour* (Chicago: University of Chicago Press, 1996).

46. At 376 paragraphs in 11,439 words, episode 11 would seem an outlier but only if we don't factor in the fifty-nine bits of text, each one its own paragraph, contained in the overture.

47. Kenner, "Gabler Era," 17.

48. A. M. Klein, "The Oxen of the Sun," *Here and Now* 1 (1949): 28–48.

49. See, for instance, Sarah Davison, "Joyce's Incorporation of Literary Sources in 'Oxen of the Sun,'" *Genetic Joyce Studies* 9 (2009) https://www.geneticjoy-cestudies.org/articles/GJS9/GJS9_Davison; Ronan Crowley, "Earmarking 'Oxen of the Sun': On the Dates of the Copybook Drafts," *Genetic Joyce Studies* 18 (Spring 2018) https://www.geneticjoycestudies.org/articles/GJS18/GJS18_Crowley

50. In this table, I am using the breakdown provided by Jeri Johnson in her edition
     of the 1922 *Ulysses* (Oxford: Oxford University Press, 2008), the one that she
     checks against the information already provided by Robert Janusko, *Sources and
     Structure of James Joyce's Oxen* (Ann Arbor, MI: UMI Research Press, 1983); and
     Stuart Gilbert's *"Ulysses": A Study*.
51. Saintsbury, *History of English Prose Rhythm*, 53.

2. WORDS IN PROGRESS

1.   "Graphic unit" is the term preferred by Gabler and his team because it empha-
     sizes the fact that words, though made up of strings of letters, can also be num-
     bers, initials, symbols, sounds, etc.
2.   Vladimir Nabokov, "*Ulysses*," in *Lectures on Literature*, ed. Fredson Bowers (New
     York: Harcourt, Brace, Jovanovich, 1982), 285.
3.   Only three issues of the *Little Review* appeared without any installments from
     Ulysses between March 1918 and December 1920. Because of the length, it is
     possible that episode 14 could have fit into three different installments, but
     based on the two or three long episodes that preceded it, I suspect that four
     would have been more likely.
4.   See *The Little Review "Ulysses*," ed. Mark Gaipa, Sean Latham, and Robert
     Scholes (New Haven, CT: Yale University Press, 2014).
5.   Pound wrote one particularly animated letter complaining about the typos
     in the December 1918 number of the *Little Review*: "What the ensanguined
     lllllllllllllllllllllll is the matter with this BLOODY goddamndamnblastedbas-
     tardbitchbornsonofaputridseahorse of foetid and stinkerous printer???????????
     Is his serbo-croatian optic utterly impervious to the twelfth letter of the alpha-
     bet ?????"; *The Letters of Ezra Pound to Margaret Anderson: "The Little Review"
     Correspondence*, ed. Thomas Scott, Melvin Friedman, and Jackson Bryer (New
     York: New Directions, 1988), 181.
6.   For a discussion of these errors, see Amanda Sigler, "Archival Errors: *Ulysses*
     and the *Little Review*," in *Errears and Erroriboose: Joyce and Error*, ed. Matthew
     Creasy, European Joyce Studies 20 (Amsterdam: Rodopi Press, 2011), 73–88.
7.   The most comprehensive history of the *episode* can be found in Matthew
     Garrett's *Episodic Poetics: Politics and Literary Form after the Constitution*
     (Oxford: Oxford University Press, 2014).
8.   Forrest Read, ed., *Pound/Joyce: The Letters of Ezra Pound to James Joyce* (New
     York: New Directions, 1970), 143, 158.
9.   *Oxford English Dictionary* Online, s.v. "episode," accessed May 5, 2020, https://
     www-oed-com.ccl.idm.oclc.org/view/Entry/63527?redirectedFrom=episode#eid
10. Gabler's theory of the lost manuscript is based on the careful comparison of
     extant manuscripts. The typescript for some episodes, then, may correspond with

the Rosenbach manuscript, but there are too many differences to suggest that another source was being consulted. This point was clarified to me by Gabler via email after he read a version of this chapter when published in *Representations*.

11. Lost in the wood, I finally contacted Michael Groden, who, after patiently considering the possibilities, wrote to me in an email: "I'd stay with words."

12. Anthony Burgess, not entirely thrilled with the whole idea of counting words, joked that "innumerable Ph.D. candidates yet unborn have their thesis subjects waiting for them—an Old Norse word-count of *Finnegans Wake*, II. iii." See *ReJoyce* (New York: Norton, 1965), xi. He's more than likely referring to Frank Budgen's word-count free "James Joyce's Work in Progress and Old Norse Poetry," in *Our Exagmination Round His Factification for Incamination of Work in Progress* (Paris: Shakespeare & Co., 1929), 37–46. As far as I know, the subject is still wide open for any enterprising PhD candidates with an interest in the subject.

13. Hugh Kenner, "Reflections on the Gabler Era," *James Joyce Quarterly* 26, no. 1 (Fall 1988): 14.

14. Hugh Kenner, *Ulysses* (London: George, Allen, & Unwin, 1980), 67; emphasis added.

15. Kenner, "Reflections," 19.

16. For more on word counts, see Duncan Harkin, "The History of Word Counts," *Babel* 3, no. 3 (1957): 113–24 and James E. DeRocher, *The Counting of Words: A Review of the History, Techniques, and Theory of Word Counts with Annotated Bibliography* (New York: Syracuse University Research Corp, 1973).

17. Miles Hanley, *Word Index to James Joyce's "Ulysses"* (Madison: University of Wisconsin Press, 1937), 384. Another early application of the word count can be found in Erwin Steinberg's *The Stream of Consciousness and beyond in "Ulysses"* (Pittsburgh, PA: University of Pittsburgh Press, 1973). See also Leslie Hancock, *Word Index to James Joyce's "Portrait of the Artist"* (Carbondale: Southern Illinois University Press, 1967); Wilhelm Füger, *Concordance to James Joyce's "Dubliners"* (Hildesheim: G. Olds, 1980); Clive Hart, *A Concordance to "Finnegans Wake"* (Minneapolis: University of Minnesota Press, 1963); and Ruth Bauerle, *Word List to James Joyce's "Exiles"* (New York: Garland, 1981).

18. Wolfhard Steppe and Hans Walter Gabler, *A Handlist to James Joyce's* Ulysses: *A Complete Alphabetical Index to the Critical Reading Text* (New York: Garland Publishing, 1986), vii.

19. Jacques Derrida, "*Ulysses* Gramophone: Hear Say Yes in Joyce," in *Acts of Literature*, ed. Derek Attridge (New York: Routledge, 1992), 305–6.

20. Though it does include by breakdown: Yes (195), *Yes* (2), yes (161), and *yes* (1). In the *Word-Index*, Hanley lumps them all together under a single entry for "yes" and gets 354.

21. Pound to Joyce, March 1917, in Read, *Pound/Joyce*, 104. In December 1918, while still serving as foreign editor of the *Little Review*, Pound had the idea of starting

up a quarterly, writing to Joyce that he wouldn't be able to "serialize novels," but he'd be willing to accept contributions of "up to let us say 10,000 words of story or essay. 10,000 not an absolute limit, but a general estimate"; Pound to Joyce, December 1918, in Read, *Pound/Joyce*, 104, 148.

22. Joyce to Pound, August 1917, *SL*, 227.

23. In *Serial Encounters: "Ulysses" and the "Little Review"* (Oxford: Oxford University Press, 2019), Clare Hutton argues that these negotiations were "vague," which I assume means nonbinding and less than urgent (144). She rests her claim on two letters (one from June 1919, another from January 1920), but the first one was written after ten episodes had already appeared and the second when the thirteenth was drafted. It's difficult to reconcile any broader claims about lack of urgency when more than half the novel was written.

24. On 27 November 1917, Joyce writes to Claud Sykes about episode 2 and episode 3: "In the other two episodes (which are not so long) it will depend on whether he [Rudolph Goldschmidt, the one they're borrowing typewriter from] disposes of his place or not. I take it you could do what I sent quickly. There is no use losing time." On December 12, 1917, Joyce reminds Sykes: "This episode [2] is only half as long as the other"; *L* I, 109; *L* II, 412.

25. In "The Development of *Ulysses* in Print, 1918–22," Hutton also generates a "rough snapshot" of word counts (using Microsoft Word) but makes the erroneous claim that "the algorithm of what counts as a word and what counts as a space would be different in another programme." Why? Computers count the spaces between and not the words as individual units. *Dublin James Joyce Journal* 6/7 (2013–2014): 121.

26. Pound was confused when he received the first seventeen pages of typescript, thinking it was intended for the first three installments instead of one. "Your 17 pages have no division marks," he wrote Joyce on December 19, 1917. "Unless this is the first month's lot, instead of the first three months, as you wrote it would be, I shall divide on page 6. After the statement that the Sassenach wants his bacon. And at the very top of page 12." Read, *Pound/Joyce*, 129. An unpublished letter reveals that Joyce was, in fact, to blame because of he repeatedly elided *episode* and *chapter*: "The first chapter of *Ulysses* is being typed in Zurich and will send as soon as possible. There are three episodes in it. To save time I shall send on each as it is finished. This chapter should run for three months—the Telemachia. There are in all three chapters in the book, the other two being Odyssey (in twelve episodes) and the Nostos (in three episodes). The chapter of the wooers falls out. Of course, these names are not to be prefixed to the chapters"; Ezra Pound Papers, YCAL MSS 43, Box 26, folder 1112, Beinecke Rare Book and Manuscript Library, Yale University. There's no date on the letter but it must have been written some time in November or December 1917 when Joyce was staying at the Pension Daheim in Locarno.

27. For a fascinating discussion about line length in all three canticles of the *Commedia*, see Joan Ferrante, "A Poetics of Chaos and Harmony," in *The Cambridge Companion to Dante*, ed. Rachel Jacoff (Cambridge: Cambridge University Press, 1993), 181–200. For an early account of the length of Shakespeare's plays, see A. Hart, "The Length of Elizabethan and Jacobean Plays," *Review of English Studies* 8, no. 30 (April 1932): 139–54. For details regarding installment size in Charles Dickens, see Robert L. Patten, "The Composition, Publication, and Reception of *Our Mutual Friend*," UC Santa Cruz, Our Mutual Friend: The Scholarly Pages (website), March 20, 2012, http://omf.ucsc.edu/publication /comp-and-pub.html. For a more general discussion of word count as a tool for literary analysis, see Mendenhall, "A Mechanical Solution," 97–105.

28. Budgen: "As a work of reference for his *Ulysses* he used the Butcher-Lang translation of the *Odyssey*." "*James Joyce and the Making of* Ulysses," 323. I am very grateful to Jim Shapiro for suggesting that I go back to Homeric translations Joyce consulted for this information.

29. Stanislaus Joyce's comment was relayed by W. B. Stanford, *The Ulysses Theme* (Oxford: Blackwell, 1954), 76. Kenner agreed with this assessment in 1969 but recanted a decade later on the grounds that Stanislaus would have had access to Joyce only *before* Zurich, since he was interned during the war, therefore making it possible that his brother would have consulted other editions, the Butler translation included. See Hugh Kenner, "Homer's Sticks and Stones," *James Joyce Quarterly* 6 (1969): 285–98 and *Joyce's Voices* (Berkeley, CA: University of California Press, 1978), 110–11.

30. Henry Fielding, *Joseph Andrews*, in *The Works of Henry Fielding: With a Life of the Author* (London: Otridge & Rackham, et al., 1824), 5:91. "Numbers" might have also signified metrical verse to Fielding's contemporaries.

31. An interesting point of comparison: the average word count per line in Elizabethan blank verse was eight. See Hart, "The Length of Elizabethan and Jacobean Plays," 141.

32. Franco Moretti: "Adventures expand novels by opening them to the world: a call for help comes—the knight goes. Usually, without asking questions; which is typical of adventure, the unknown is not a threat here, it's an opportunity, or more precisely: there is no longer any distinction between threats and opportunities." See "The Novel: History and Theory," *New Left Review* 52 (July–August 2008): 5.

33. There's another possibility: I also suspect that Joyce may have sent along his typescript to Pound, waiting for the arrival of the issue of the *Little Review* before moving ahead. Since his issues, which Pound passed on to him from London, were always delayed, it is more than likely that he would have been receiving them up to half a year after he sent the typescript to Pound, sometimes more when the publication of an issue was delayed. "As 'them females,'" he wrote to

Joyce on November 24, 1919, "dont [*sic*] send me the little Review I cant [*sic*] forward it to you I will ask Rodker to do so, and suggest that a note from you to N.Y. office might help"; Read, *Pound/Joyce*, 162.

34. Episode 8 could easily have fit into a single issue. It's unclear who decided where it should be divided. Pound and Jane Heap, once again, are the most likely candidates.

35. He never mentions this in his letters to Margaret Anderson, and there are no distinguishable marks on the batch of *Little Review* typescript pages that survive: seventeen and a half of them from episode 14 that begin with page 10. A copy of the first ten typescript pages can be found in the copy used by Maurice Darantière when preparing the proofs for *Ulysses* and reveal that the first serial installment of episode 14 was made from seven pages (with about three lines continuing on to page 8), making it possible to generate three more at roughly the same length. See *The Letters of Ezra Pound to Margaret Anderson*; *James Joyce Archive* (New York: Garland, 1977), 14:141–59, 171–98.

36. On August 6, 1919, he explained his method to an increasingly frustrated Harriet Shaw Weaver: "I understand that you may begin to regard the various styles of the episodes with dismay and prefer the initial style much as the wanderer did who longed for the rock of Episode 17. But in the compass of one day to compress all these wanderings and clothe them in the form of this day is for me possible only by such variation which, I beg you to believe, is not capricious." Joyce, *SL*, 242.

37. Groden, Ulysses *in Progress*, 33.

38. Wyndham Lewis, "The Revolutionary Simpleton," in *The Enemy: A Review of Art and Literature* (January 1927). Reprinted in Wyndham Lewis, *Time and Western Man*, ed. Paul Edwards (Santa Rosa, CA: Black Sparrow Press, 1993), 27–30. Referring specifically to a single sentence from episode 8, Kenner was in agreement. "'The year marked on a dusty bottle,'" he argues, "seems too many words for Bloom's swift thought; seven words have evidently been supplied for what passed before Bloom as a visual fancy." Seven words for a single impression may have been too long for Kenner, but he was quick to remind everyone that Bloom is "a creation of words, which sometimes overlay and amend 'his' words and are also sometimes shut off, as when he came through his front door and later could not remember what the words did not record, what he had done with his hat." Kenner, *Ulysses*, 70.

39. Gilbert, *James Joyce's "Ulysses,"* 26.

40. Kenner, *Ulysses*, 67.

41. Groden, Ulysses *in Progress*, 115.

42. Paul Ricoeur, *Time and Narrative*, vol. 2, trans. Kathleen McLaughlin and David Pellauer (Chicago: University of Chicago Press, 1984), 78.

43. A quantitative analysis of sentence length in *Ulysses* still remains to be done.

44. For a more detailed discussion of this middle stage, see Groden, Ulysses *in Progress*, 37–52.

45. Groden, Ulysses *in Progress*, 49.

46. Pound to Joyce, June 10, 1919, in Read, *Pound/Joyce*, 158.

47. For some reason or other, Joyce informed Budgen on January 3, 1920 that episode 13 was "not so long as the others." Because he uses the plural here, "others," I'm assuming he had episode 11 and episode 10 in mind as well. He was well off the mark: episode 13 is longer than both of them by more than 2,000 words; Joyce, *SL*, 246.

48. These word counts vary slightly from other published counts due to the ambiguities in the language and typesetting. In every case, though, the differences are very minor, between two and twenty words, with only one of them reaching seventy. These small differences do not affect the ratios I am presenting here.

49. *Aristotle's Poetics: The Argument*, trans. Gerald F. Else (Cambridge: Cambridge University Press, 1957), 286.

50. In the revised 1986 *Handlist*, the number of graphic units, which was generated automatically from the TUSTEP typesetting program, is 264,448. In the word counts for the 1984 edition personally given to me by Gabler, the total is 266,601. Since I do not have access to the TUSTEP program, I am unable to explain the reason for these differences. That said, they are very slight and do not affect the point I am making here. However, the differences I keep encountering in word counts of *Ulysses* as a book and as a collection of serialized episodes reveals that a final, exact number remains to be found.

51. Groden, Ulysses *in Progress*, 169.

52. For these numbers, I compared the serial word counts I compiled using Word Counter with the book word counts provided to me by Gabler.

53. It's a response the man himself had, making sure that everyone knew that the serial version was rotten to the core. James Pinker, for instance, was informed in December 1919 that "the text hitherto published in *Little Review* is *not* my text as sent on in typescript," and on March 11, 1920 John Quinn was told that the "the version in *The Little Review* is, of course, mutilated"; *L* II, 456, 459.

54. Driver points out that the greatest number of additions were reserved for episode 5, episode 8, episode 13, and episode 12; Clive Driver, "Bibliographical Preface," in *Ulysses: A Facsimile of the Manuscript* (New York: Octagon, 1975)

55. To Harriet Shaw Weaver on November 10, 1920, Joyce described it as "about twice as long as the longest episode hitherto, Cyclops [episode 12]." To Claud Sykes in early 1921, he explained that it would run "to nearly 200 pages of typescript," adding that "it is as intricate as it is long." *L* I, 149, 158.

56. Joyce to Robert McAlmon: "I shall give Molly another 2000 word spin, correct a few more episodes and write all over them and then begin to put the spectral penultimate *Ithaca* into shape." Joyce to Budgen on August 16, 1921: "Penelope is the clou of the book. The first sentence contains 2500 words. There are

8 sentences in the episode." Joyce to Weaver on August 7, 1921: he had "written the first sentence of *Penelope* but as this contains about 2500 words the deed is more than it seems to be"; *SL*, 285; *L* III, 48; *L* I, 168. It appears Joyce knew early on that episode 18 would be shorter than episode 15. On November 24, 1920, he wrote to Quinn: "I must have a few month's leisure after January to write *Ithaca* and *Penelope* episodes [17 and 18] which, however, have been sketched since 1916 and are very short in comparison with the *Circe* episode." *L* III, 31.

57. Ezra Pound, *Literary Essays* (New York: New Directions, 1968), 407.

3. ONE OR HOW MANY?

The epigraph to this chapter comes from Balzac's preface to his 1842 edition of the *Comédie humaine* (10). I am grateful to Peter Brooks for reminding me of the number (c. 2400) contained in the six-volume catalogue compiled by Anatole Cerfberr and Jules François Christophe. See *Repertory of the Comédie humaine: Complete A-Z* (Philadelphia: Avil Publishing Co., 1912).

1. See Groden, Ulysses *in Progress*, 181; Character list reproduced in *Joyce's "Ulysses" Notesheets in the British Museum*, ed. Philip Herring (Charlottesville: University Press of Virginia, 1972), 526–27.

2. And in a long line of characters *not on the list* is Mina Purefoy's newborn baby boy from episode 14, Mortimer Edward Purefoy.

3. In *Joyce's "Ulysses" Notesheets*, Herring confuses the "1" with an apostrophe, transcribing it as " '38" instead of "138" (366).

4. Pedro J. Miranda, Murilo S. Baptista, and Sandro E. de Souza Pinto, "Analysis of Communities in a Mythological Social Network," *ArXiv* abs/1306.2537 (2013), n. pag. Curtius, *European Literature*, 365. Moretti points out that there are over "600 characters in *The Scholars*, 800 in *The Water Margin* and the *Jin Ping Mei*, 975 in *The Story of the Stone*." See Franco Moretti, "History of the Novel, Theory of the Novel," *Novel: A Forum on Fiction* 43, no. 1 (2010): 5.

5. All of them listed in Anatole Cerfberr and Jules François Christophe, *Repertory of the Comédie humaine: Complete A-Z* (Philadelphia: Avil, 1912).

6. Balzac, *Comédie humaine* (1842), 18.

7. Franco Moretti, *Atlas of the European Novel, 1800–1900* (London: Verso, 1998), 68.

8. The original line reads: "Most novels are in some sense knowable communities." See Raymond Williams, "The Knowable Community in George Eliot's Novels," *Novel: A Forum on Fiction* 2, no. 3 (Spring 1969): 255–68.

9. Even influencing the naming of children in ancient Rome (first four sons in a family get names, the rest numerals). See Georges Ifrah, *The Universal History of Numbers*, trans. David Bellos, E. F. Harding, Sophie Wood, and Ian Monk (London: John Wiley & Sons, 2000), 9.

10. Ifrah, *Universal History*, 7.

11. Richard Kain, *Fabulous Voyager: A Study of James Joyce's "Ulysses"* (New York: Viking, 1959), 252.

12. Shari Benstock and Bernard Benstock, *Who's He When He's at Home: A James Joyce Directory* (Urbana: University of Illinois, 1980).

13. All of them are listed in Benstock and Benstock, *Who's He When He's at Home*, 373.

14. In the Legend, the Benstocks identify the need to include some animals and objects as characters: "Although this directory is limited to 'human' characters, the unusual nature of *Ulysses* dictates that (1) all dogs (like Garryowen) and horses (like Throwaway) must necessarily be included, provided that they have names, (2) that those inanimate objects that have speaking roles in *Circe* be included—as hallucinations." Benstock and Benstock, *Who's He When He's at Home*, xii.

15. Alex Woloch, *The One vs. the Many: Minor Characters and the Space of the Protagonist in the Novel* (Princeton, NJ: Princeton University Press, 2003).

16. In order for these divisions to work at all, the reappearance of characters in episode 15 from previous episodes does not count as a reappearance. This is particularly relevant to a large quantity of characters who would fall in the minor minor category. In addition, by using speaking as part of the criteria for distinguishing types of characters, I am not including those characters who shout or yell unless they are addressing someone in particular. There will be places where arguments can be made for the appearance of characters in more than one category, but this is what I've come up with based on these four criteria. The most important distinction involves identifying the different between minor and minor minor for the analysis that follows.

17. Woloch, *The One vs. the Many*, 122, 117, 124.

18. The data for the network visualizations would not have been possible without the directory the Benstocks compiled. Like so many others, I am grateful to them for this valuable service even though I never expected to need it long ago when I first acquired a copy.

19. Bloom: "'Twentyfour solicitors in that one house" (*U*, 237). This line was immediately followed by "Counted them" but did not appear in the 1922 edition. It did, however, appear in the Rosenbach manuscript and was reinserted by Gabler.

20. "The importance of the number [12] is made evident by the choice of another apostle to complete the number when one was lost. Or again, Noah, the tenth generation, had 3 sons, but one fell into sin to preserve the number. The tribe of Levi also made thirteen tribes in actuality, but they are always spoken of as 12, thus demonstrating that the idea of the number is more important than the actuality." Hopper, *Medieval Number Symbolism*, 86.

21. And there's also the added irony that the twelve characters may correspond with the twelve disciples, but there's really no room for the Jew.

22. Joyce put Paddy on his list along with Rudy Bloom and Dodd & Son.

23. Curtius, *European* Literature, 509; Gunnar Qvarnström, *Poetry and Numbers: On the Structural Use of Symbolic Numbers* (Lund, Sweden: Gleerup, 1966), 36.

24. "Between the original work on Cyclops in summer 1919 and the pulling of the episode's first proofs in October 1921, he began to write a new kind of book." Groden, Ulysses *in Progress*, 158.

25. Michael Groden, Philip Herring, David Hayman, and Karen Lawrence.

26. Four of them begin with the adverb *so*, two with the conjunction *and*, one with a car pulling up, and another with a character popping in.

27. David Hayman, "Cyclops," in *James Joyce's* Ulysses: *Critical Essays*," ed. Clive Hart and Hugh Kenner (Berkeley: University of California Press, 1974), 253.

28. Hayman,"Cyclops," 253. See also Phillip Herring, *Joyce's Notes and Early Drafts for "Ulysses"* (Charlottesville: University Press of Virginia, 1977), 146.

29. Groden, Ulysses *in Progress*, 135.

30. "Scenes and Fragmentary Texts for 'Cyclops,'" NLI II. ii. 4 'Partial Draft: Cyclops". MS 36, 639/10. There's a line preceding the lineup that reads: "Michan's: Bloom + ? [question mark Joyce's] Woman." This list is different from the one Groden discusses from later in the process (Ulysses *in* Progress, 122).

31. See *Parliamentary Papers House of Commons and Command*, vol. 68 (Dublin: Cahill & Co., 1901), 1.

32. Clive Hart and Ian Gunn, with Harald Beck, *A Topographical Guide to the Dublin of* Ulysses (London: Thames & Hudson, 2004).

33. In his excellent article on the census, Sam Alexander arrives at the number 108. Using the phrase "by my count," shows that he is acutely aware of the difficulty of figuring out who counts but also how to count (several figures together are one?). See "Joyce's Census: Character, Demography, and the Problem of Population in *Ulysses*," Novel: *A Forum on Fiction* 45, no. 3 (2012), 448.

34. See Leo Knuth, "A Bathymetric Reading of Joyce's *Ulysses*, Chapter X," *James Joyce Quarterly*, vol. 8, no. 4 (Summer 1972), 405–22.

35. Curtius, *European Literature*, 505.

36. Stanislaus Joyce, *Recollections of James Joyce*, trans. Ellsworth Mason (New York: James Joyce Society, 1950), 19.

37. Gilles Deleuze and Félix Guattari, "One or Several Wolves?" in *A Thousand Plateaus: Capitalism and Schizophrenia*, trans. Brian Massumi (Minneapolis: University of Minnesota Press, 1987), 29.

38. In an interesting twist, M'Coy also asks Bloom to add his name to the list at the funeral, even though he plans to go to Sandycove to wait and see if the body of the drowned man is found. After his departure, Bloom's thoughts, inspired by M'Coy's reminder about Dignam, turn to his own dead father, leading him to remark, "Wish I hadn't met that M'Coy fellow" (*U*, 63).

39. In their quantitative analysis of character networks in a corpus of sixty different nineteenth-century British novels, Nicholas Dames, David Elson, and Kathleen

McKeown were curious to know if urban novels were more crowded than rural ones. They were surprised to discover that urban settings did not correspond with an increase in the number of characters. Instead, they concluded that the narrative standpoint from which they were imagined (whether omniscient or not) was a more significant factor in the population increase. "Extracting Social Networks from Literary Fiction," *Proceedings of the 48th Annual Meeting of the Association for Computational Linguistics*, Uppsala, Sweden, 11–16 July 2010, 138–47.

40. Groden, Ulysses *in Progress*, 55.

41. None of the characters from episode 16 appear.

42. For these numbers, I am relying on Benstock's lists, which include both a straight-forward "Directory of Names" but also an Appendix with "Molly's Masculine Pronouns" and another decoding the many "Anonymous Listings." Benstock and Benstock, *Who's He When He's at Home*, 229–33, 169–216.

43. It was the first edition of *Thom's Irish Who's Who: A Biographical Book of Reference of Prominent Men and Women in Irish Life at Home and Abroad* (Dublin: Alexander Thom, 1923). The rough estimate, "upwards of 2,500," is given in the preface.

44. February 26, 1923, *L* III, 73.

4. GIS JOYCE

The epigraphs to this chapter are from two of the earliest reviews of *Ulysses*: Sisley Huddleston, in the March 1922 issue of *Observer*; Joseph Collins in a May 1922 issue of the *New York Times*. Reprinted in *James Joyce: Critical Heritage*, vol. I, ed. Robert Deming (New York: Barnes & Noble, 1970).

1. The last documented copy was sold to Lewis Galantière on July 1, 1922 (Beach writing "Only the Dutch and verge d'Arche lists are complete and have been kept up to date until July 1, 1922"), but others were still being made available into the fall of that same year, which indicates that some were held back. I am very grateful to Ted Bishop for sharing his materials with me for this chapter and his many valuable insights in "The 'Garbled History' of the First Edition of *Ulysses*," *Joyce Studies Annual* 9 (1998): 3–36. Thanks also to Laura Barnes for generously answering my questions about the messy business of documenting the who, what, and where of this first edition.

2. The original number Joyce reported to Weaver in April 1921 was 1,020. *L* I, 162. As late as February 3, when the final bill was presented to Beach, Darantière was planning to print 1,047 copies (770 vergé à barbes, 155 arches, 102 hollandes, and 20 ordinaires) but never followed through, in part, because it was already too costly, and a second edition was already in the works for October. The number 1,020 was eventually arrived at, but the story is not so straightforward.

On March 16, 1922, Darantière explained to Beach that he was unable to print all twenty press copies because of the ones that were damaged along the way. His revised total broke that number down to 754 vergé à barbes, 151 arches, 100 hollandes, 13 exemplaires de presse along with "deux paquets de defets." In the catalogue she compiled for Glenn Horowitz, Laura Barnes, using Beach's notebook, pins it down to an extra nineteen copies (fourteen for review and five for family and friends) but there's another "unnumbered press copy" that she discovered in the Bibliothèque Nationale de France that was deposited by Darantière for copyright. In addition, there are the retained printer's copies, an unnumbered one given to Henry Kaeser by Joyce from the one hundred pile and another one inscribed to Darantière by Joyce on October 12, 1922 from the 150 pile. Some of the numbered copies were erased and rubber stamped with "Unnumbered Press Copy," including the three mentioned by Slocum and Cahoon, *A Bibliography of James Joyce: From the Yale University Libraries Collection* (New Haven, CT: Yale University Press, 1953), 25.

3.   Ten percent then 20 percent discount was a problem. The cheaper edition sold out before the more expensive ones, but there were also some booksellers who used the discount to their advantage.

4.   As reported by Sylvia Beach on August 7, 1922: "I got all the copies of 'Ulysses' to the subscribers (in all states except New York) through the post without any trouble." *The Letters of Sylvia Beach*, ed. Keri Walsh (New York: Columbia University Press, 2010), 101. A majority of the subscription forms, along with the relevant address books and correspondence, can be found online in the Sylvia Beach Papers at Princeton University: https://findingaids.princeton.edu/collections/C0108/. Some of them can also be found in the Sylvia Beach papers in the Poetry Collection, Capen Library, University at Buffalo, New York.

5.   I say *allegedly* since Joyce, prone to exaggeration in these matters, was the one to report it: "A second edition of *Ulysses* was published on the 12 October. The entire edition of 2000 copies at 2.2.0 [missing pound sign] a copy was sold out in four days" (*L* I, 191). In a letter dated October 9, 1922, Darantière informed Beach that 108 copies were being sent.

6.   The names and addresses used in these maps come from a variety of sources that include address books, subscription forms, lists, cards, letters, and censuses. Beach was very inconsistent with her tracking methods, so a lot of this material had to be checked against multiple sources whenever possible. Only confirmed subscriptions are included in this data set, though others will certainly be found. What makes all of this even more difficult is the fact that some subscribers ordered through bookstores and agents, and Beach was less than thorough with her documentation of the copies that would have sold through her store for those who never actually filled out subscriptions. Anyone interested in the subscription forms and orders received can access the digital reproductions. See "Slips with Names of Subscribers," Sylvia Beach Papers, C0108, Manuscripts

Division, Department of Rare Books and Special Collections, Princeton University Library.

7. Beach uses this phrase in "The Ulysses Subscribers," an essay she submitted to two different journals in 1950, but it was turned down. That same year she signed a contract for the book version with Harcourt, Brace, and Jovanovich, and portions of this essay were revised for her memoir. See "The *Ulysses* Subscribers" Sylvia Beach Papers, C0108, Manuscripts Division, Department of Rare Books and Special Collections, Princeton University Library. A digital reproduction can be found at https://figgy.princeton.edu/catalog/11e13587-f477-48f8-9b31-3ae7623d96e0

8. The total was divided in different amounts between December 1921 and June 1922. The first installment required using any profit from the business, and possibly loans, but subsequent ones were to be covered by subscribers. "My business is going well and I could tackle the carpenter bill if I didn't have to put every single centime aside to pay the printer of *Ulysses* five thousand francs on the 1st of December. He requires it and naturally *the cheques from subscribers will not arrive in* time for that first payment." Beach, *Letters of Sylvia Beach*, 88; emphasis added.

9. Rachel Potter, *Obscene Modernism: Literary Censorship and Experiment* (Oxford: Oxford University Press, 2013), 73.

10. Egmont Arens was a notable exception, paying only 1,620 francs out of 3,000. Beach sent her father to pick up the balance four years later (in 1926) without interest or the addition of shipping costs. Bishop, "The 'Garbled History,' " 20. For a history of the common reader, see William Powell Jones, *James Joyce and the Common Reader* (Norman: University of Oklahoma Press, 1955). For an account of the common reader after Hans Walter Gabler's 1984 edition, see Julie Sloan Brannon, *Who Reads "Ulysses"? The Rhetoric of the Joyce Wars and the Common Reader* (New York: Routledge, 2003).

11. Potter, *Obscene Modernism*, 62.

12. Information about the ban in the United States was used for the promotional material, including the prospectuses announcing that it was "suppressed four times during serial publication in *The Little Review.*"

13. Potter, *Obscene Modernism*, 65.

14. Lawrence Rainey argues that the subscriptions were one way to make *Ulysses* a desirable commodity for collectors, but Potter explains that he downplays the novel's status as pornography that would need subscriptions to circulate. "It is only in retrospect," she writes, "that the distinctions between *Ulysses* and pornographic texts, and the literary market and the pornography trade, are straightforward. It did not look so clear-cut to lawyers, judges, vice crusaders, publishers, customs officials, or others at the time." Potter, *Obscene Modernism*, 69.

15. For the "unnumbered press copies" of the second edition, Joyce instructed Weaver to have a stamp made that would be applied "in the space left for no. . . ?" (*L* I, 194).

16. The most detailed census was sponsored by Glenn Horowitz, a rare book dealer in New York City, and overseen by Barnes. Cataloguing subscribers, not mapping them, was the primary concern. See note 3.

17. Read, *Pound/Joyce*, 123.

18. Beach, *Shakespeare and Company*, 48, 96.

19. Febvre and Martin, *The Coming of the Book*, 111.

20. Ezra Pound, *The Selected Letters of Ezra Pound, 1907–1941*, ed. D. D. Paige (New York: New Directions, 1971), 262–63.

21. On April 10, 1921, Joyce provides an account to Weaver with a breakdown of the edition, adding that there would be "1,000 copies, with 20 extra copies for libraries and press" (*L* I, 162). On April 18, 1921, Darantière sends a full cost breakdown for one thousand copies with "la justification du tirage." On April 23, 1921, Beach mentions to her sister that "It [*Ulysses*] will appear in October—a thousand copies—subscriptions only" (85).

22. April 19, 1921, *L* III, 40.

23. Vergil to Dante: "and he pointed out and named to me more than a thousand shades" (Canto V, 67–68); See Hopper, *Medieval Number Symbolism*, 29.

24. *L* I, 196. In his journal, Stuart Gilbert also recalls Joyce throwing out a rough calculation about his losses to Roth: eight thousand copies at seven or eight dollars apiece of which an unspecified percentage should go to him. Quoted in Alastair McCleery, "The Reputation of the Odyssey Press Edition of *Ulysses*," *Papers of the Bibliographical Society of America* 100, no. 1 (2006): 96.

25. Quoted in Robert Spoo, *Without Copyrights: Piracy, Publishing, and the Public Domain* (Oxford: Oxford University Press, 2013), 217.

26. The United States Census of 1920 was 106,021,537 and the one for 1930 was 122,775,046. Joyce, in 1927, three years before census statistics were updated, must have received this speculative assessment from a reliable source. See https://www.census.gov/library/publications/1921/dec/vol-01-population.html and https://www.census.gov/content/census/en/library/publications/1930/compendia/statab/52ed.html

27. *L* I, 196.

28. If we follow the paid subscription trail between May 19, 1921 and July 1, 1922, we discover that with 142,000 francs Beach more than covered the costs of Darantière's bill. If Beach sold every copy without a discount and did not give any away, the total would have been 185,000 francs. Maurice Saillet, "List of Subscribers, ca. 1921," Harry Ransom Center, University of Texas at Austin, box 262, folder 10.

29. Beach, "The *Ulysses* Subscribers." The American subscribers had to wait the longest. In a letter to Marion Peter (owner of the *Sunwise Turn* bookshop) dated August 7, 1922, Beach explains how copies can be brought by bookleggers to avoid customs officials, but that was six months *after* the printing was completed. See *Letters of Sylvia Beach*, 101.

30.   The names and addresses for these letters were taken from two separate lists. The first, entirely in Joyce's hand, the second also in Joyce's hand but with additions from Lucia Joyce and notations from Sylvia Beach. Originals can be found in the James Joyce Collection at the University at Buffalo, XXVIII Miscellaneous Material Related to Joyce's Works, "*Ulysses*: The First Edition," folders 7 and 8.

31.   I got this number from the orders logged in Darantière letters to Beach. With his usual exaggeration, Joyce informed Weaver on August 7, 1921 that "5000 prospectuses" had gone out with "the capture" of a mere "260." Original letter in the Harriet Shaw Weaver collection at the British library.

32.   Quoted in Beach, *Shakespeare and Company*, 85. Discussing her tactics for enlisting subscribers, Beach claimed that "no one escaped from the rue de l'Odéon without subscribing." But there was also Robert McAlmon, who would collect subscriptions from night clubs, leaving many people "surprised to find themselves subscribers." That may help to explain the large number that didn't pay up when the copies actually arrived (50, 51).

33.   The original plan was for seventeen uncovered press copies to be sent out: five for the Continent, six for England, and six for the United States. The two unnumbered copies retained by Darantière were signed by Joyce on October 12, 1922: one was given to the printer, the other to Henry Kaeser. See Sarah Funke, Glenn Horowitz, and Laura Barnes, *James Joyce* Ulysses: *An Exhibition of Twenty-Four Inscribed Copies of the First Edition* (New York: Glenn Horowitz Bookseller, 1998), 28, 34.

34.   Ellmann, "*Ulysses" on the Liffey*, 531.

35.   Four hundred subscriptions may have been sent in by November 1921, but in Beach's papers, there are only twenty separate payments, some of them for multiple copies.

36.   *L* II, 182; *L* II, 145; *L* III, 61. Pound repeated this exact number to Alice Corbin Henderson on March 12, 1922. See *The Letters of Ezra Pound to Alice Corbin Henderson*, ed. Ira Nadel (Austin: University of Texas Press, 1993), 224.

37.   "The Novel of the Century," Lilly Library at Indiana University (website), accessed March 26, 2020, http://www.indiana.edu/~liblilly/joyce/manuscripts .html.

38.   September 30, 1924, *SL*, 302.

39.   *L* I, 173.

40.   He may never have ordered a copy of the first edition, but he kept the original prospectus (and in mint condition). A reproduction can be found here: https:// www.bl.uk/collection-items/g-b-shaws-order-form-for-ulysses.

41.   One of them included a personal note asking if the edition was "in English" (George Daugherty).

42.   Beach, "The *Ulysses* Subscribers": "I was still busy delivering the 1st edition of *Ulysses* to places all over the globe."

43.   In one of her lists for potential subscribers she also included a "miscellaneous" section lumping together subscribers from Ireland, Scotland, Holland, Jerusalem, Belgrade, Spain, Italy, Czechoslovakia, Germany, India, Belgium, Sweden, Norway, Brazil, Argentina, Austria, Norway, Luxembourg, and South Africa. See note 4.

44.   Beach, *Shakespeare and Company*, 62. Though there is evidence that a subscription form was sent to Sarawak Straits and orders came in from China for the second and third edition. There's also a curious anecdote about his Chinese readers that Joyce reported to Weaver in October 1923: "A friend of his [John Quinn] told me that there is a club in the far east where Chinese ladies (not American as I supposed) meet twice a week to discuss my mistresspiece. Needless to say the said club is in—shavole Shanghai!" (*L* I, 206).

45.   Kenner, *Joyce's Voices*, 1.

46.   I've taken this phrase from an unsigned article that appeared in the *Nation*, December 20, 1933.

47.   There was also the pirated edition that Samuel Roth printed in the United States in 1929. David Magorlick points out though that a majority of the copies were personal imports from Paris: "Illicit copies of *Ulysses* bound in light-blue paper, became nearly as available in the late 1920s as bootleg gin. It became commonplace for Americans in Europe to bring copies back with them, and the supply was sufficient for T. S. Eliot to include it as required reading for a course on modern literature he taught at Harvard in the late 1920's." See David Magorlick, "Judge's Ruling Still a Landmark 50 Years Later," *New York Times*, December 6, 1983. A year later, Eliot would complain to Dorothea Richards (who kept a record in her diary) "how the young don't now get anything out of *Ulysses* now its notoriety is gone." *Letters of T.S. Eliot*, ed. Valerie Eliot and Hugh Haffenden, vol. 6, 1932–33 (New Haven, CT: Yale University Press, 2016), 697.

48.   Forty to fifty booksellers also received a letter asking them a similar question: "If the book were declared legal would you stock it for sale, and cooperate in effecting its general circulation." See Michael Moscato and Leslie Le Blanc, eds. *The United States of America v. One Book Entitled "Ulysses" by James Joyce: Documents and Commentary—A 50 Year Retrospective* (Frederick, MD: University Publications of America, 1984), (henceforth *U v. u*). For a discussion of the role librarians played in this case, see William Brockman, "American Librarians and Early Censorship of *Ulysses*: Aiding the Cause of Free Expression?" *Joyce Studies Annual* 5 (1994): 56–74.

49.   Moscato and Le Blanc, *The United States of America v. One Book Entitled "Ulysses" by James Joyce*, 124; emphasis added.

50.   *U v. u*, Ernst, Appendix 4, 421. The full results of this questionnaire, "Re: *Ulysses*, Answers from Librarians and Booksellers," complete with the map and tally of answers collected by Ernst's team, can be found in the Morris Ernst Papers at the Harry Ransom Center, University of Texas at Austin

51. U *v. u*, 141. Ernst had wanted the data presented in an "easy form" to the court, as he told Cerf, suggesting further that "they might even be analyzed as to number of states in which libraries are anxious for the book." A carefully chosen sequence of "comments of librarians on *Ulysses*" was also used as Exhibit C, many of them with dramatic critical flourishes (196).

52. The map does not indicate the locations or libraries where copies already existed. Twenty-four of the librarians were willing to admit the presence of copies in their collections, only two of them from 1922.

53. Ernst, "Brief for Claimant Appellee," appendix 3, 66.

54. Without citing any sources, Herbert Gorman claimed that the number climbed to 50,000 by the time he was writing his biography some time in 1937 or 1938 (323).

55. Edwin McDowell, "Publishing: Cheaper Corrected: *Ulysses* Awaited," *New York Times*, June 22, 1984, 26.

56. An article in the *New York Times* provides a further breakdown of this number. For the Random House edition there were 544,000; in the Modern Library Giant Edition, 69,000; in the regular edition, and since 1967, 275,000 in the Vintage paperback. The Bodley Head includes the 350,000 hard-cover copies, including the original edition of one thousand, and a new edition in 1960, and soft-cover sales of 300,000 after Penguin bought paperback rights in 1967. See Richard Shephard, "U.S. Sales of the Book at 880,000," *New York Times*, February 2, 1972, 41.

57. This dataset was collected from Darantière's letters. Each shipment was accompanied by a summary of the contents, but there are copies missing and duplicates. At least thirty-three copies slipped by and were left unaccounted for. I haven't come across any document on Beach's side that would indicate she was keeping track. See the "Correspondence from Imprimerie Darantière to Sylvia Beach" in the James Joyce Collection at the University at Buffalo.

58. Gorman, *James Joyce*, 304.

59. Gorman, *James Joyce*, 306.

60. Noel Riley Fitch provided one of the earliest and most erroneous lists of first subscribers: "The book ledger for England, Ireland, and Scotland was slowly filling with familiar names: Bennett, two Huxleys, three Sitwells, Woolf, Churchill, Wells, Walpole, and Yeats." *Sylvia Beach and the Lost Generation: A History of Literary Paris in the Twenties & Thirties* (New York: W. W. Norton, 1985), 105. Only Woolf and Yeats subscribed: the others may have sent in subscription forms without paying, but it's doubtful.

61. Andrew Shyrock and Daniel Lord Smail, eds., *Deep History: The Architecture of Past and Present* (Berkeley: University of California Press, 2011), 247.

62. Febvre and Martin, "Geography of the Book," in *The Coming of the Book*, 167–215.

63. Reinhart Koselleck, *Futures Past: On the Semantics of Historical Time*, trans. Keith Tribe (New York: Columbia University Press, 2004), 260.

64. Hans Robert Jauss, "Literary History as a Challenge to Literary Theory," *New Literary History* 2, no. 1 (Autumn 1970): 12.

65. In her memoir, Monnier has a chapter devoted exclusively to "Joyce's *Ulysses* and the French Public." In Monnier, *The Very Rich Hours of Adrienne Monnier*, 112–26.

66. As indicated by Beach to Weaver on June 26, 1922: "Adrienne Monnier . . . took over a number and is beginning to sell them at Fr 500 (edition at Fr 150) and will give the proceeds to Mr. Joyce. Perhaps you will give that address to people who inquire where they can obtain 'Ulysses.'" *Letters of Sylvia Beach*, 97.

67. Though Beach is often prone to exaggeration in her memoir, I find this particular account believable not least because of the degree of detail. See Beach, "The *Ulysses* Subscribers."

68. Rainey identified the one hundred copies of William Jackson, a number that is found in Beach's UK address book for the 150 trade copies, but there is no proof of payment. The census compiled by Laura Barnes, however, shows that at least three copies from the 350 version were purchased. What complicates it further is the presence of two payments in Maurice Saillet's notebook (May 5 and June 8), each one for 5,200 francs. Given the total 10,400 franc payment, and the possibility of the trade discount from Beach, it appears that one hundred copies at 100 or 120 francs could have been the original plan—that is, until copies sold out, forcing Jackson to purchase the more expensive option. Proof that only eighty-seven copies were bought by Jackson can be found in the receipt housed in Beach's papers identifying that he bought eighty-five at 150 francs, and two at 250 francs. See "Order Forms J," in Beach Papers, Princeton University.

69. Lawrence Rainey, "Consuming Investments," *James Joyce Quarterly* 33, no. 4 (1996), 541.

70. Edward Bishop, "The Garbled First Edition of *Ulysses*," *Joyce Studies Annual*, vol. 9 (Summer 1998): 4.

71. Beach, *Shakespeare & Company*, 85.

72. Beach claimed that the first copies to arrive in the United States were "confiscated at the Port of New York" forcing her to suspend shipments. If true, this may suggest that the copies confiscated had been replaced by the ones already printed (86).

73. Margaret Anderson, *My Thirty Years' War: An Autobiography* (New York: Covici, 1930), 175.

74. Locations of librarians in New York State on the map of library responses include Buffalo, Rochester, Ithaca, Binghamton, Schenectady, Albany, and New York.

75. In 1939, Vivian Mercier, who smuggled a copy past "two customs barriers" in 1922, provided one characteristic response: "It would be natural to assume that the

book [*Ulysses*] was banned in the Irish Free State under the Censorship of Publications Act, 1929, but in fact it never was: even the customs prohibition order
against it was withdrawn in 1932." See "Literature in English, 1892–1921," in *A
New History of Ireland*, vol. 6, ed. W.E. Vaughan (Oxford: Oxford University
Press, 1989), 505.

76.   James Joyce, *Exiles* (New York: B. W. Huebsch, 1918), 38.
77.   Beach, 86. The recipients include Mrs. Murray (unnumbered), John Joyce
       (unnumbered), Michael Healy (unnumbered), C. P. Curran (unnumbered),
       Charles Rowe (#?), MJ McManus (#313), John Nolan (#609), Thomas Kiersey
       (#?), Lennox Robinson (#751), L. A. Waldron (#378), Hodges and Figgis (seven
       copies), Fred Hanna (six copies), Irish Book Shop (thirteen copies), Combridge
       & Co. (four copies), National Library of Ireland (press copy).
78.   James Douglas, "Beauty and the Beast," *Sunday Express*, May 28, 1922, 5.
79.   Beach had her own wish list, but it was complemented by the ones collected
       by Sherwood Anderson, Robert McAlmon, and Alfred Kreyemborg. In these
       counts, I have not included the names of Ezra Pound, John Quinn, Baron
       Ambrogio Ralli, and Harriet Shaw Weaver because they were crossed out. I sus-
       pect that indicates they were already on Beach's list and/or had already commit-
       ted. The original "List of Clients Interested in *Ulysses*" is housed in the Sylvia
       Beach Papers, Manuscripts Division, Department of Rare Books and Special
       Collections, Princeton University and has been digitally reproduced here:
       https://findingaids.princeton.edu/collections/C0108/c00747.
80.   Beach, *Shakespeare and Company*, 62.
81.   Spoo, *Without Copyrights, 183*.
82.   Ellmann, *"Ulysses" on the Liffey*, 159.
83.   At least that was the number originally planned on in April 1921. Larbaud to
       Joyce, as reported in interview with Hoffmeister: "He compared it to a starry
       sky: when you look at it long and carefully, it becomes more beautiful as new,
       uncounted stars reveal themselves." *L* I, 162.
84.   It was printed with a batch of one hundred others in vergé à barbes and 8 verge
       d'Arches a month after the first copy arrived and with hundreds of others still left
       to do.
85.   Jauss, "Literary History as a Challenge to Literary Theory," 9.

5. DATING *ULYSSES*

1.   *Dubliners*, for instance, is dateless. And while it is true that *Portrait* also ends
      with a series of cities and dates (Dublin, Trieste, 1904–1914), there's no evidence
      to prove that Joyce was responsible for the addition or the way it was formatted.
      It's more than likely that it was taken for book publication from the final serial
      installment in the *Egoist*. Gorman, however, claims that Joyce "added the dates

Dublin, 1904, Trieste, 1914," but he also mentions that there was a *finis* at the end (which there is not). Gorman, *James Joyce*, 221.

2. September 7, 1915, Read, *Pound/Joyce*, 364; emphasis mine.

3. Seven is one option for counting 1914–1921, and it is based on a more generalized quantity since the composition does not include ALL the months in these years. Joyce keeps the ambiguity, but for those who work through the evidence, as I will in what follows, the beginning for him was in March 1914 and the end in October 1921. The fact that there are only years and not months or days is central to understanding that the concept of compositional time was elastic and could be bent in many directions depending upon the different meanings that Joyce and others have wanted to assign to it.

4. Joseph Priestley, "A Description of a Chart of Biography," in *A Chart of Biography* (Warrington: William Eyres, 1764), 5.

5. The exact day in June was recently established by two Texas Astronomers. See Tim Radford, "Frankenstein's Hour of Creation Identified by Astronomers," *Guardian*, September 25, 2011, https://www.theguardian.com/books/2011/sep /26/frankenstein-hour-creation-identified-astronomers.

6. Margaret McBride, "The Ineluctable Modality: Stephen's Quest for Immortality," in *James Joyce*, Harold Bloom, ed. (Philadelphia: Chelsea House, 2009), 117.

7. It was definitely a more common practice for poets who would use dates to mark the day or month of composition.

8. The 1932 Odyssey Press is an exception. "The End" was inserted after the final inscription.

9. Edward Said, *Beginnings: Intention and Method* (New York: Columbia University Press, 1985), 49; Frank Kermode, *The Sense of an Ending: Studies in the Theory of Fiction* (Oxford: Oxford University Press, 1967); October 7, 1921. L I, 172.

10. Edward Said, *Beginnings: Intention and Method* (New York: Columbia University Press, 1985), 49; Frank Kermode, *The Sense of an Ending: Studies in the Theory of Fiction* (Oxford: Oxford University Press, 1967); October 7, 1921. *L* I, 172.

11. Alain Robbe-Grillet, "The Use of Theory," in *For a New Novel: Essays on Fiction* (Evanston, IL: Northwestern University Press, 1992), 10.

12. A wonderful coincidence that this particular letter was written on the same day that the plot of *Ulysses* is set. "Written in the land of the living, on the right bank of the Adige, in Verona, a city of Transpadane Italy; on the 16th of June, and in the year of that God whom you never knew the 1345th." Quoted. in Anthony Grafton, *Cartographies of Time: A History of the Timeline* (Princeton, NJ: Princeton University Press, 2012), 16.

13. Other signoffs can be found as early as his 1903 "Epiphanies" (JAJ 13/2/03) and his 1904 "Portrait of the Artist" essay (Jas. A. Joyce 7/1/1904).

14. Critics have suggested the possibility of counting eight years, but that would require including ALL the months. So, for instance, if Joyce began writing on January 1, 1914 and ended on January 31, 1921, that would be eight years. Anything

less would be seven plus the months added. Others count from 1914 to 1915, 1915 to 1916, 1916 to 1917, 1917 to 1918, 1918 to 1919, 1919 to 1920, 1920 to 1921. Based on comments from Joyce, Nora, and the others he primed with information, including Gilbert and Gorman, we know that Joyce preferred seven.

15. William James, *Meaning of Truth* (New York, 1909; Project Gutenberg, 2002), 92–93, https://www.gutenberg.org/files/5117/5117-h/5117-h.htm.

16. He compiled another holograph notebook entitled "Shakespeare Dates" between 1916 and 1917. It is housed in The James Joyce collection at the University at Buffalo, James Joyce Collection, V.A.4.

17. The Joyce Papers, National Library of Ireland, NB MS 36, 639/5/B, p. 10 [v.].

18. John Henry Raleigh, *The Chronicle of Leopold and Molly Bloom: "Ulysses" as Narrative* (Berkeley: University of California Press, 1978), 4–5.

19. Here are two of them: on August 16, 1921 Joyce tells Budgen that "Molly Bloom was born 1871" (*L* I, 170), and in episode 17 the Narrator identifies "1870" (*U*, 605).

20. As evidenced from a letter dated September 3, 1921, in which he prepares to "give Molly another 2,000 word spin." *L* III, 48.

21. See Peter Costello, *Leopold Bloom: A Biography* (New York: Harper Collins, 1983); Raleigh, *Chronicle of Leopold and Molly Bloom*, 51, 97.

22. Ellmann makes a point of mentioning that Joyce is thirty-eight years old when arriving in Paris in 1920, partly to identify that he had matured significantly since his years in Trieste and Zurich. "Joyce, the artist," he writes, "now thirty-eight, completed *Circe* and then the final three episodes of *Ulysses*." Ellmann, *James Joyce*, 486.

23. Wyndham Lewis, *Time and Western Man*, Book One (London: Chatto & Windus, 1927), 83.

24. Henri Bergson, *Time and Free Will: An Essay on the Immediate Data of Consciousness* (Mineola, NY: Dover, 2001), 104

25. The connection between 1914 and World War I is suggested but not confirmed, as it would be with Lukács in his 1962 preface to *Theory of the Novel*: "The first draft of this study was written in the summer of 1914 and the final version in the winter of 1914–15. . . . The immediate motive for writing was supplied by the outbreak of the First World War."

26. Rodney Wilson Owen, *James Joyce and the Beginnings of "Ulysses"* (Ann Arbor: UMI Research Press, 1983), 3

27. Gorman, *James Joyce*, 224.

28. November 1, 1921, *L* III, 52.

29. Gorman, *James Joyce*, 224

30. In one of his reminiscences of the *Ulysses* origin myth, Georges Borach recorded the following conversation with Joyce on 1 August 1, 1917: "I first wished to choose the title *Ulysses in Dublin*, but gave up the idea. In Rome, when I had finished about half the *Portrait*, I realized that the *Odyssey* had to be the sequel, and I began to write *Ulysses*" (*Portraits of the Artist in Exile*, 69–70). Crispi agrees:

"Given its cast of characters and relatively simple style (before Joyce overhauled the episode in 1921), it is possible that as early September 1906 to 1907 he had written some sketches or one or more proto-drafts of at least some of the scenes that appear in this episode." Luca Crispi, "A *Ulysses Manuscript Workbook*," *Genetic Joyce Studies*, issue 17 (Spring 2017), https://www.geneticjoycestudies. org/static/issues/GJS17/GJS17_Crispi_Appendix.pdf

31. See *L* II, 168, Joyce to Stanislaus Joyce, Postmark September 30, 1906, when Joyce first mentioned his plans for a new short story. See also *L* II, 190, Joyce to Stanislaus Joyce on November 13, 1906; *L* II, 190, Joyce to Stanislaus Joyce on February 6, 1907; *L* I, 98, Joyce to Harriet Shaw Weaver on November 8, 1916; *L* II, 392, Joyce to C. P. Curran on March 15, 1917; Owen, *James Joyce and the Beginnings of "Ulysses,"* 3–6.

32. And even though it is the year in which he wrote the essay "Portrait of the Artist," the actual writing of *Portrait* would not start until 1907. It's more likely that 1904 is significant as a date because this is the year he left Dublin.

33. Ezra Pound, "James Joyce et Pécuchet," *Mercure de France*, June 1, 1922: "Novelists like to spend only three months, six months on a novel. *Joyce spent fifteen years on his*. And *Ulysses* is more condensed (732 pages) than any whole work whatsoever by Flaubert; more architecture is discovered"; emphasis added.

34. Ellmann, *James Joyce*, 524.

35. Owen is skeptical that Joyce could have had done much writing at all during that busy year, guessing that he could not have written more "than two dozen pages." The last word is a mystery as well, though Gorman claims that for *Finnegans Wake* "it was in mid-November, 1938." Owen, *James Joyce and the Beginnings of "Ulysses,"* 111, 347.

36. Ellmann, *James Joyce*, 357, 383. Owen: "Of the seven letters that are implied by Pound's correspondence, only two from Joyce survive, and neither mentions *Ulysses*; unfortunately missing are Joyce's replies to Pound's questions about the novel in August 1915 and 1916." Owen, *James Joyce and the Beginnings of "Ulysses,"* 117. Some of these unpublished letters can be found in the Pound Collection at the Beinecke Library.

37. *SL*, 209. The first and earliest known reference to the day was made to Weaver on October 10, 1916: "I am writing it as well as I can. It is called *Ulysses* and the action takes place in Dublin in 1904. . . . I hope to finish it in 1918." *L* II, 387.

38. July 14, 1915. This letter is unpublished. Joyce had sent it to Pound so that he could, then, pass it on to Yeats, who was helping to secure money from the Royal Literary Fund. The portion I am quoting here was not included in Pound's edited version as reprinted in *L* II, 352.

39. As was the case on 12 July 1915, when he corrected Weaver: "May I point out that there is a slight mistake in your advertisement columns. My novel did not begin in your paper on the 1 March 1914 but on the 2 February 1914—which, strange to say, is also my birthday." *L* I, 83.

40. September 14, 1916 (it is mistakenly dated 14 October at the top by someone else). Unpublished letter. Ezra Pound Papers, YCAL MSS 43, box 26, folder 1112, Beinecke Rare Book and Manuscript Library, Yale University.

41. Joyce to Pound, July 24, 1917, unpublished. Quoted in Ellmann, "*James Joyce*, 416. Ezra Pound Papers, YCAL MSS 43, box 26, folder 1112, Beinecke Rare Book and Manuscript Library, Yale University; Joyce to Weaver on November 8, 1916: "I began this in Rome six years [ago] (or seven) and am writing it *now*. I hope to finish it in 1918" (*SL*, 223). Joyce to Curran on March 15, 1917: "I am writing *Ulysses* which I began six or seven years ago in Rome and hope I shall be able to finish it in 1918" (*L* II, 392). The notes he made from this visit were incorporated into the final chapter of *Portrait* and various episodes of *Ulysses*, indicating that at one point, at least, this was reason enough to revise the date. In Jane Lidderdale's *Dear Miss Weaver: Harriet Shaw Weaver 1876–1961* (New York: Viking, 1971), Joyce's confusing timeline about the time and place of the beginning of *Ulysses* remained intact: "she [Weaver] knew no more about the book than the odd scraps gleaned from letters: that Mr Joyce had begun it in Rome in 1909 or 1910" (146).

42. See Walton Litz, "Early Vestiges of Joyce's *Ulysses*," *PMLA* 71, no. 1 (March 1956), 59. Using evidence from the "Alphabetical Notebook" Joyce compiled in 1910 for *Portrait*, Luca Crispi even goes so far as to identify the episodes: episode 3, episode 5, episode 6.

43. Gabler, "Rocky Road," 3.

44. Budgen, *Making of* Ulysses, 22.

45. He wanted *Portrait* published before the end of 1916 because it was his lucky year. Ellmann, *"Ulysses" on the Liffey*, 406. A much earlier precedent for this practice of counting the sum of yearly numbers can be found in Giovanni Boccaccio, whose *Decameron* is set in 1348 during the black plague: 1+8=9, the number of the trinity squared, and 3+4 add up to 7, the number of virtues and days of creation. See Aldo S. Bernardo, "The Plague as Key to Meaning in Boccaccio's *Decameron*," in *The Black Death*, ed. Daniel Williman (Binghamton, New York: Medieval & Renaissance Texts & Studies, 1982), 39–64.

46. Joyce to Weaver on April 3, 1921, *L* I, 160.

47. Joyce to Quinn on November 24, 1920, *L* III, 30.

48. Thomas Hardy, *Poems of Thomas Hardy: A New Selection*, ed. T.R.M. Creighton (London: MacMillan Press, 1977), 318; For a discussion of numerical thinking in Hardy, see Kent Puckett, "Hardy's 1900," *Modern Language Quarterly* vol 75, no. 1 (March 2014): 57-75.

49. As reported to Weaver on June 24, 1921. *L* I, 166.

50. Tom Stoppard, *Travesties* (London: Faber & Faber, 1975), 44.

51. *L* III, 51. He continued: "I have still a lot of proofreading and revising to do *but the composition is at an end*. . . . About 3 weeks more stewing over proofs and *all is finished*. So three cheers for Bloom!" (*L* I, 175; emphasis added). A day later, and he wrote to Larbaud: "I finished *Ithaca* last night so that now the writing of

Ulysses is ended, though I have still some weeks of work in revising the proofs."
Another day later, and he informed Weaver as if it had just happened: "I have
now finished the *Ithaca* episode and with that the writing of *Ulysses*" (*L* III, 52).

52. Gabler, *Ulysses: A Critical and Synoptic Edition*, 1890.

53. Richard Madtes, *A Textual and Critical Study of the "Ithaca" Episode of James Joyce's "Ulysses"* (New York: Columbia University Press, 1961), 9.

54. Madtes, *Textual and Critical Study of the "Ithaca"* [*Episode* 17]. According to Madtes, eighty-three of the 309 questions were added after the basic manuscript was written. That makes up 9,380 of the 22,421 words in the episode. He also calculated the number of additions: twenty-four in the manuscript, thirty-one in the first typescript, two in the second typescript, four in the first galley proof, fourteen in the second galley proof, and eight in page proof (44).

55. Michael Groden first pointed out that two hundred pages of *Ulysses* still needed to be set in page proofs in the final month as the process carried over into 1922 (Ulysses *in Progress*, 191).

56. "He was doing something that he had not done in the case of his previous books, actually composing, for his voluminous additions were no less than that, while his manuscript went through the press and came out in the form of galley and page proofs" (Herbert Gorman, *James Joyce*, 288).

57. Darantière to Joyce, August 31, 1921.

58. The first flyer printed July 5, 1921, another one in September 19/20, 1921.

59. In a letter to Weaver dated November 1, 1921, he wonders "on whose [birthday] it will be published." In a footnote Ellmann suggests that "Joyce had already made up his mind that it should appear on 2 February 1922, his own birthday," but other letters written at the same time suggest that Joyce was still thinking the end of November, possibly early December (*L* I, 175). Joyce may have had fantasies about his book appearing on February 2, but he also was at the mercy of the printers, to whom he was sending copious corrections. This coincidence was a late development in the process. In fact, by January 23, he was still thinking that *Ulysses* would appear on the 28th (Saturday) or the 30th (Monday) of the month. *L* III, 57.

60. The last set of proofs for episode 18 was sent to Joyce between January 16 and 20.

61. Both Groden and Gorman use eight years when calculating the amount of time Joyce spent writing *Ulysses* (Ulysses *in Progress*, 3; *James Joyce*, 223). Adrienne Monnier arrives at the same count in her memoir: "we had been waiting eight years" (*Very Rich Hours of Adrienne Monnier*, 114). Gilbert Seldes, in his review of the novel, arrives at the same calculation: "It has stood for eight years as the pledge of Joyce's further achievement." Gilbert Seldes, *The Nation*, August 30, 1922, 211–212.

62. In an interview with Adolf Hoffmeister in 1930, Joyce identified a few historical precedents for his numerical superstitions: "Dante was obsessed by the number three: he divided his verse into three *cantiche*, each written in thirty-three cantos

and in terza rima. Why do we depend on the number four? Four legs on a table, four legs on a horse, four seasons and four provinces of Ireland? Why are there twelve pillars of the law, twelve apostles, twelve months, twelve of Napoleon's marshalls? Why was the armistice of the Great War sounded at the eleventh hour of the eleventh day of the eleventh month? Number as a measure of time is indeterminable. The ratio of these numbers is relative to place and content." See Adolf Hoffmeister, "The Game of Evenings," trans. Michelle Woods, *Granta* 89 (April 2005).

63. Kenner, *Joyce's Voices*, 59–60. When revising page 77 in the proof stage, D. F. McKenzie points out that Joyce added the phrase "seventh heaven." See McKenzie, *Bibliography and Sociology of Texts*, 59.

64. Don Gifford and Robert J. Seidman, Ulysses *Annotated: Notes for James Joyce* Ulysses (Berkeley: University of California Press, 1988), 194.

65. William Shakespeare, *As You Like It*, Act II, Scene VII, accessed on May 6, 2020 at https://shakespeare.folger.edu/shakespeares-works/as-you-like-it/. In his lecture on Shakespeare, Stephen adapts this very line: "Every life is many days, day after day. We walk through ourselves, meeting robbers, ghosts, giants, old men, young men, wives, widows, brothers-in-love, but always meeting ourselves" (*U*, 175).

66. Ellmann, *James Joyce*, 519. Gorman, *James Joyce*, 289. Ellmann, like Gorman before him, understood, and he even used Nora's testimony as backup in his biography. She may have never read the novel, but she was certainly aware of how long the process took, even making the distinction between the time spent thinking (sixteen years) and the time spent writing (seven years) (*James Joyce*, 524).

67. Ford Madox Ford, *Critical Essays*, ed. Max Saunders and Richard Stang (Manchester: Carcanet, 2002), 217.

68. Virginia Woolf, *The Diary of Virginia Woolf*, vol. 5: 1936–41 (New York: Houghton, Mifflin, Harcourt, 1985), 353.

69. F. R. Leavis contended that the variety of styles in *Ulysses* may have been the reason for so much praise from the "cosmopolitan literary world," but like Pound, concluded that this novel was a "dead end." *The Great Tradition: George Eliot, Henry James, Joseph Conrad* (London: Faber, 2008), 36.

70. *The Letters of Ezra Pound, 1907–1941*, ed. D. D. Paige (New York: New Directions, 1971), 174.

71. In one of the great dating ironies in literary history, it's also the case that October 29/30 anticipated by a full year, the first date of the Fascist calendar after Mussolini's March on Rome.

72. Ezra Pound, "James Joyce to His Memory," Ezra Pound Papers, Yale University, Beinecke Rare Book and Manuscript Library, YCAL MSS 43, box 31, folder 5540.

73. Peter de Voogd is more precise: it's a "quadrilateral six-point typesetter's 'em.'" See "Joycean Typeface," *Aspects of Modernism: Studies in Honour of Max Nanny*, eds.

A. Fischer, M. Heusser, and T. Hermann (Tübingen, Germany: Gunter, Narr, Verlag, 1997), 213. Less concerned with the compositor's dilemma, Joyce referred to it as "un point" when revising the typescript: "La réponse à la dernière demande est un point." *Ulysses: A Facsimile of the Manuscript*, ed. Clive Driver, vol. 2, Episode 17 (New York: Rosenbach Foundation, 1975), 32.

74. In 1926, Joyce tells Weaver: "The book really has no beginning or end. . . . It ends in the middle of a sentence and begins in the middle of the same sentence." *L* I, 246.

75. Contrary to what Margot Norris argues, Molly does not seem to be "drift[ing] off to sleep." See Margot Norris, "Character, Plot, and Myth," in *The Cambridge Companion to "Ulysses,"* ed. Sean Latham (Cambridge: Cambridge University Press, 2014), 78. Compare with Bloom's drifting off at the end of episode 17.

76. In 1930, Joyce admitted to Adolf Hoffmeister, "I never finish any of my work" adding, "*Ulysses* is the most unfinished." See Hoffmeister, "The Game of Evenings."

77. 13. Rabaté and Ferrer agree: "It is likely that *Ulysses* would never have been finished, or at least that it would have been much longer than it is, if Joyce, by superstition, had not decided that it should be finished the day of his 40th birthday." Jean-Michel Rabaté and Daniel Ferrer, "Paragraphs in Expansion," 139.

78. See James Ramsey Wallen, "What is an Unfinished Work?," *New Literary History* 46, no. 1 (Winter 2015): 125–42.

79. He continues: "Accordingly, all events in the history of a people, a nation, or a civilization which take place at a given moment are supposed to occur and there for reasons bound up, somehow, with that moment." See Siegfried Kracauer, "Time and History," *History and Theory* 6 (1966): 66.

80. Budgen, *James Joyce and the Making of* Ulysses, 17.

81. Gorman, *James Joyce*, 289.

82. Joyce to Weaver, March 11, 1922, *L* I, 183. Nora was no exception. A frustrated Joyce kept close watch of her progress, informing his aunt that "She [Molly] has got as far as page 27 counting the cover." Joyce to Mrs. William Murray, *L* I, 193. When the fourth edition came out in 1924, he tried again: "The edition you have is full of printers' errors. Please read it in this. I cut the pages. There is a list of mistakes at the end" (*SL*, 299).

83. *L* I, 202.

84. Claude Lévi-Strauss, *La pensée sauvage* (Paris: Librairie Plon, 1962), 342.

85. In *Theory of Literature*, René Wellek and Austin Warren describe the shift from calendar centuries to periods in literary history, but they argue that instead of following periods that mirror the "cultural history of man," we'd be better served by establishing literary periods by literary criteria. "But our starting point," they write, "must be the development of literature as literature. . . . A period is thus a time section dominated by a system of literary norms, standards, and conventions, whose introduction, spread, diversification, integration, and disappearance

can be traced." René Wellek and Austin Warren, *Theory of Literature* (New York: Harcourt, Brace, 1942), 255.

86.   Lévi-Strauss: "Dates may not be the whole of history, nor what is most interesting about it, but they are its *sine qua non*, for history's entire originality and distinctive nature lie in apprehending the relation between *before* and *after*, which would perforce dissolve if its terms could not, at least in principle, be dated." See Claude Lévi-Strauss, *The Savage Mind*, trans. George Weidenfeld (Chicago: University of Chicago Press, 1966), 258.

87.   See, for instance, Clément Moisan, *Qu'est-ce que l'histoire littéraire?* (Paris: Presses Universitaires de France, 1987).

88.   Hayden White, "Interpretation in History," *New Literary History* 4, no. 2 (Winter 1973): 289.

89.   Grafton, *Cartographies of Time*, 19–20.

90.   Alan Liu, *Wordsworth: The Sense of History* (Stanford, CA: Stanford University Press, 1989), 154.

91.   Liu, *Wordsworth: The Sense of History*, 577n44.

92.   He returns to the problem thirty years later in Alan Liu, *Friending the Past: The Sense of History in a Digital Age* (Chicago: University of Chicago Press, 2018).

93.   *Oxford English Dictionary* online, s.v. "dating," accessed May 2020, https://www -oed-com.ccl.idm.oclc.org/view/Entry/47418?rskey=Ln2IJG&result=1#eid.

3PILOGUE: MISCOUNTS, MISSED COUNTS

1.   William James, *The Meaning of Truth* (New York: Longman, Green, 1911), 92–93.

2.   Ted Underwood, *Distant Horizons: Digital Evidence and Literary Change* (Chicago: Chicago University Press, 2019), 182.

3.   Underwood, *Distant Horizons*, 183.

4.   Margaret Cohen, *The Sentimental Education of the Novel* (Princeton, NJ: Princeton University Press, 2018), 23.

5.   Gertrude Stein, *Everybody's Autobiography* (New York: Random House, 1937), 100.

6.   T. S. Eliot, *Selected Prose of T.S. Eliot*, ed. Frank Kermode (London: Faber & Faber, 1975), 75.

7.   Kenner, *Dublin's Joyce*, xi.

8.   Large discrepancies exist between the document counting the responses as drafted by Ernst's team and the actual responses. In the Ernst tally, for instance, Texas, Iowa, and Utah, are added as *yeses* to the question of whether or not there is demand for *Ulysses*, even though the column in the original is blank. There are also two fewer *yeses* for New Jersey and six more for New York. See "United

States v. One Book Entitled *Ulysses* by James Joyce," Morris Leopold Ernst Papers, box 364. 2–3, Harry Ransom Center, University of Texas at Austin.

9. Alexandre Koyré, "Du monde de *l'à-peu-près* à l'univers de la précision," in *Études d'histoire de la pensée philosophique* (Paris: Gallimard 1971), 342.

10. Koyré, "Du monde de *l'à-peu-près* à l'univers de la précision," 359–60.

11. Thomas Kuhn, "The Function of Measurement in Modern Physical Science," in *The Essential Tension: Selected Studies in Scientific Tradition and Change* (Chicago: University of Chicago Press, 1977), 194.

12. P. H. Smith Jr., "The Computer and the Humanist," in *Computers in Humanistic Research: Readings and Perspectives*, ed. Edmund A. Bowles (Englewood Cliffs, NJ: Prentice-Hall, Inc., 1967), 18.

13. Da, "The Computational Case against Computational Literary Studies," 634.

14. Ezra Pound, "Date Line," *Literary Essays of Ezra Pound*, ed. T. S. Eliot (New York: New Directions, 1968), 84.

Index